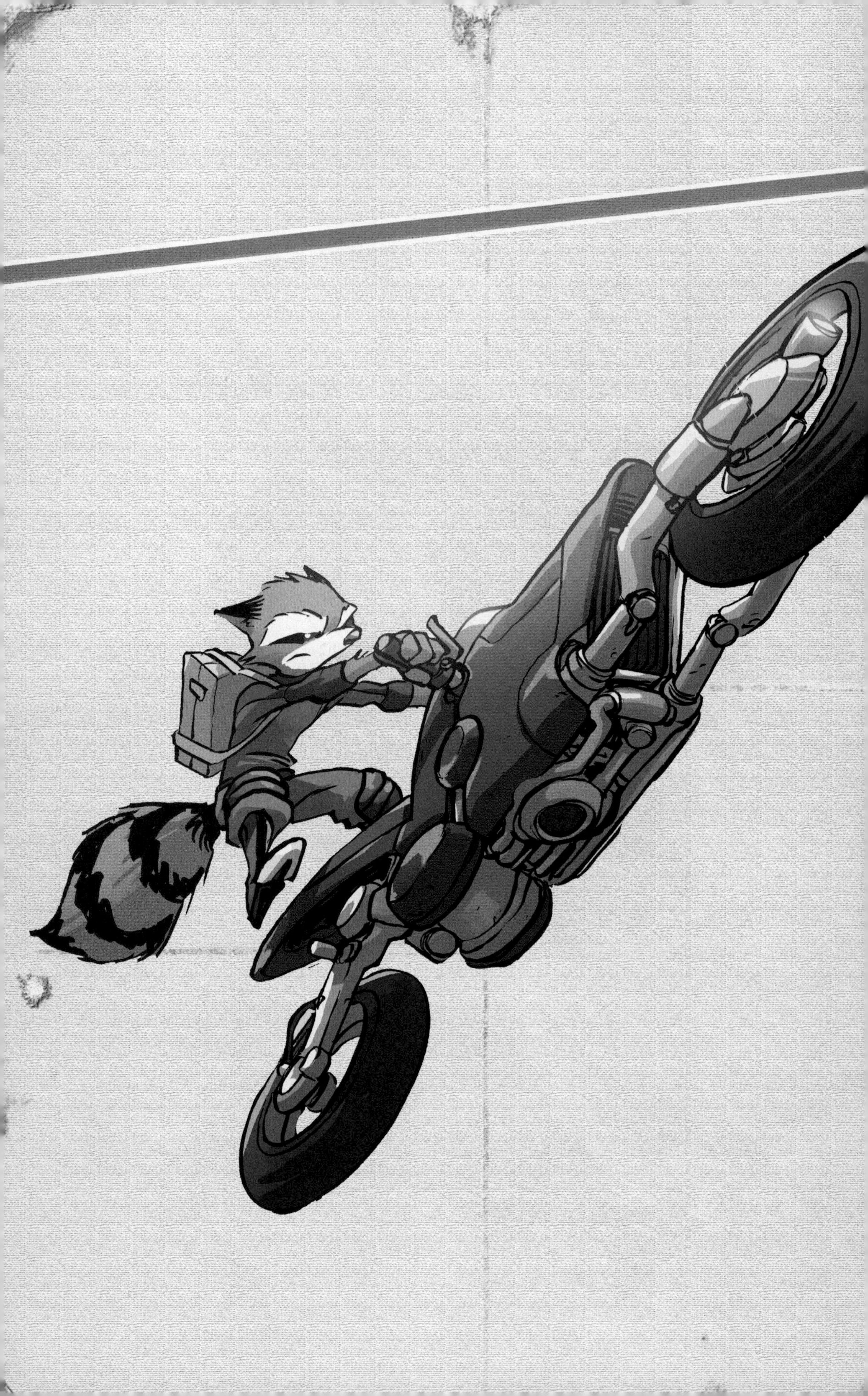

ROCKET RACCOON
STORYTAILER

WRITER
SKOTTIE YOUNG

ARTISTS
FILIPE ANDRADE (#7-8)
& JAKE PARKER (#9-11)

COLOR ARTIST
JEAN-FRANÇOIS BEAULIEU

LETTERER: **JEFF ECKLEBERRY**
COVER ART: **SKOTTIE YOUNG**
ASSISTANT EDITORS: **CHARLES BEACHAM & DEVIN LEWIS**
EDITOR: **SANA AMANAT**
SENIOR EDITOR: **NICK LOWE**

COLLECTION EDITOR: **JENNIFER GRÜNWALD** • ASSISTANT EDITOR: **SARAH BRUNSTAD**
ASSOCIATE MANAGING EDITOR: **ALEX STARBUCK** • EDITOR, SPECIAL PROJECTS: **MARK D. BEAZLEY**
SENIOR EDITOR, SPECIAL PROJECTS: **JEFF YOUNGQUIST** • SVP PRINT, SALES & MARKETING: **DAVID GABRIEL**

EDITOR IN CHIEF: **AXEL ALONSO** • CHIEF CREATIVE OFFICER: **JOE QUESADA**
PUBLISHER: **DAN BUCKLEY** • EXECUTIVE PRODUCER: **ALAN FINE**

ROCKET RACCOON VOL. 2: STORYTAILER. Contains material originally published in magazine form as ROCKET RACCOON #7-11. First printing 2015. ISBN# 978-0-7851-9390-6. Published by MARVEL WORLDWIDE, INC., a subsidiary of MARVEL ENTERTAINMENT, LLC. OFFICE OF PUBLICATION: 135 West 50th Street, New York, NY 10020. Copyright © 2015 MARVEL No similarity between any of the names, characters, persons, and/or institutions in this magazine with those of any living or dead person or institution is intended, and any such similarity which may exist is purely coincidental. **Printed in the U.S.A.** ALAN FINE, President, Marvel Entertainment; DAN BUCKLEY, President, TV, Publishing and Brand Management; JOE QUESADA, Chief Creative Officer; TOM BREVOORT, SVP of Publishing; DAVID BOGART, SVP of Operations & Procurement, Publishing; C.B. CEBULSKI, VP of International Development & Brand Management; DAVID GABRIEL, SVP Print, Sales & Marketing; JIM O'KEEFE, VP of Operations & Logistics; DAN CARR, Executive Director of Publishing Technology; SUSAN CRESPI, Editorial Operations Manager; ALEX MORALES, Publishing Operations Manager; STAN LEE, Chairman Emeritus. For information regarding advertising in Marvel Comics or on Marvel.com, please contact Jonathan Rheingold, VP of Custom Solutions & Ad Sales, at jrheingold@marvel.com. For Marvel subscription inquiries, please call 800-217-9158. Manufactured between 5/22/2015 and 7/6/2015 by R.R. DONNELLEY, INC., SALEM, VA, USA.

0 9 8 7 6 5 4 3 2 1

PREVIOUSLY IN
ROCKET

GUARDIAN OF THE GALAXY, GUNSLINGER, GALLANT?

ROCKET, THE TALKING SPACE RACCOON, AND GROOT, THE TALKING SPACE TREE, HA
BEEN BOUNCING AROUND THE GALAXY, TRYING TO MAKE GOOD ON THEIR VARIOUS
INTERSTELLAR DEBTS.

THIS IS ONE OF THOSE ADVENTURES. THERE, YOU'RE CAUGHT UP.

HERE. HAVE A RACCOON FACT.

RACCOON FACT #842: RACCOONS GENERALLY PREFER TO LIVE IN THE WETLAND
BIOME. THESE ARE MARSHY, MODERATE CLIMATES.

DID YOU KNOW: OUTER SPACE IS NOT A WETLAND BIOME? MAYBE THAT IS WHY
ROCKET IS SUCH A GROUCH.

RACCOON

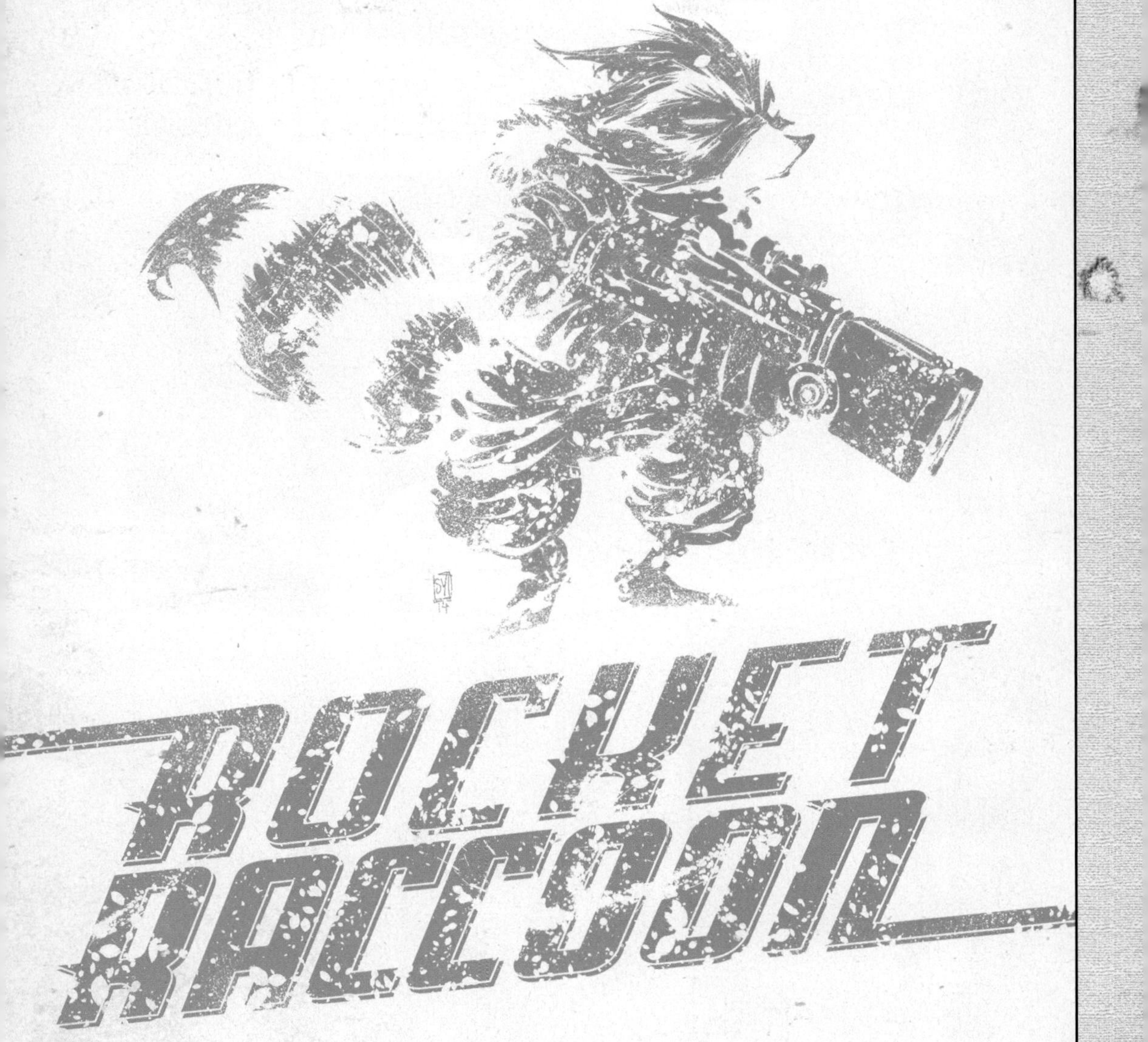

ROCKET RACCOON

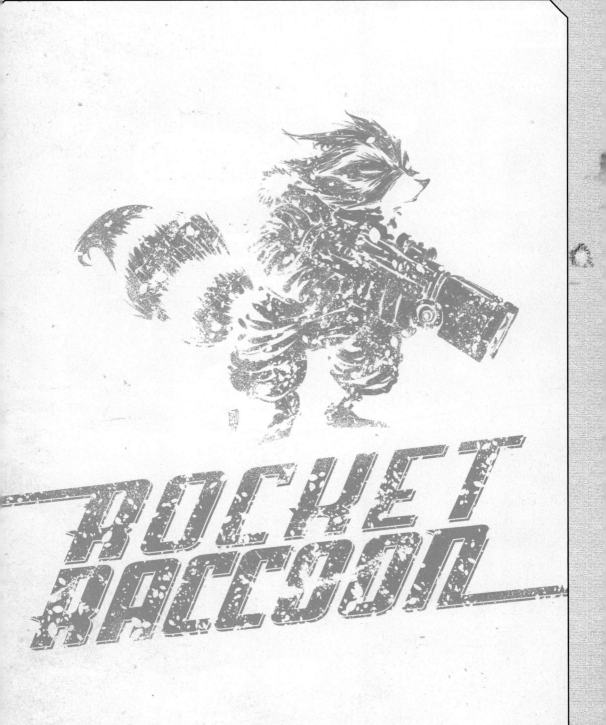

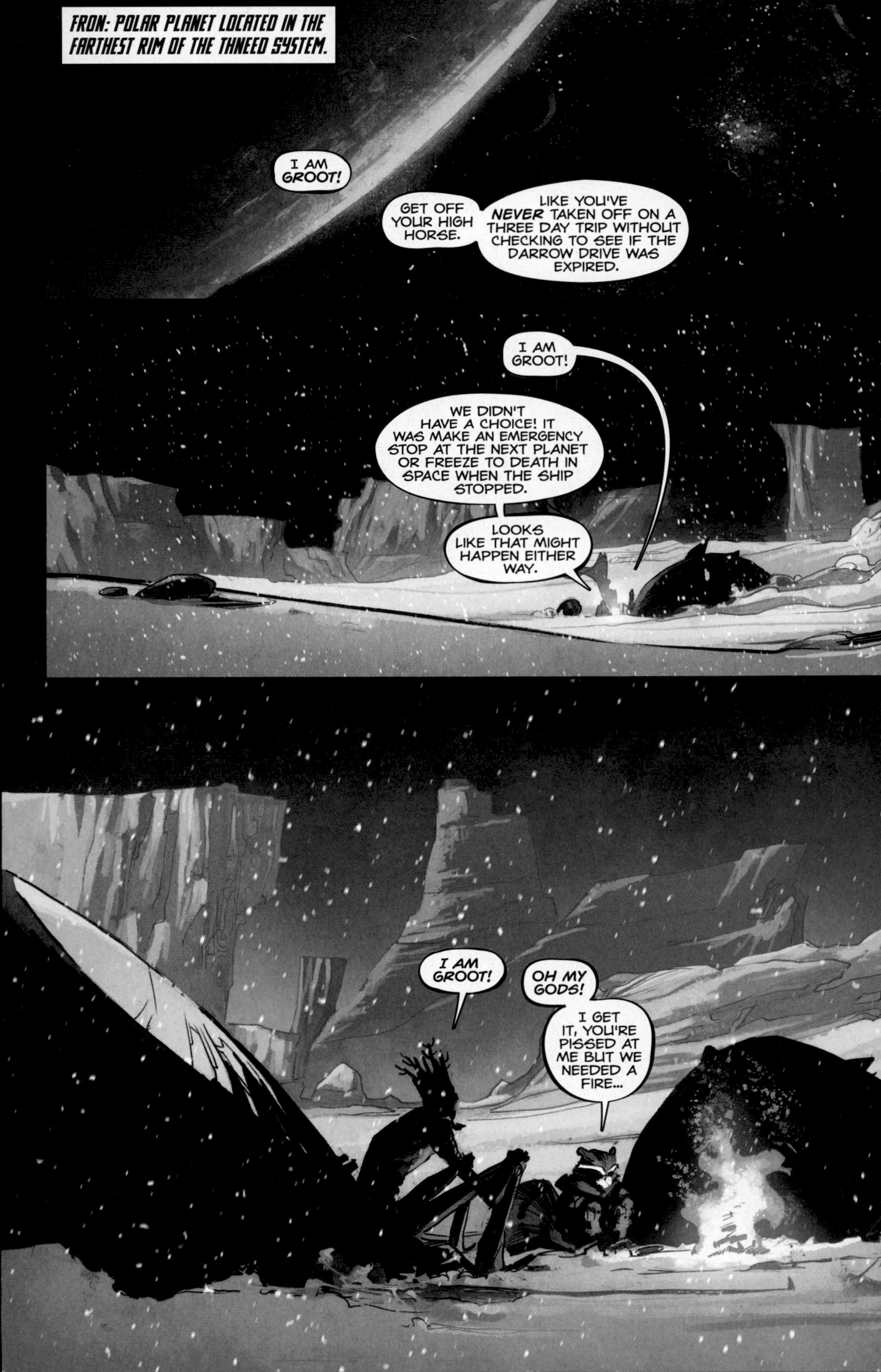
FRON: POLAR PLANET LOCATED IN THE FARTHEST RIM OF THE THNEED SYSTEM.
I AM GROOT!
GET OFF YOUR HIGH HORSE.
LIKE YOU'VE NEVER TAKEN OFF ON A THREE DAY TRIP WITHOUT CHECKING TO SEE IF THE DARROW DRIVE WAS EXPIRED.
I AM GROOT!
WE DIDN'T HAVE A CHOICE! IT WAS MAKE AN EMERGENCY STOP AT THE NEXT PLANET OR FREEZE TO DEATH IN SPACE WHEN THE SHIP STOPPED.
LOOKS LIKE THAT MIGHT HAPPEN EITHER WAY.
I AM GROOT!
OH MY GODS!
I GET IT, YOU'RE PISSED AT ME BUT WE NEEDED A FIRE...

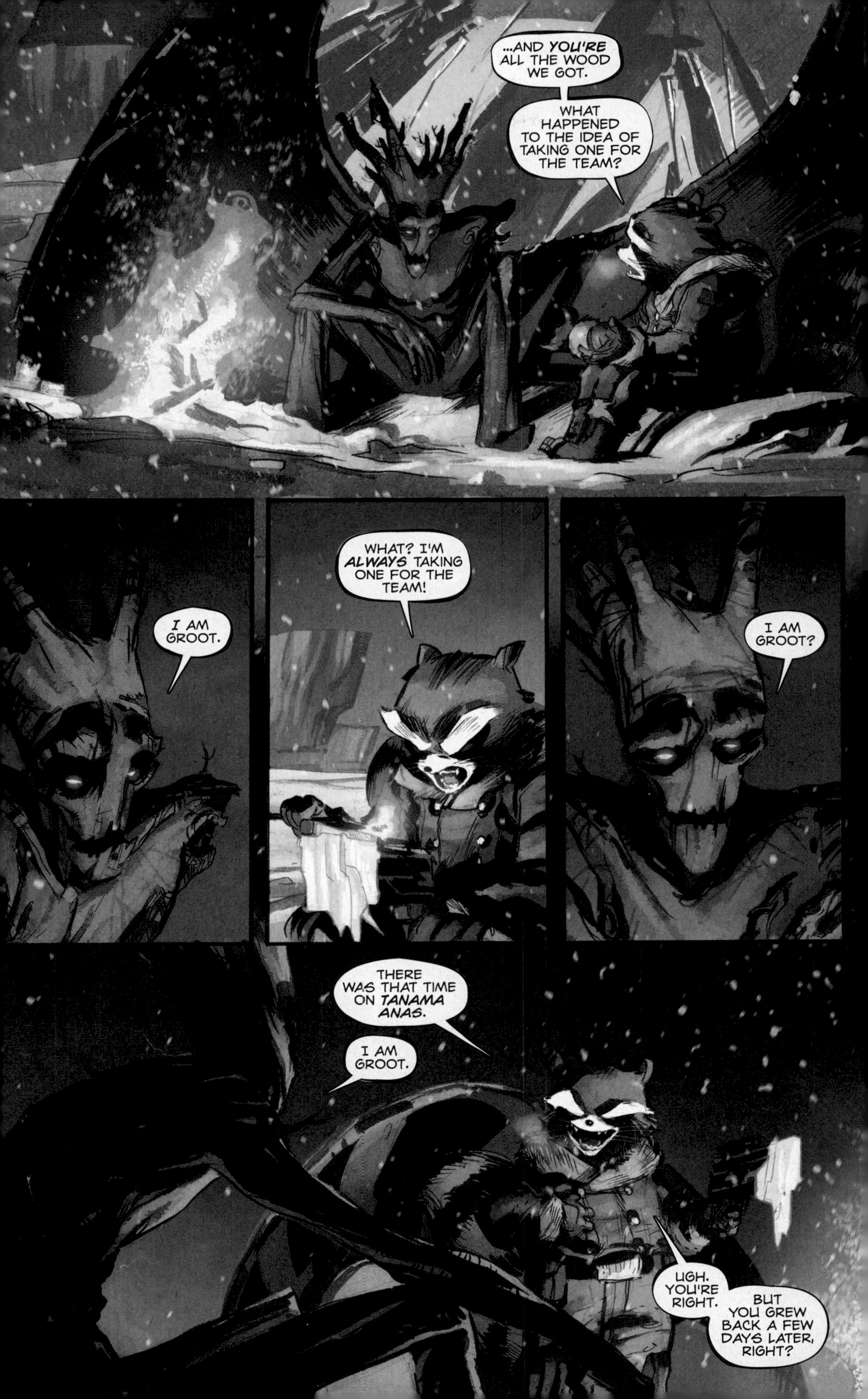
...AND YOU'RE ALL THE WOOD WE GOT.
WHAT HAPPENED TO THE IDEA OF TAKING ONE FOR THE TEAM?
I AM GROOT.
WHAT? I'M ALWAYS TAKING ONE FOR THE TEAM!
I AM GROOT?
THERE WAS THAT TIME ON TANAMA ANAS.
I AM GROOT.
UGH. YOU'RE RIGHT.
BUT YOU GREW BACK A FEW DAYS LATER, RIGHT?

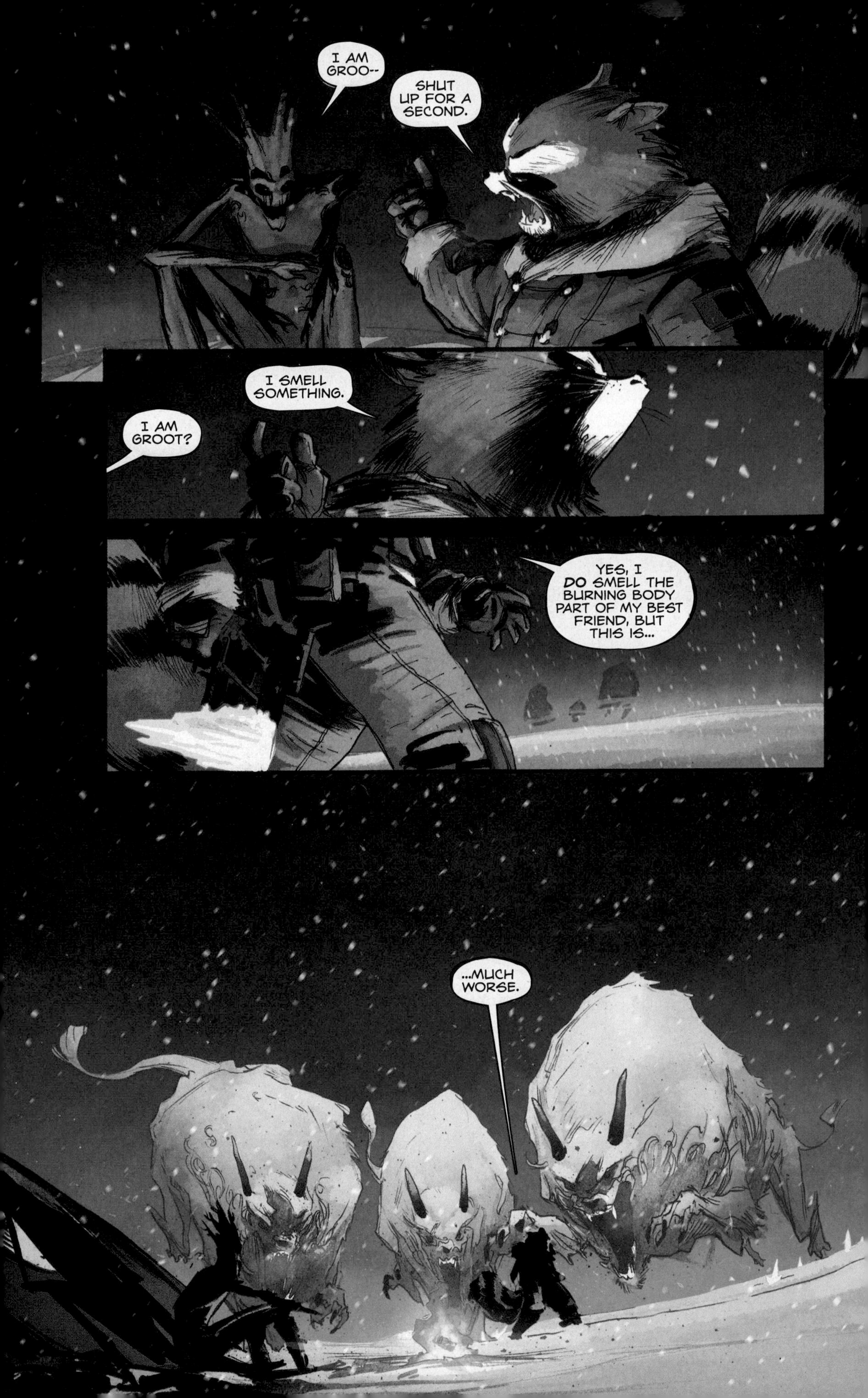
I AM GROO--
SHUT UP FOR A SECOND.
I SMELL SOMETHING.
I AM GROOT?
YES, I DO SMELL THE BURNING BODY PART OF MY BEST FRIEND, BUT THIS IS...
...MUCH WORSE.

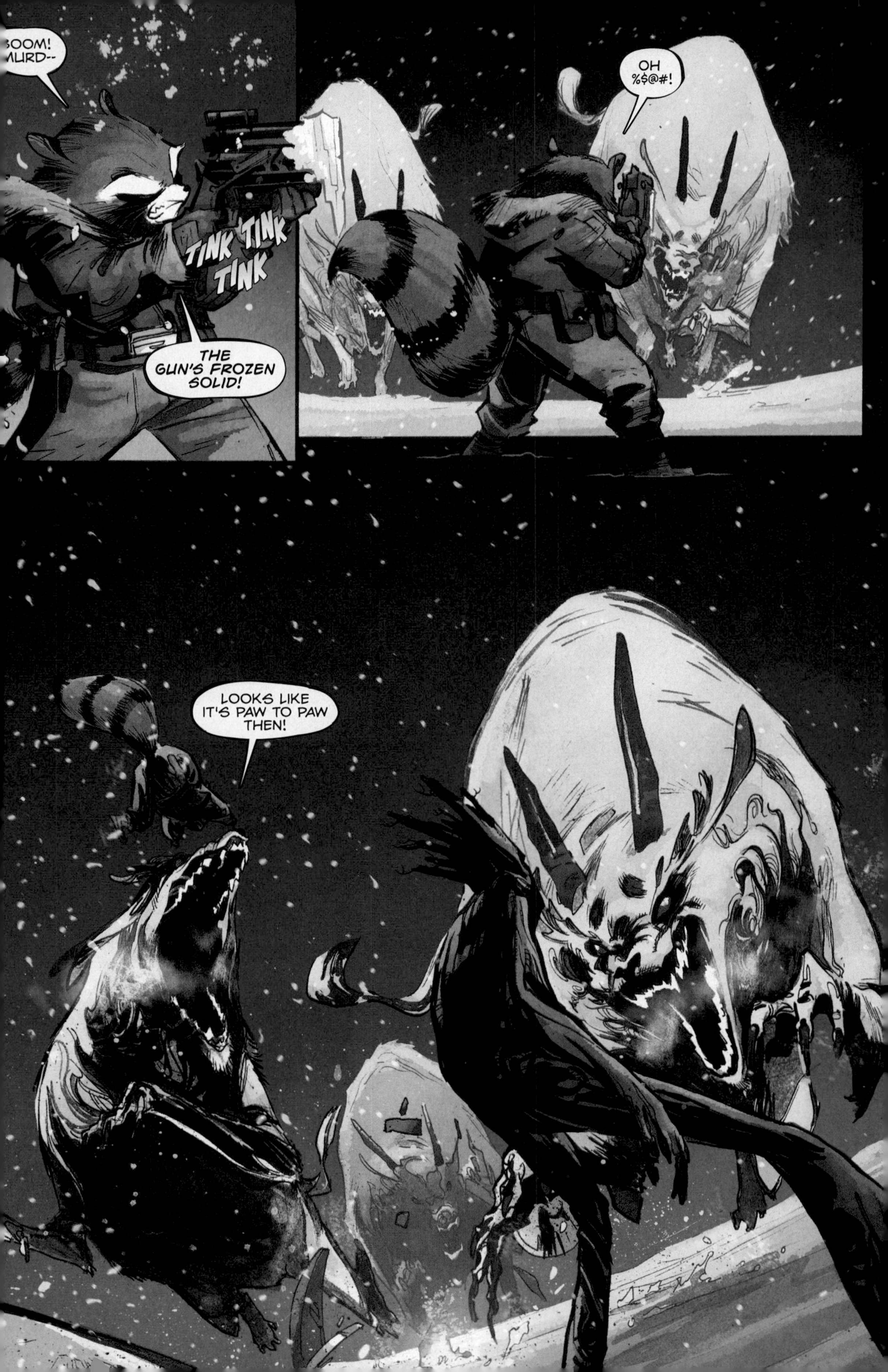
BOOM!
MURD--
TINK TINK
TINK
THE GUN'S FROZEN SOLID!
OH %$@#!
LOOKS LIKE IT'S PAW TO PAW THEN!

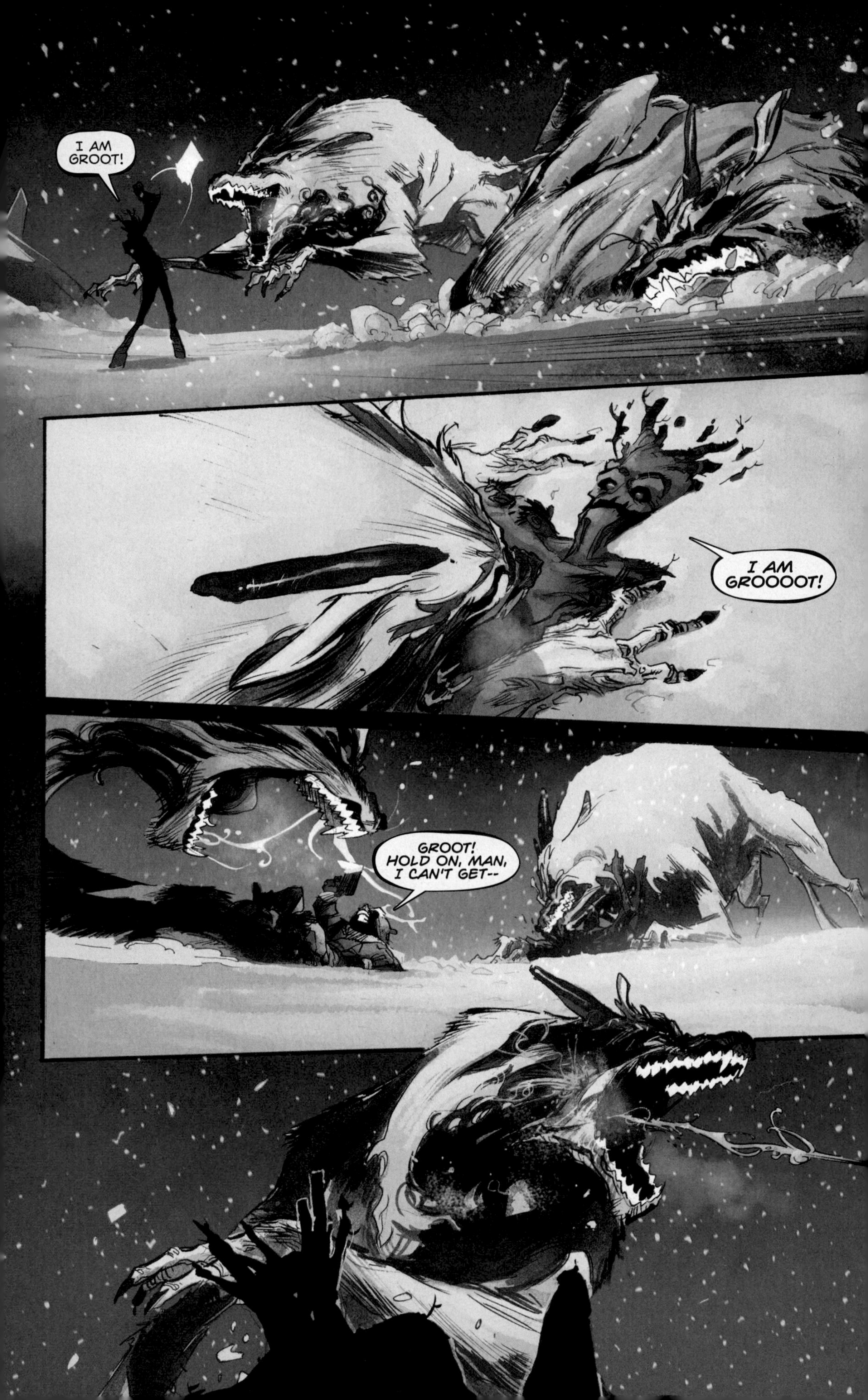
I AM GROOT!
I AM GROOOOT!
GROOT! HOLD ON, MAN, I CAN'T GET--

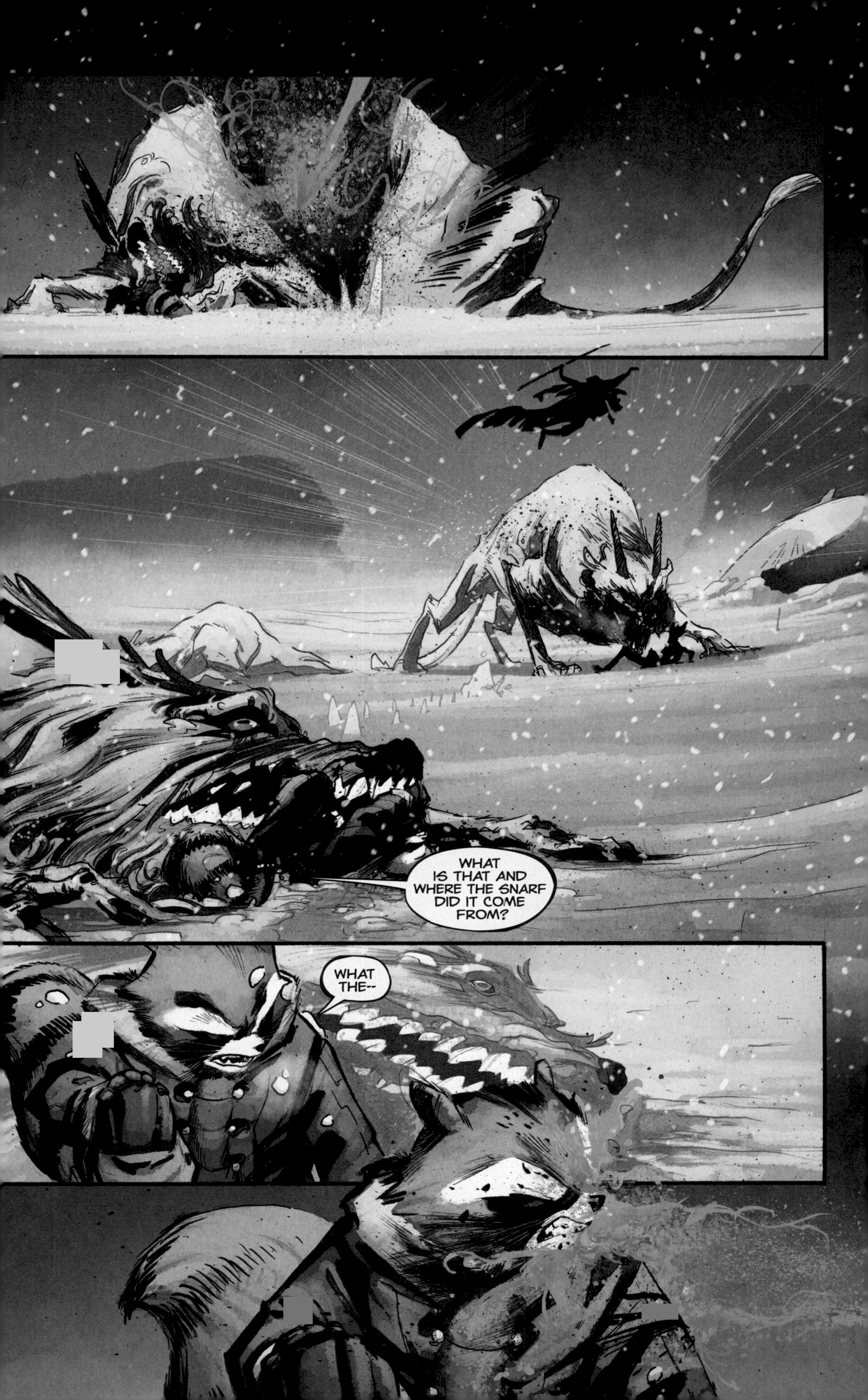
WHAT IS THAT AND WHERE THE SNARF DID IT COME FROM?
WHAT THE--

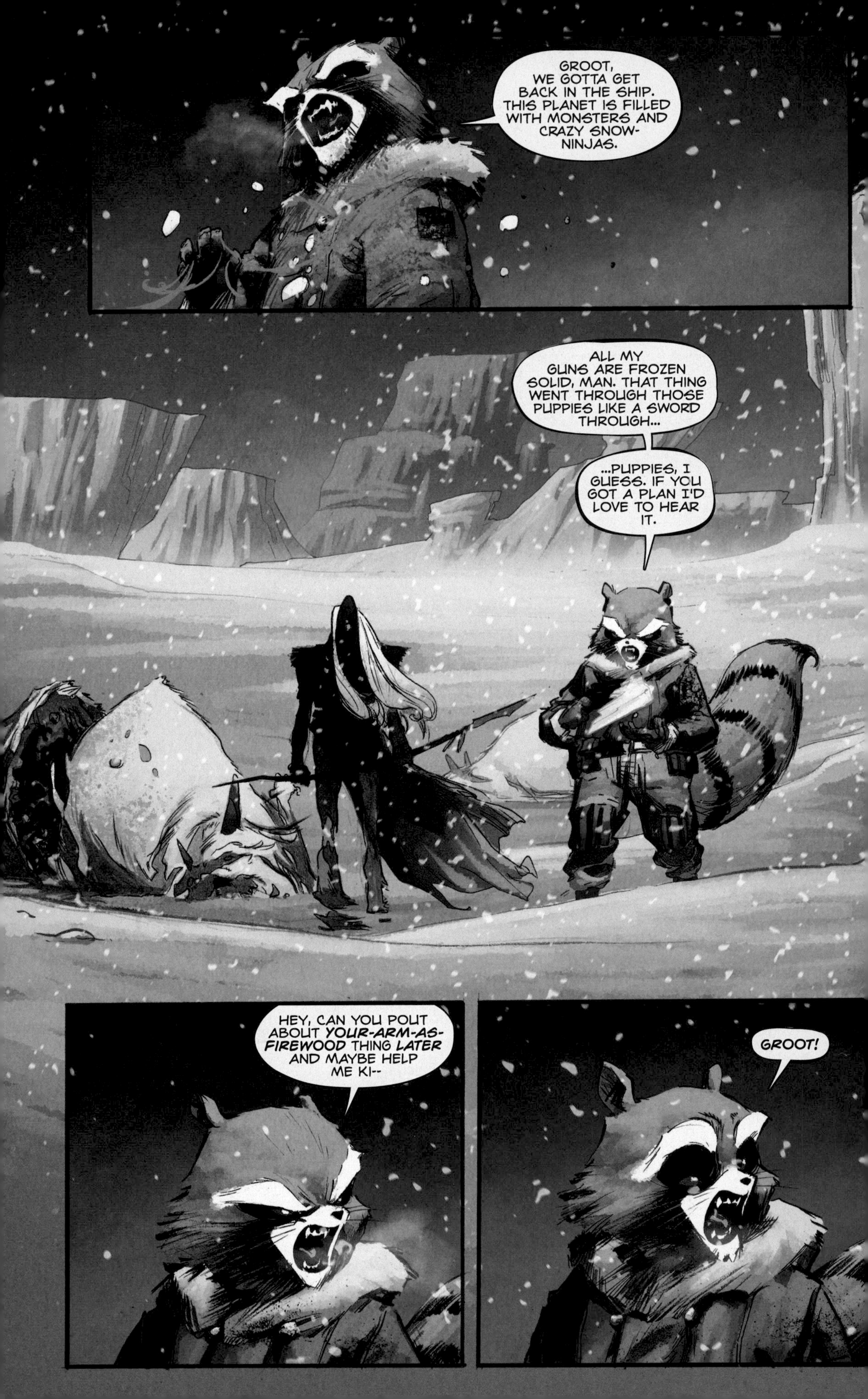
GROOT, WE GOTTA GET BACK IN THE SHIP. THIS PLANET IS FILLED WITH MONSTERS AND CRAZY SNOW-NINJAS.
ALL MY GUNS ARE FROZEN SOLID, MAN. THAT THING WENT THROUGH THOSE PUPPIES LIKE A SWORD THROUGH...
...PUPPIES, I GUESS. IF YOU GOT A PLAN I'D LOVE TO HEAR IT.
HEY, CAN YOU POUT ABOUT *YOUR-ARM-AS-FIREWOOD* THING *LATER* AND MAYBE HELP ME KI--
GROOT!

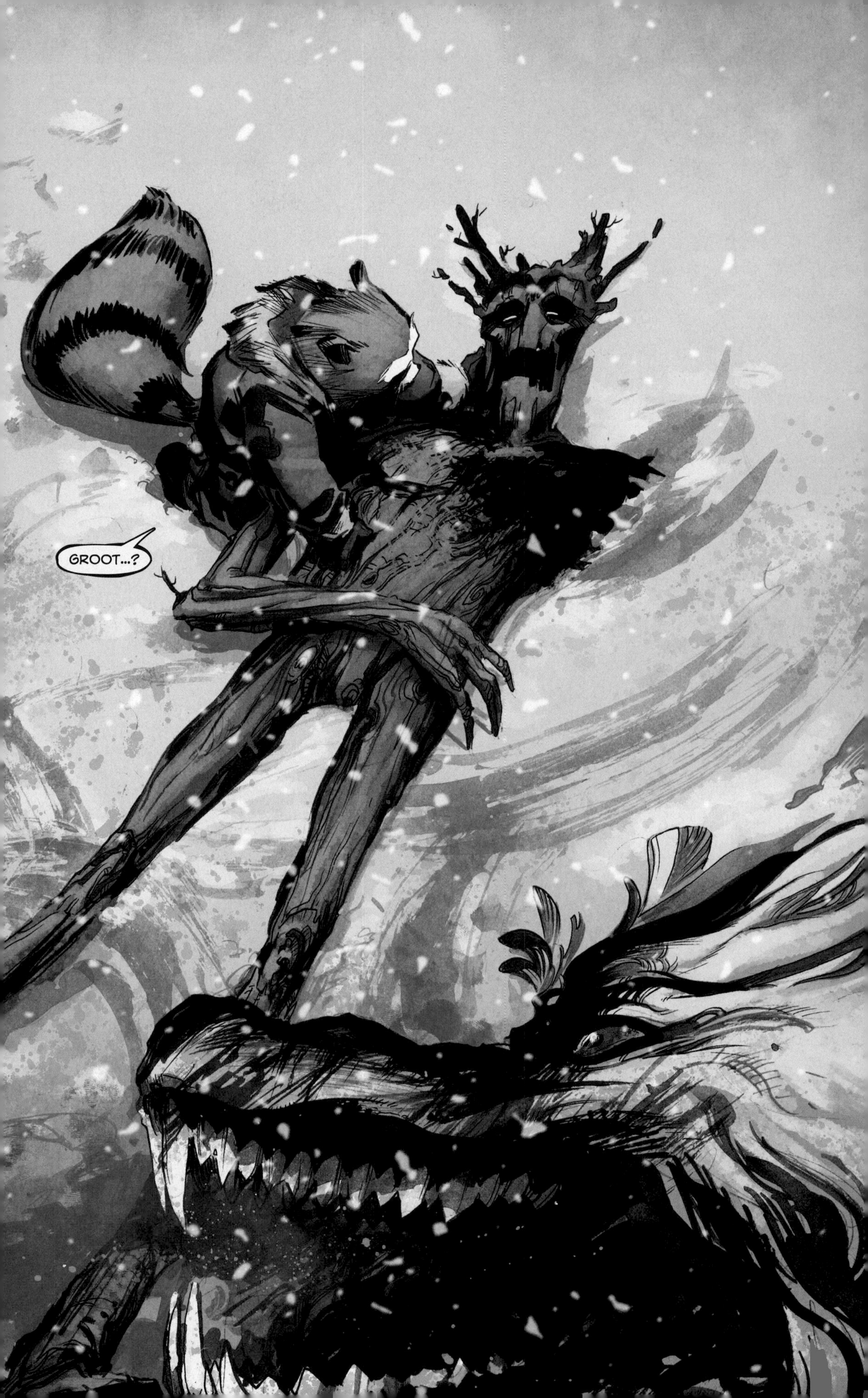
GROOT...?

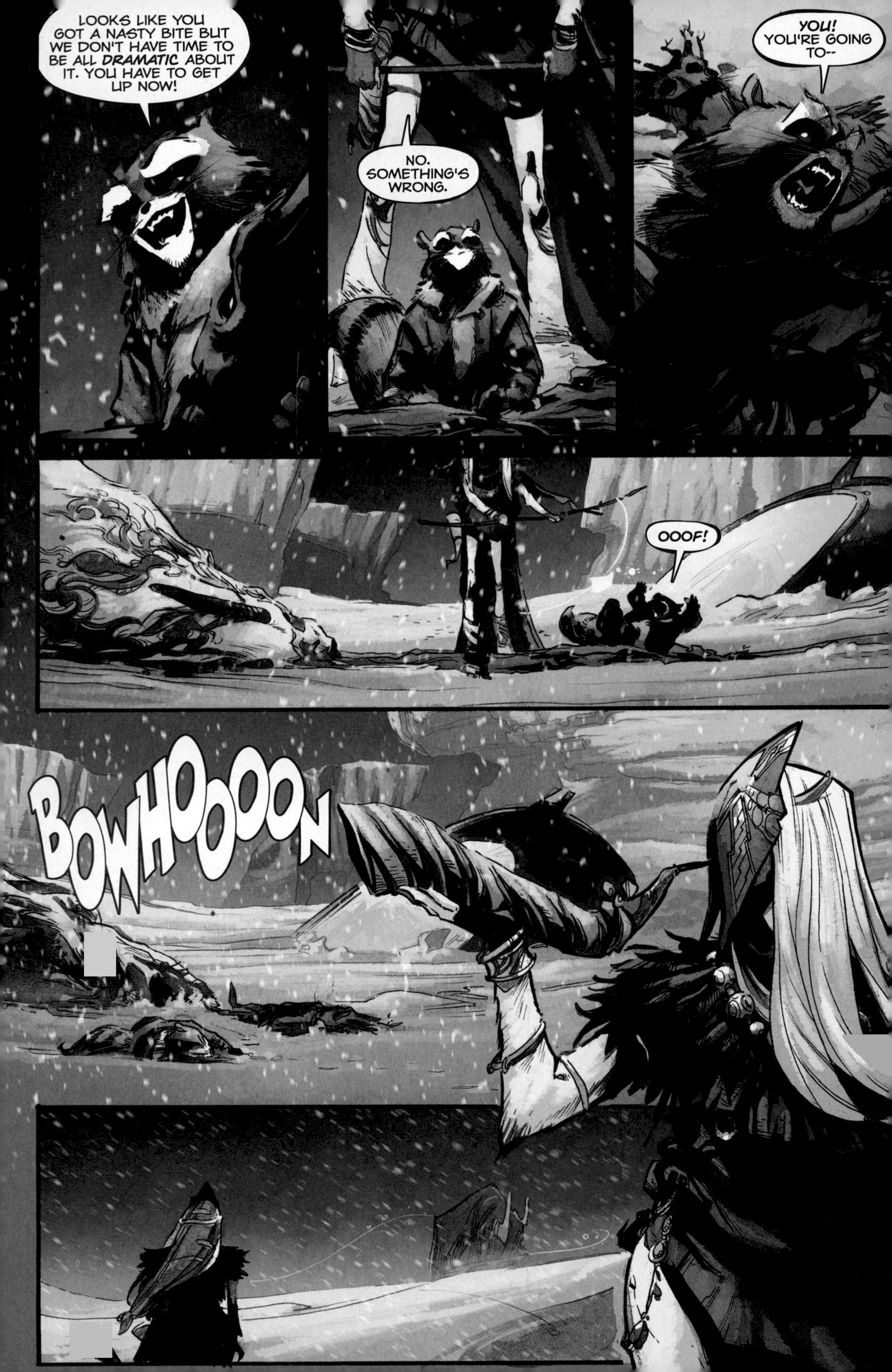
LOOKS LIKE YOU GOT A NASTY BITE BUT WE DON'T HAVE TIME TO BE ALL *DRAMATIC* ABOUT IT. YOU HAVE TO GET UP NOW!
NO. SOMETHING'S WRONG.
YOU! YOU'RE GOING TO--
OOOF!
BOWHOOOON

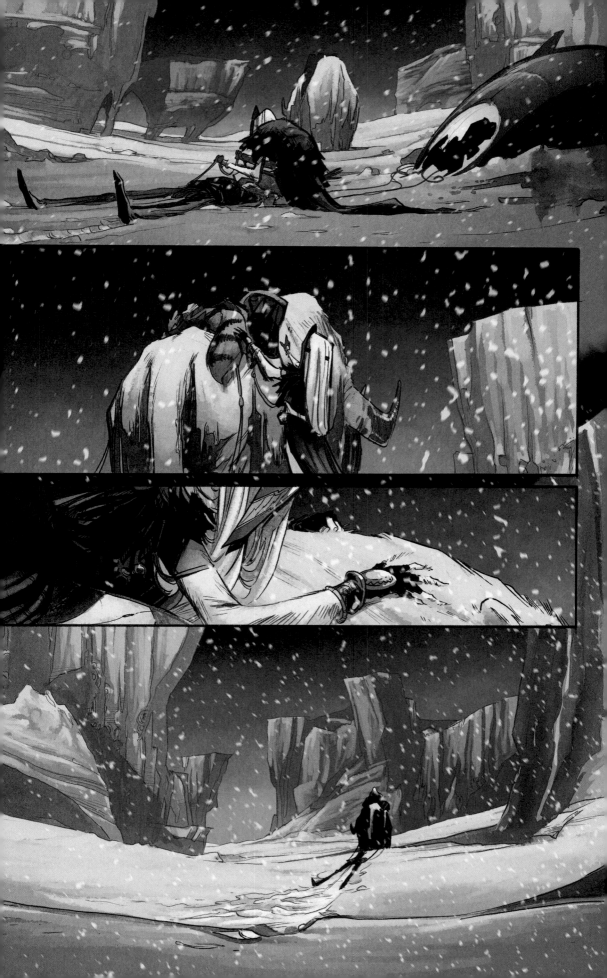

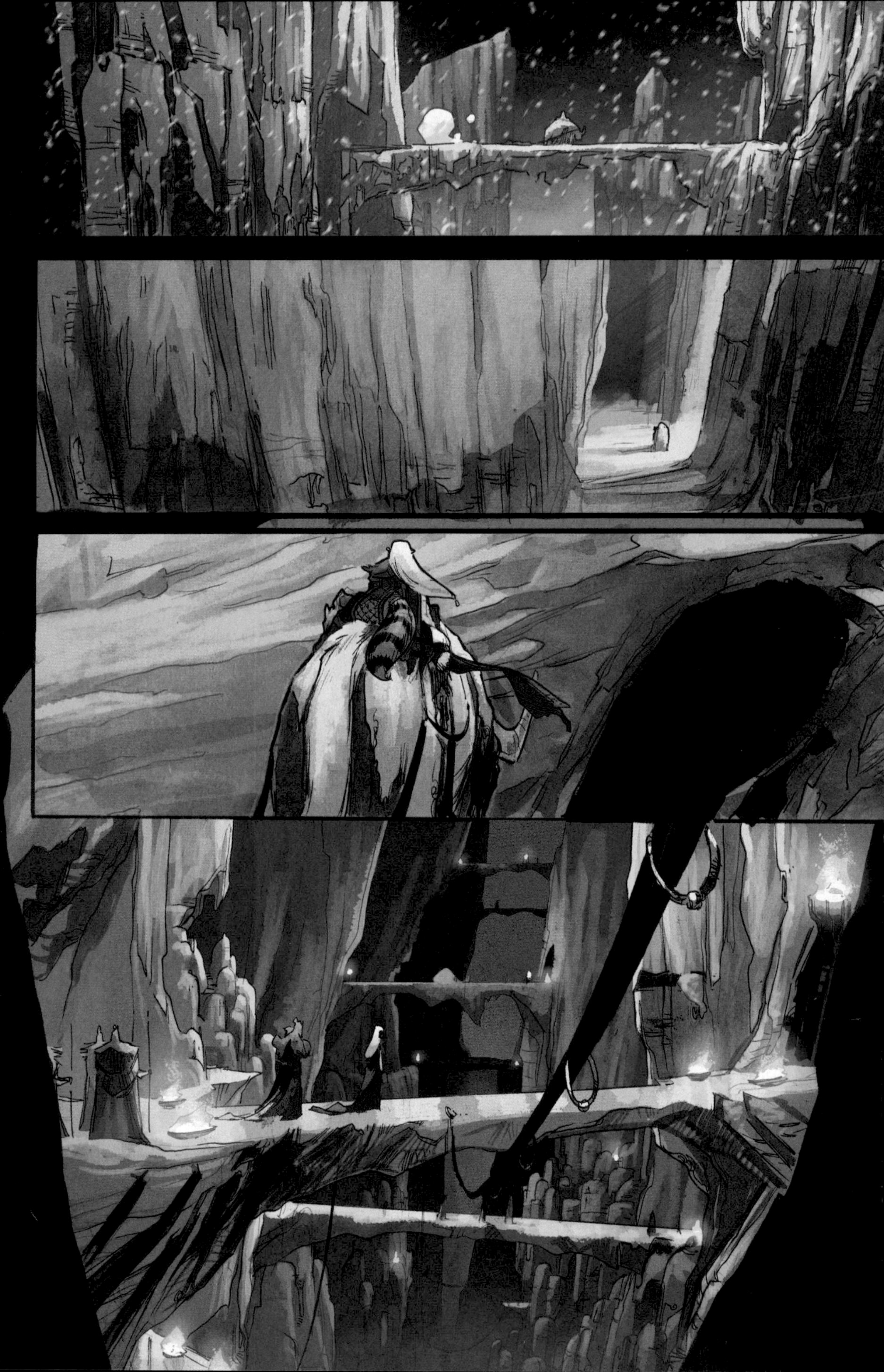

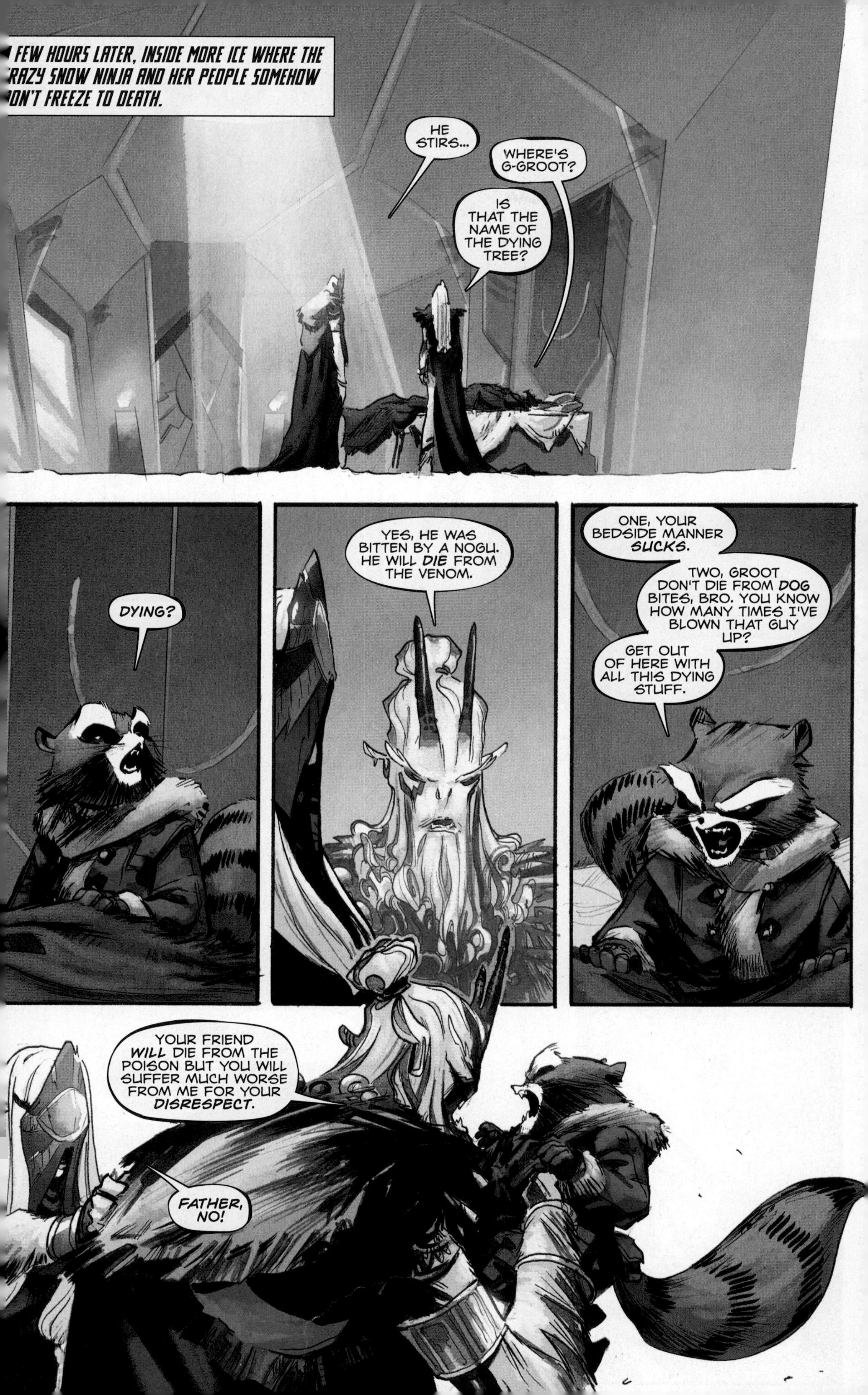
A FEW HOURS LATER, INSIDE MORE ICE WHERE THE CRAZY SNOW NINJA AND HER PEOPLE SOMEHOW DON'T FREEZE TO DEATH.
HE STIRS...
WHERE'S G-GROOT?
IS THAT THE NAME OF THE DYING TREE?
DYING?
YES, HE WAS BITTEN BY A NOGLI. HE WILL DIE FROM THE VENOM.
ONE, YOUR BEDSIDE MANNER SUCKS.
TWO, GROOT DON'T DIE FROM DOG BITES, BRO. YOU KNOW HOW MANY TIMES I'VE BLOWN THAT GUY UP?
GET OUT OF HERE WITH ALL THIS DYING STUFF.
YOUR FRIEND WILL DIE FROM THE POISON BUT YOU WILL SUFFER MUCH WORSE FROM ME FOR YOUR DISRESPECT.
FATHER, NO!

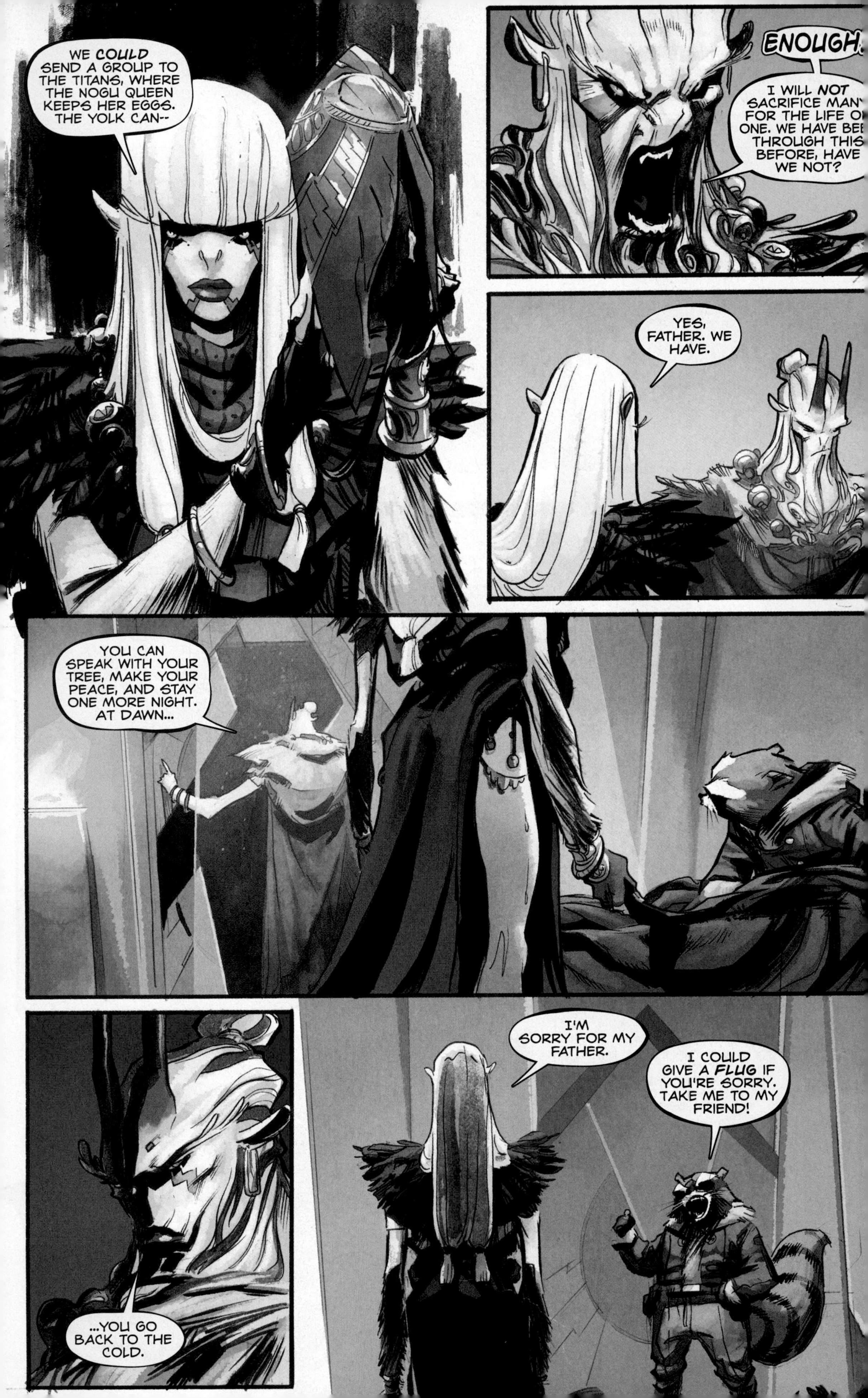

WE COULD SEND A GROUP TO THE TITANS, WHERE THE NOGU QUEEN KEEPS HER EGGS. THE YOLK CAN--
ENOUGH!
I WILL NOT SACRIFICE MANY FOR THE LIFE OF ONE. WE HAVE BEEN THROUGH THIS BEFORE, HAVE WE NOT?
YES, FATHER. WE HAVE.
YOU CAN SPEAK WITH YOUR TREE, MAKE YOUR PEACE, AND STAY ONE MORE NIGHT. AT DAWN...
...YOU GO BACK TO THE COLD.
I'M SORRY FOR MY FATHER.
I COULD GIVE A FLUG IF YOU'RE SORRY. TAKE ME TO MY FRIEND!

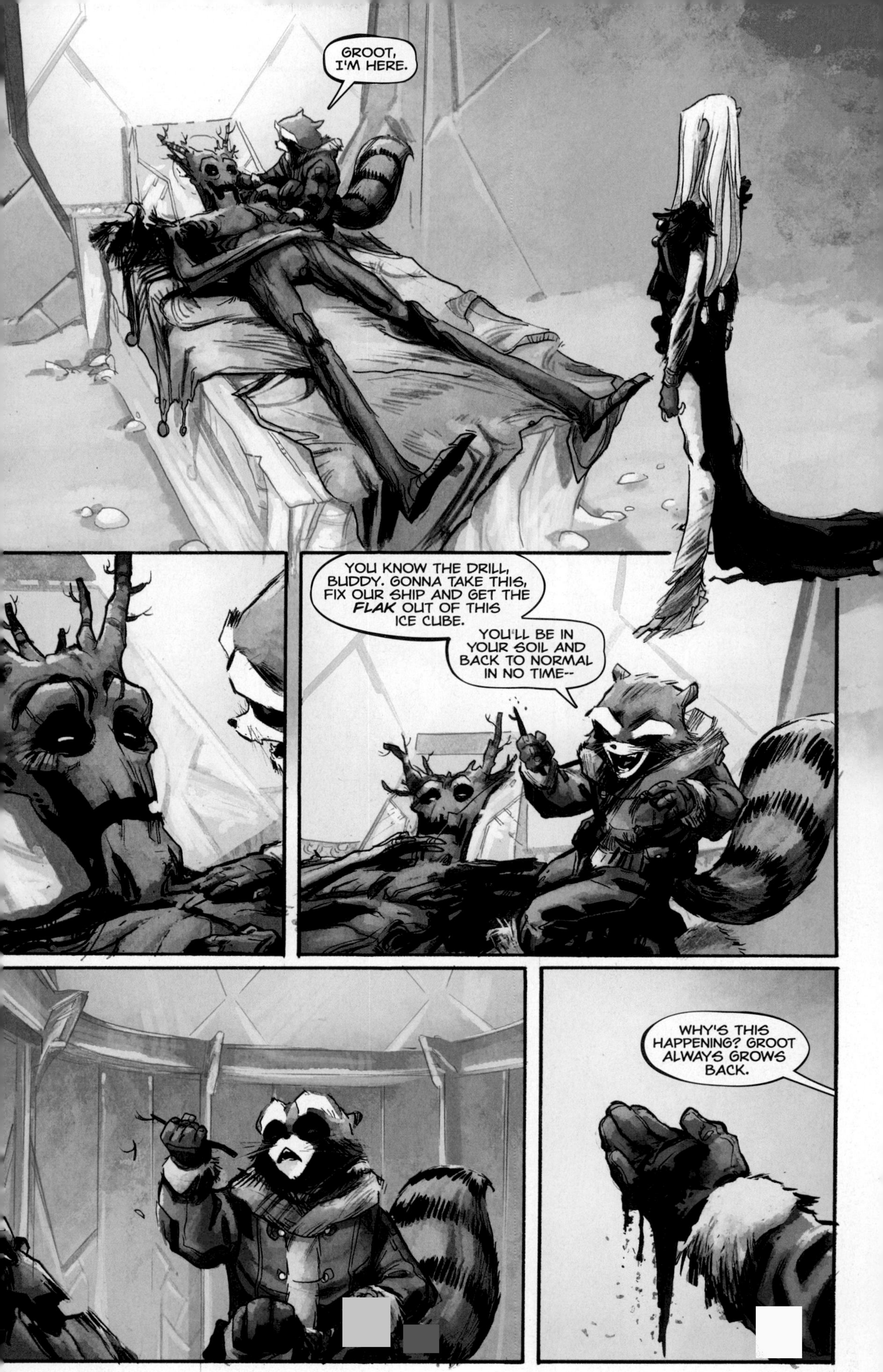
GROOT, I'M HERE.
YOU KNOW THE DRILL, BUDDY. GONNA TAKE THIS, FIX OUR SHIP AND GET THE FLAK OUT OF THIS ICE CUBE.
YOU'LL BE IN YOUR SOIL AND BACK TO NORMAL IN NO TIME--
WHY'S THIS HAPPENING? GROOT ALWAYS GROWS BACK.

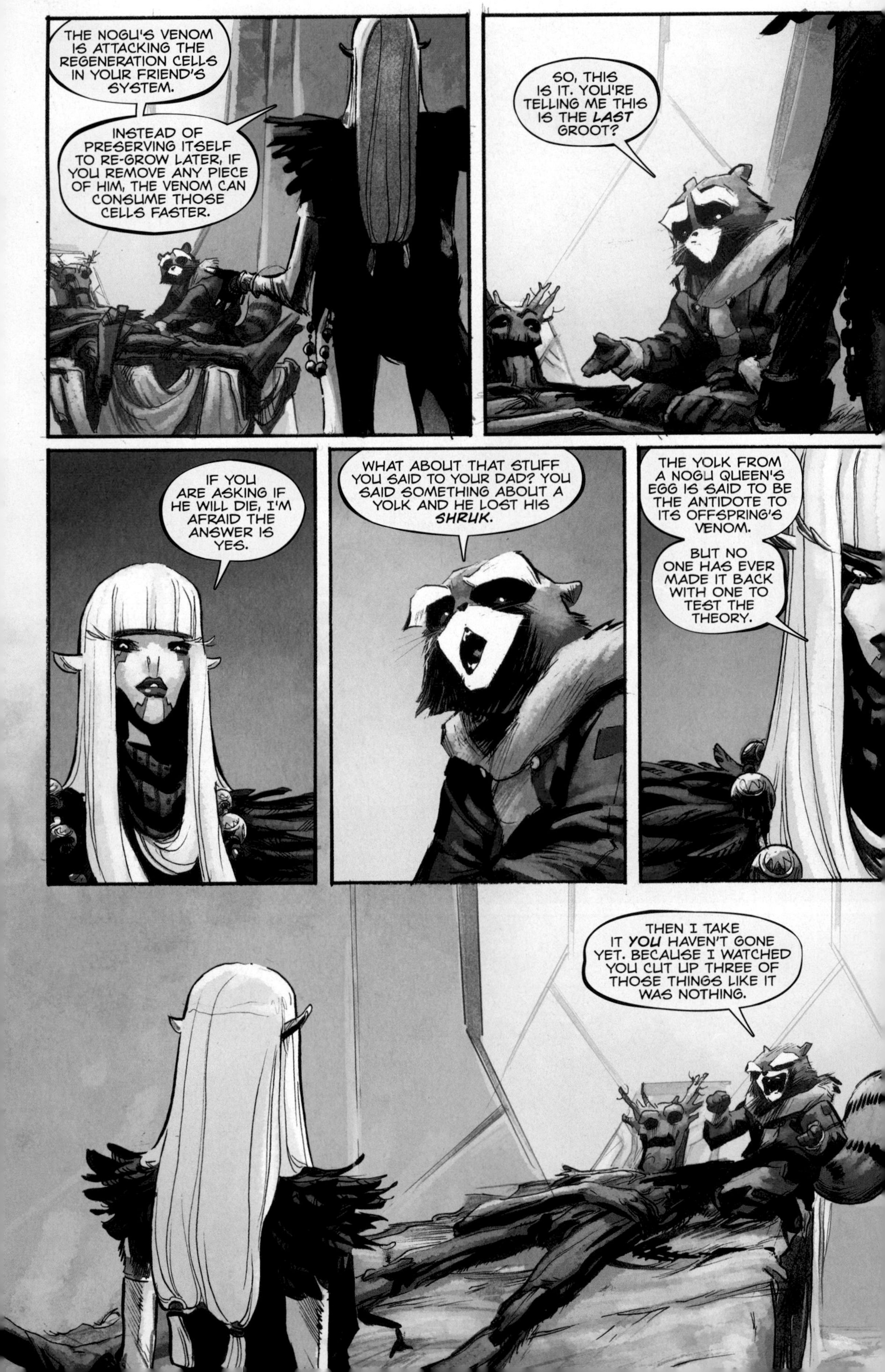
THE NOGU'S VENOM IS ATTACKING THE REGENERATION CELLS IN YOUR FRIEND'S SYSTEM.
INSTEAD OF PRESERVING ITSELF TO RE-GROW LATER, IF YOU REMOVE ANY PIECE OF HIM, THE VENOM CAN CONSUME THOSE CELLS FASTER.
SO, THIS IS IT. YOU'RE TELLING ME THIS IS THE ***LAST*** GROOT?
IF YOU ARE ASKING IF HE WILL DIE, I'M AFRAID THE ANSWER IS YES.
WHAT ABOUT THAT STUFF YOU SAID TO YOUR DAD? YOU SAID SOMETHING ABOUT A YOLK AND HE LOST HIS ***SHRUK***.
THE YOLK FROM A NOGU QUEEN'S EGG IS SAID TO BE THE ANTIDOTE TO ITS OFFSPRING'S VENOM.
BUT NO ONE HAS EVER MADE IT BACK WITH ONE TO TEST THE THEORY.
THEN I TAKE IT ***YOU*** HAVEN'T GONE YET. BECAUSE I WATCHED YOU CUT UP THREE OF THOSE THINGS LIKE IT WAS NOTHING.

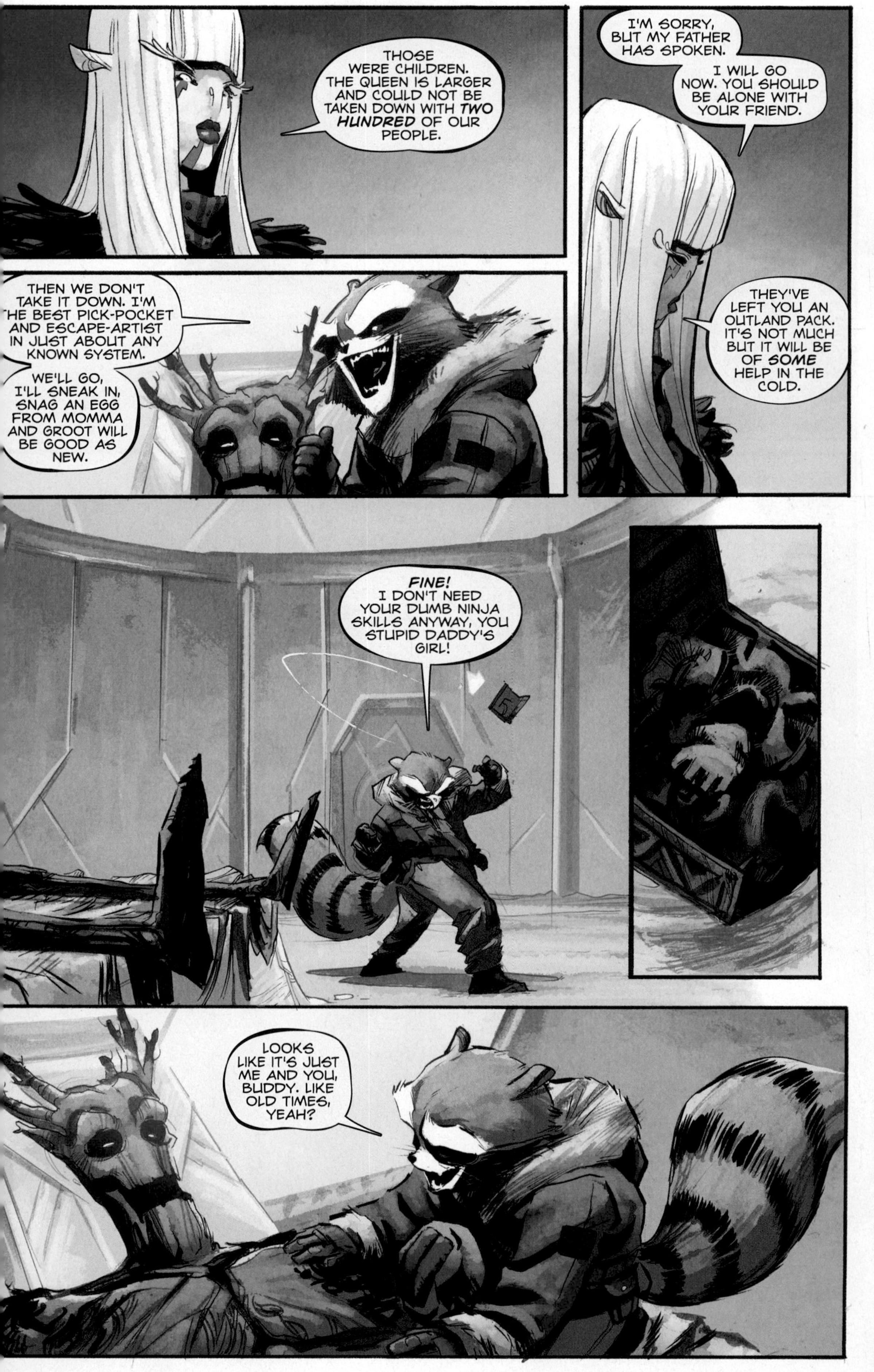
THOSE WERE CHILDREN. THE QUEEN IS LARGER AND COULD NOT BE TAKEN DOWN WITH *TWO HUNDRED* OF OUR PEOPLE.
I'M SORRY, BUT MY FATHER HAS SPOKEN.
I WILL GO NOW. YOU SHOULD BE ALONE WITH YOUR FRIEND.
THEN WE DON'T TAKE IT DOWN. I'M THE BEST PICK-POCKET AND ESCAPE-ARTIST IN JUST ABOUT ANY KNOWN SYSTEM.
WE'LL GO, I'LL SNEAK IN, SNAG AN EGG FROM MOMMA AND GROOT WILL BE GOOD AS NEW.
THEY'VE LEFT YOU AN OUTLAND PACK. IT'S NOT MUCH BUT IT WILL BE OF *SOME* HELP IN THE COLD.
FINE! I DON'T NEED YOUR DUMB NINJA SKILLS ANYWAY, YOU STUPID DADDY'S GIRL!
LOOKS LIKE IT'S JUST ME AND YOU, BUDDY. LIKE OLD TIMES, YEAH?

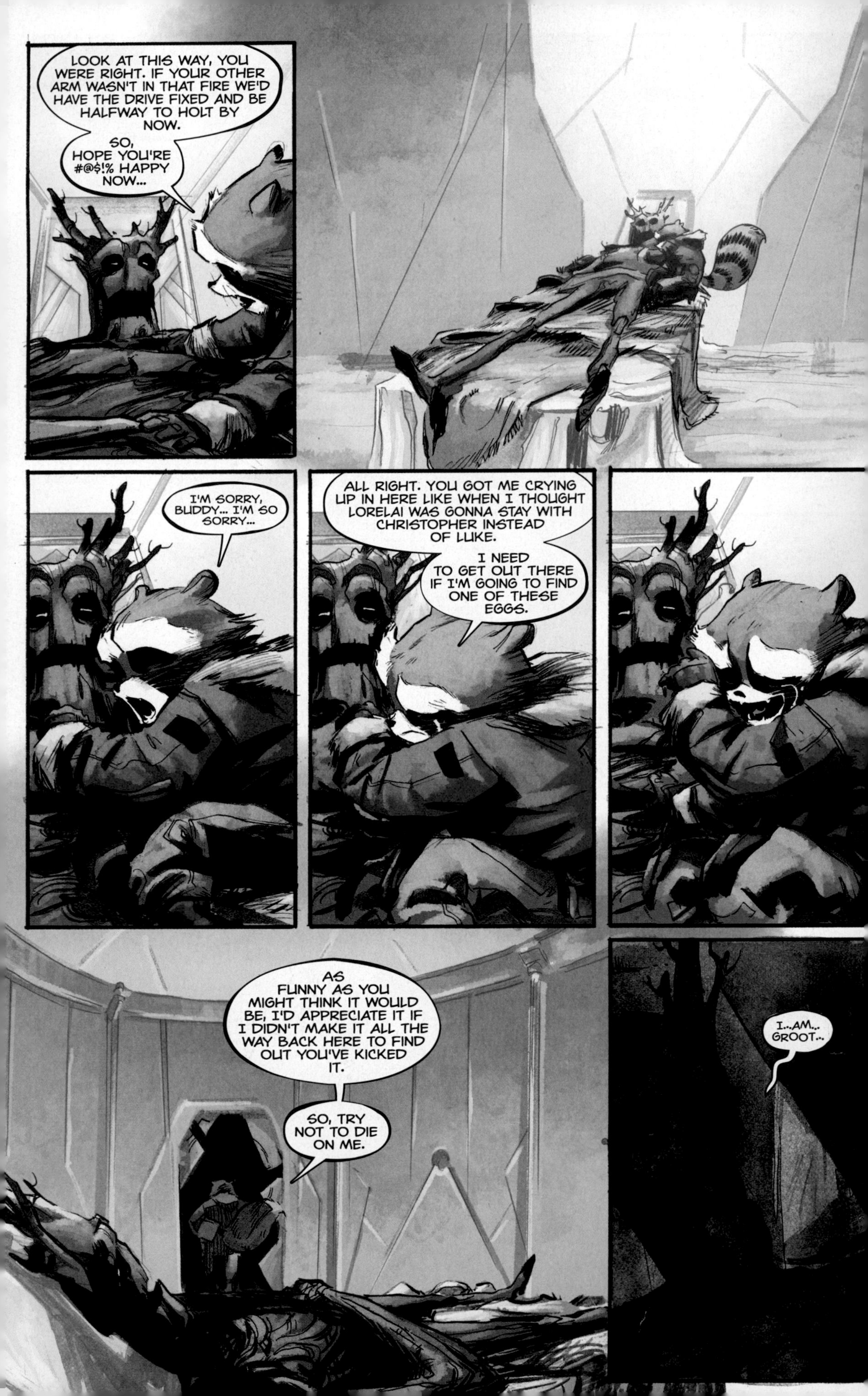
LOOK AT THIS WAY, YOU WERE RIGHT. IF YOUR OTHER ARM WASN'T IN THAT FIRE WE'D HAVE THE DRIVE FIXED AND BE HALFWAY TO HOLT BY NOW.
SO, HOPE YOU'RE #@$!% HAPPY NOW...
I'M SORRY, BUDDY... I'M SO SORRY...
ALL RIGHT. YOU GOT ME CRYING UP IN HERE LIKE WHEN I THOUGHT LORELAI WAS GONNA STAY WITH CHRISTOPHER INSTEAD OF LUKE.
I NEED TO GET OUT THERE IF I'M GOING TO FIND ONE OF THESE EGGS.
AS FUNNY AS YOU MIGHT THINK IT WOULD BE, I'D APPRECIATE IT IF I DIDN'T MAKE IT ALL THE WAY BACK HERE TO FIND OUT YOU'VE KICKED IT.
SO, TRY NOT TO DIE ON ME.
I...AM... GROOT...

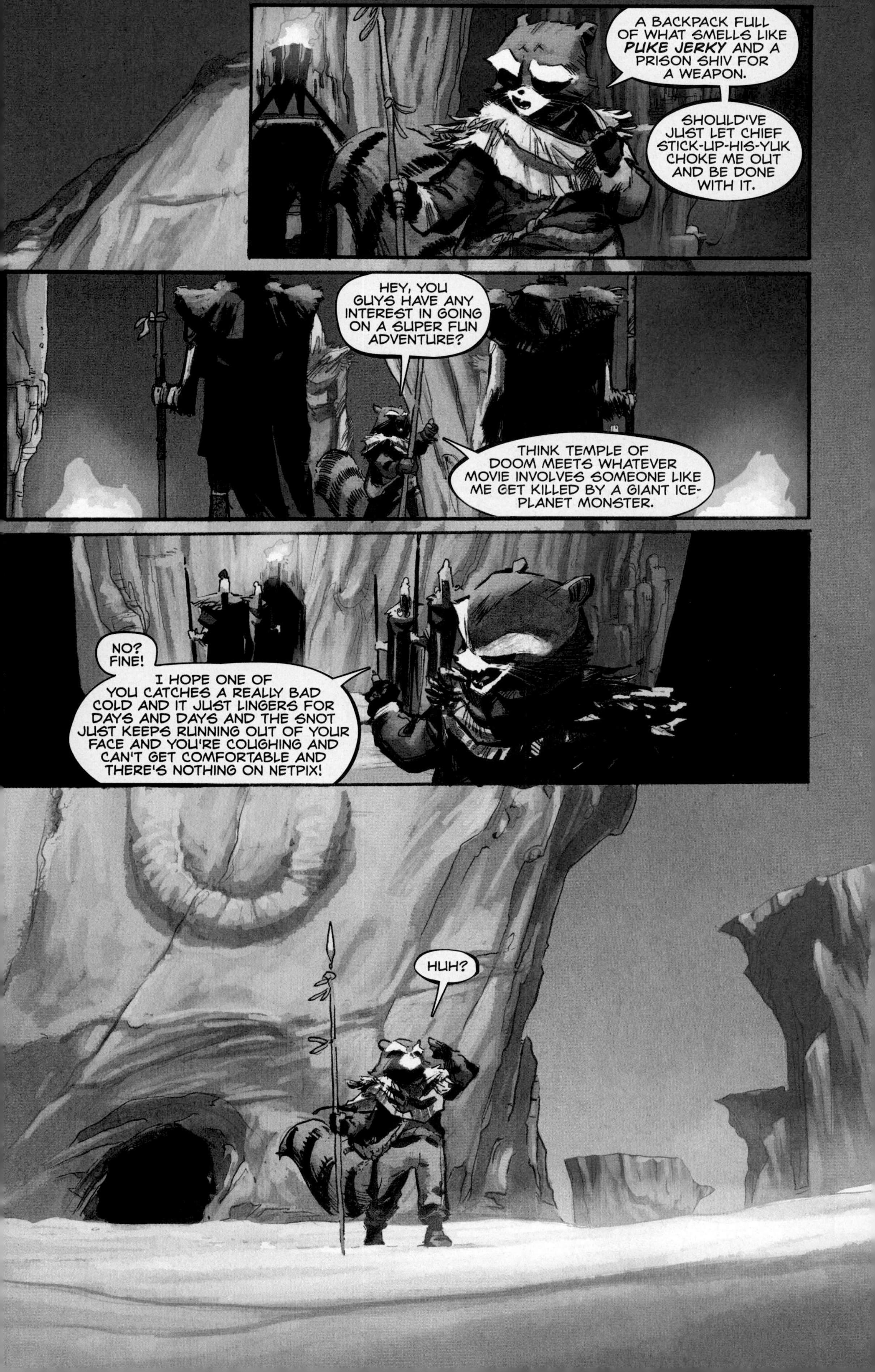

A BACKPACK FULL OF WHAT SMELLS LIKE **PUKE JERKY** AND A PRISON SHIV FOR A WEAPON.
SHOULD'VE JUST LET CHIEF STICK-UP-HIS-YUK CHOKE ME OUT AND BE DONE WITH IT.
HEY, YOU GUYS HAVE ANY INTEREST IN GOING ON A SUPER FUN ADVENTURE?
THINK TEMPLE OF DOOM MEETS WHATEVER MOVIE INVOLVES SOMEONE LIKE ME GET KILLED BY A GIANT ICE-PLANET MONSTER.
NO? FINE!
I HOPE ONE OF YOU CATCHES A REALLY BAD COLD AND IT JUST LINGERS FOR DAYS AND DAYS AND THE SNOT JUST KEEPS RUNNING OUT OF YOUR FACE AND YOU'RE COUGHING AND CAN'T GET COMFORTABLE AND THERE'S NOTHING ON NETPIX!
HUH?

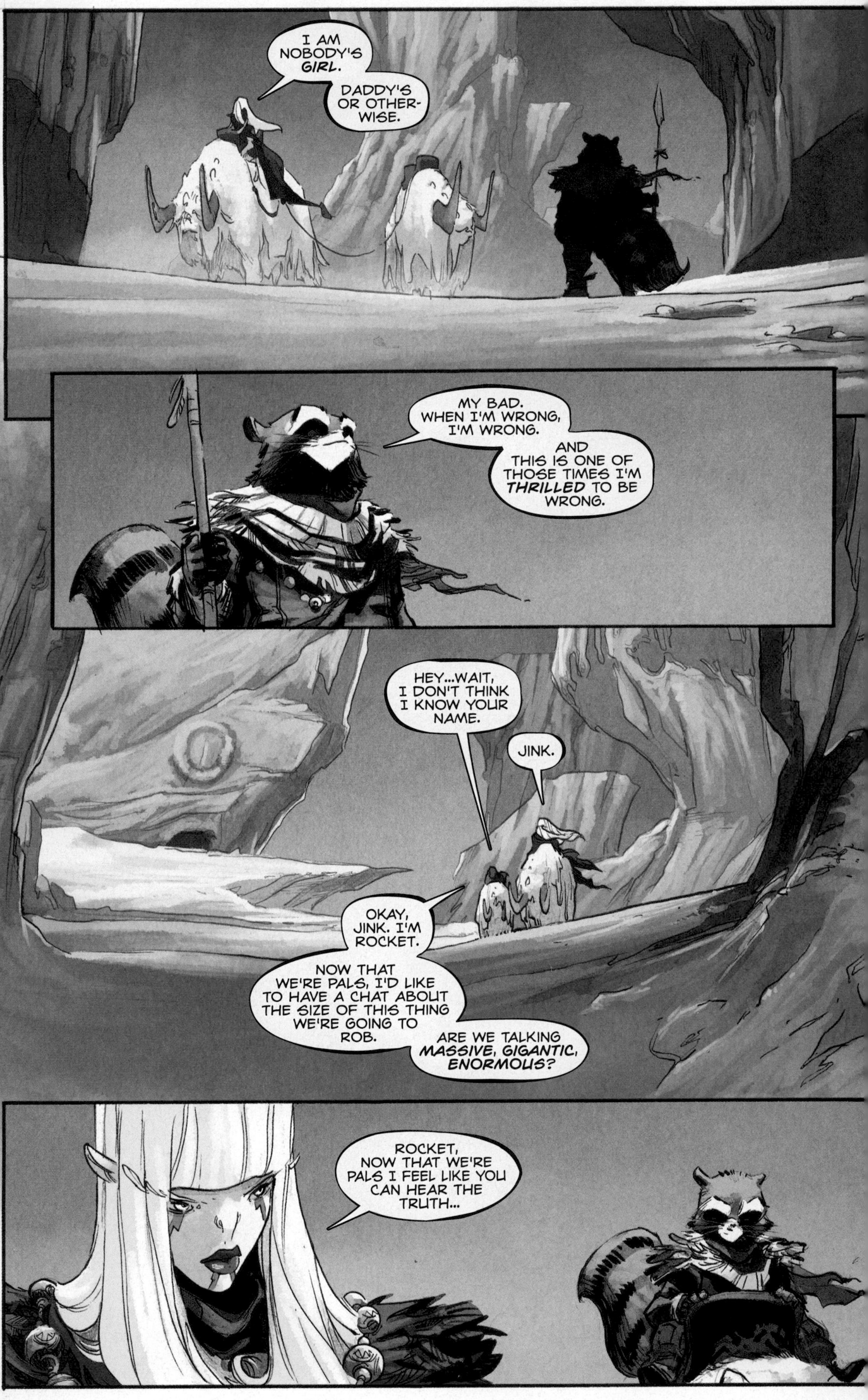
I AM NOBODY'S GIRL.
DADDY'S OR OTHER-WISE.
MY BAD. WHEN I'M WRONG, I'M WRONG.
AND THIS IS ONE OF THOSE TIMES I'M THRILLED TO BE WRONG.
HEY...WAIT, I DON'T THINK I KNOW YOUR NAME.
JINK.
OKAY, JINK. I'M ROCKET.
NOW THAT WE'RE PALS, I'D LIKE TO HAVE A CHAT ABOUT THE SIZE OF THIS THING WE'RE GOING TO ROB.
ARE WE TALKING MASSIVE, GIGANTIC, ENORMOUS?
ROCKET, NOW THAT WE'RE PALS I FEEL LIKE YOU CAN HEAR THE TRUTH...

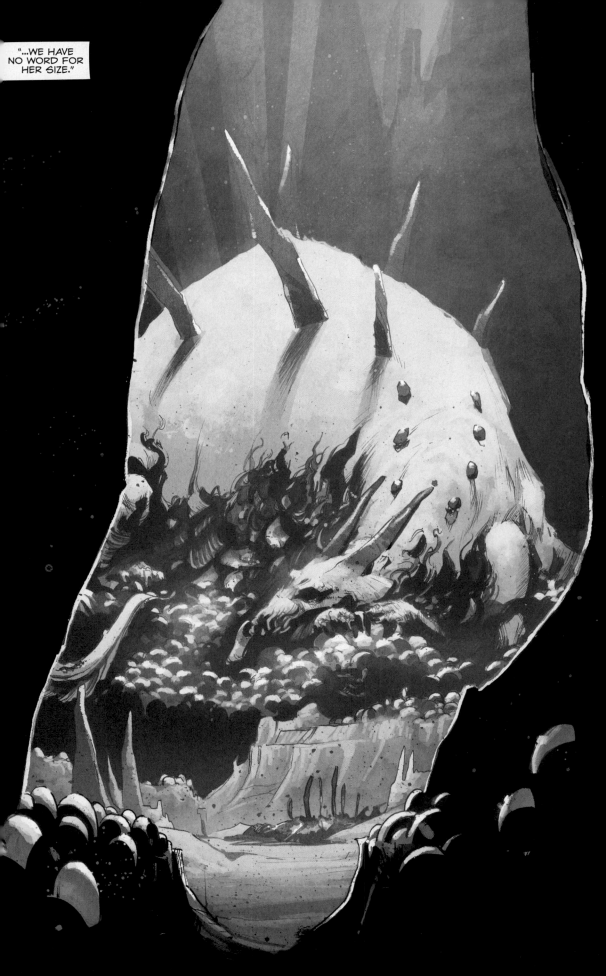

"...WE HAVE NO WORD FOR HER SIZE."

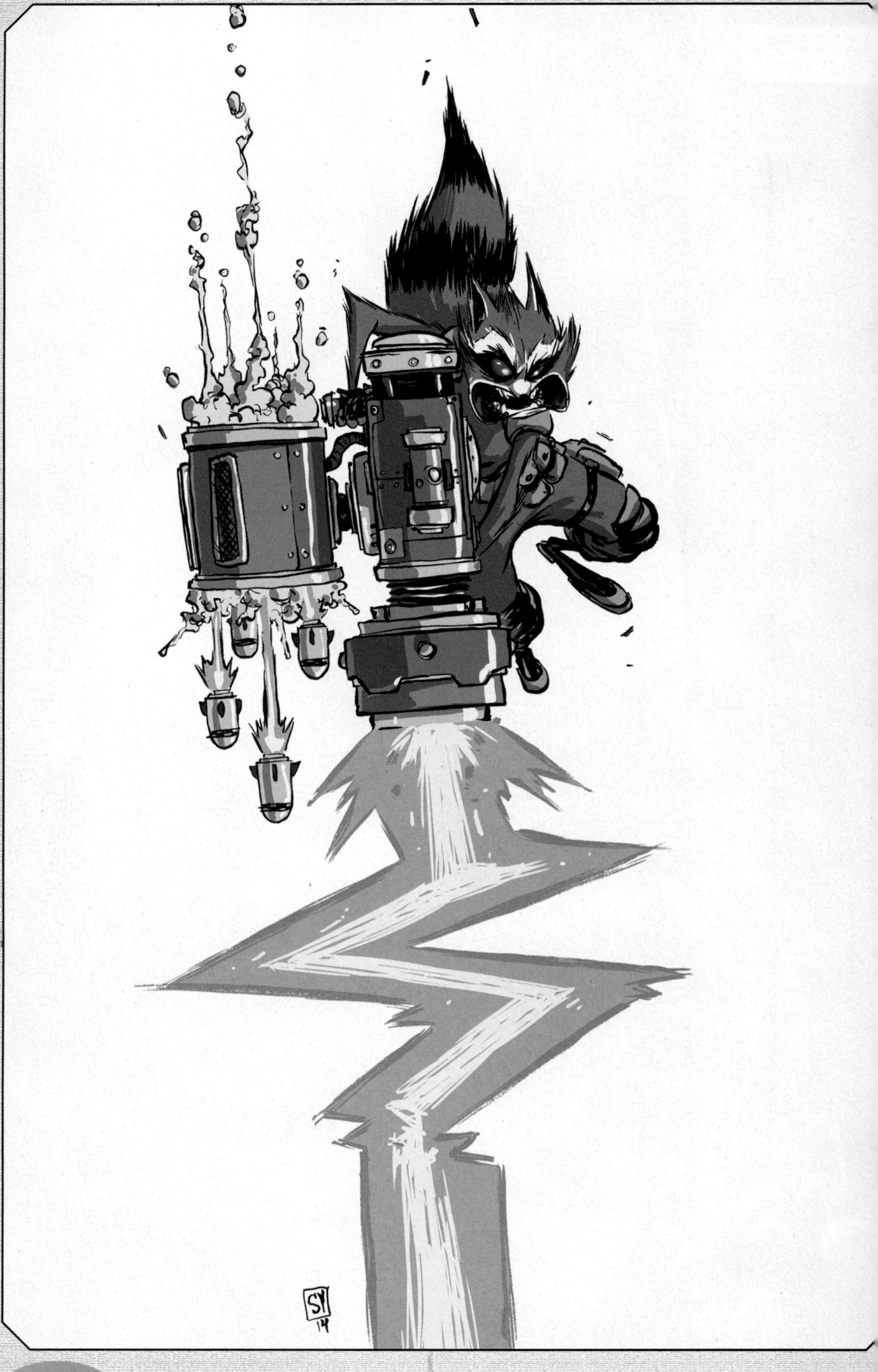

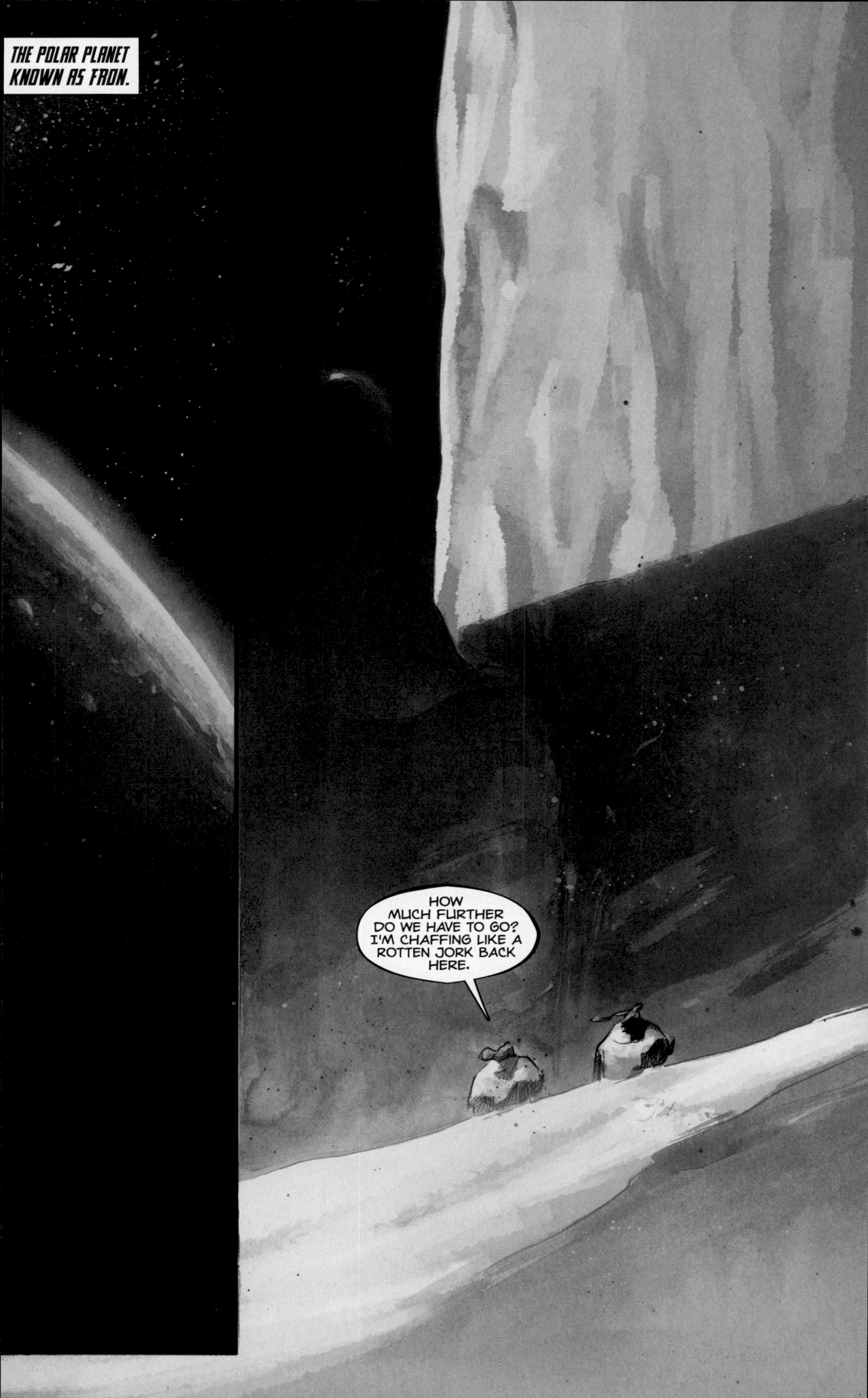
THE POLAR PLANET KNOWN AS FRON.
HOW MUCH FURTHER DO WE HAVE TO GO? I'M CHAFFING LIKE A ROTTEN JORK BACK HERE.

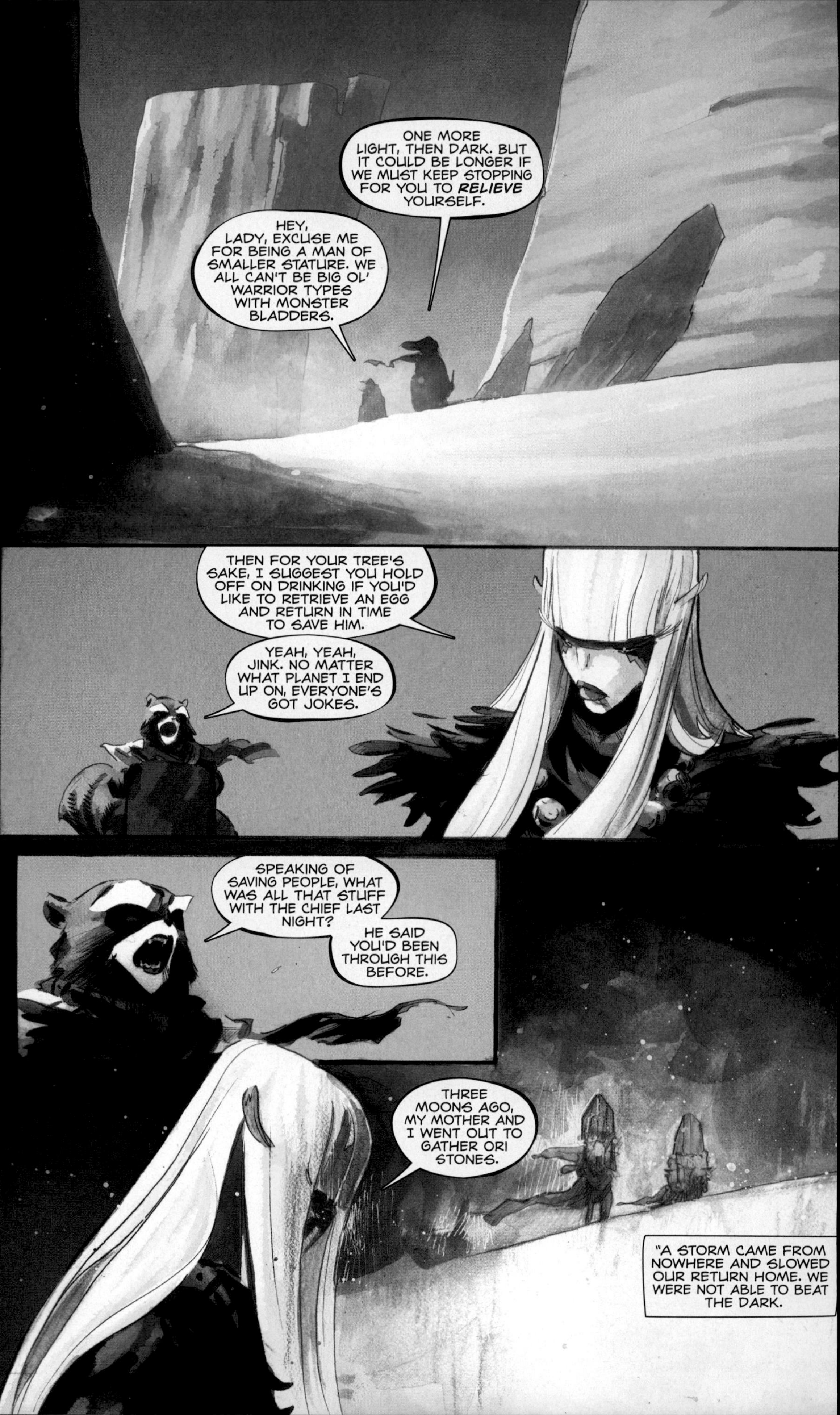
ONE MORE LIGHT, THEN DARK. BUT IT COULD BE LONGER IF WE MUST KEEP STOPPING FOR YOU TO ***RELIEVE*** YOURSELF.
HEY, LADY, EXCUSE ME FOR BEING A MAN OF SMALLER STATURE. WE ALL CAN'T BE BIG OL' WARRIOR TYPES WITH MONSTER BLADDERS.
THEN FOR YOUR TREE'S SAKE, I SUGGEST YOU HOLD OFF ON DRINKING IF YOU'D LIKE TO RETRIEVE AN EGG AND RETURN IN TIME TO SAVE HIM.
YEAH, YEAH, JINK. NO MATTER WHAT PLANET I END UP ON, EVERYONE'S GOT JOKES.
SPEAKING OF SAVING PEOPLE, WHAT WAS ALL THAT STUFF WITH THE CHIEF LAST NIGHT?
HE SAID YOU'D BEEN THROUGH THIS BEFORE.
THREE MOONS AGO, MY MOTHER AND I WENT OUT TO GATHER ORI STONES.
"A STORM CAME FROM NOWHERE AND SLOWED OUR RETURN HOME. WE WERE NOT ABLE TO BEAT THE DARK.

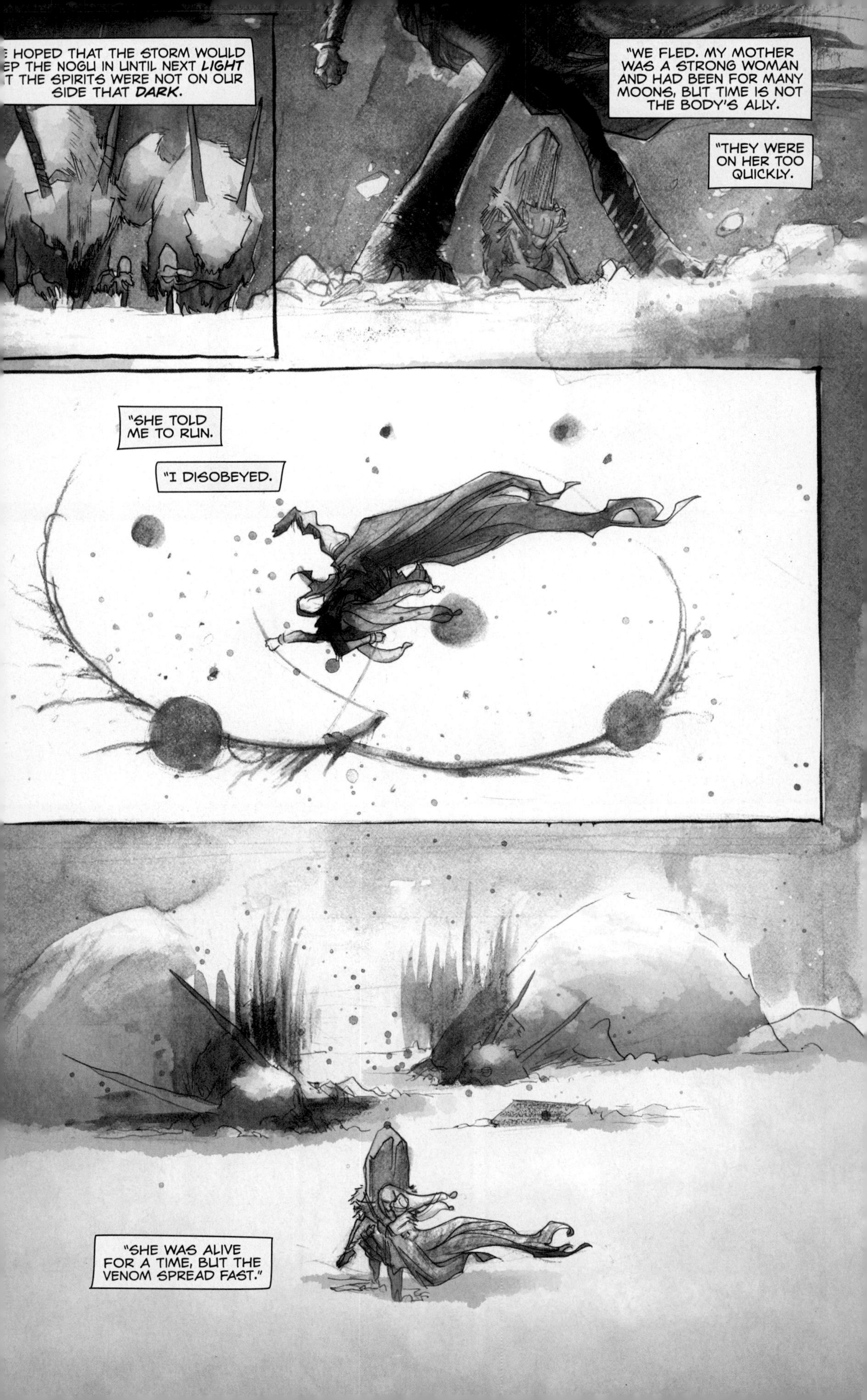
E HOPED THAT THE STORM WOULD EP THE NOGU IN UNTIL NEXT LIGHT T THE SPIRITS WERE NOT ON OUR SIDE THAT DARK.
"WE FLED. MY MOTHER WAS A STRONG WOMAN AND HAD BEEN FOR MANY MOONS, BUT TIME IS NOT THE BODY'S ALLY.
"THEY WERE ON HER TOO QUICKLY.
"SHE TOLD ME TO RUN.
"I DISOBEYED.
"SHE WAS ALIVE FOR A TIME, BUT THE VENOM SPREAD FAST."

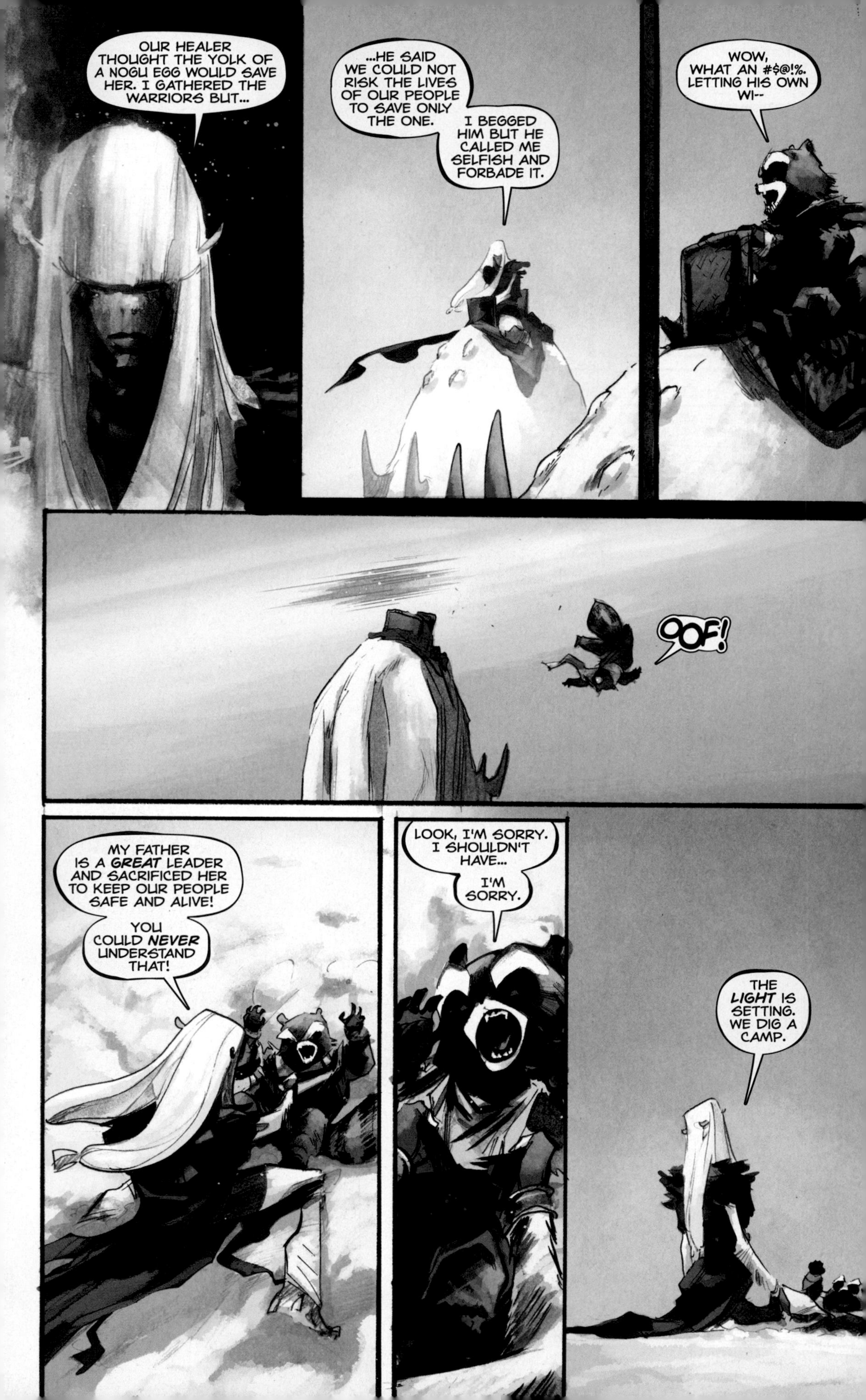
OUR HEALER THOUGHT THE YOLK OF A NOGU EGG WOULD SAVE HER. I GATHERED THE WARRIORS BUT...
...HE SAID WE COULD NOT RISK THE LIVES OF OUR PEOPLE TO SAVE ONLY THE ONE.
I BEGGED HIM BUT HE CALLED ME SELFISH AND FORBADE IT.
WOW, WHAT AN #$@!%. LETTING HIS OWN WI--
OOF!
MY FATHER IS A GREAT LEADER AND SACRIFICED HER TO KEEP OUR PEOPLE SAFE AND ALIVE!
YOU COULD NEVER UNDERSTAND THAT!
LOOK, I'M SORRY. I SHOULDN'T HAVE...
I'M SORRY.
THE LIGHT IS SETTING. WE DIG A CAMP.

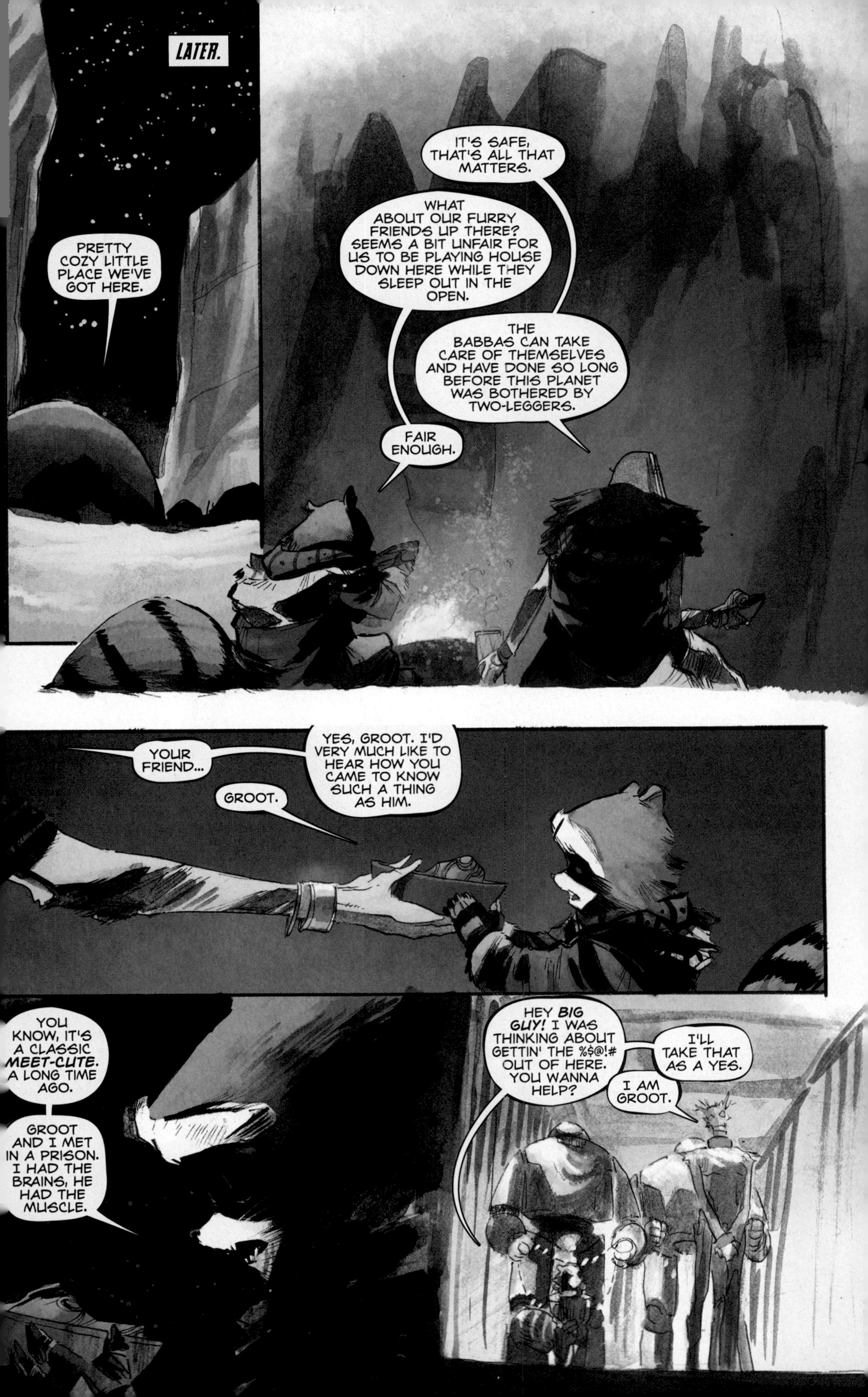
LATER.
PRETTY COZY LITTLE PLACE WE'VE GOT HERE.
IT'S SAFE, THAT'S ALL THAT MATTERS.
WHAT ABOUT OUR FURRY FRIENDS UP THERE? SEEMS A BIT UNFAIR FOR US TO BE PLAYING HOUSE DOWN HERE WHILE THEY SLEEP OUT IN THE OPEN.
THE BABBAS CAN TAKE CARE OF THEMSELVES AND HAVE DONE SO LONG BEFORE THIS PLANET WAS BOTHERED BY TWO-LEGGERS.
FAIR ENOUGH.
YOUR FRIEND...
GROOT.
YES, GROOT. I'D VERY MUCH LIKE TO HEAR HOW YOU CAME TO KNOW SUCH A THING AS HIM.
YOU KNOW, IT'S A CLASSIC MEET-CUTE. A LONG TIME AGO.
GROOT AND I MET IN A PRISON. I HAD THE BRAINS, HE HAD THE MUSCLE.
HEY BIG GUY! I WAS THINKING ABOUT GETTIN' THE %$@!# OUT OF HERE. YOU WANNA HELP?
I AM GROOT.
I'LL TAKE THAT AS A YES.

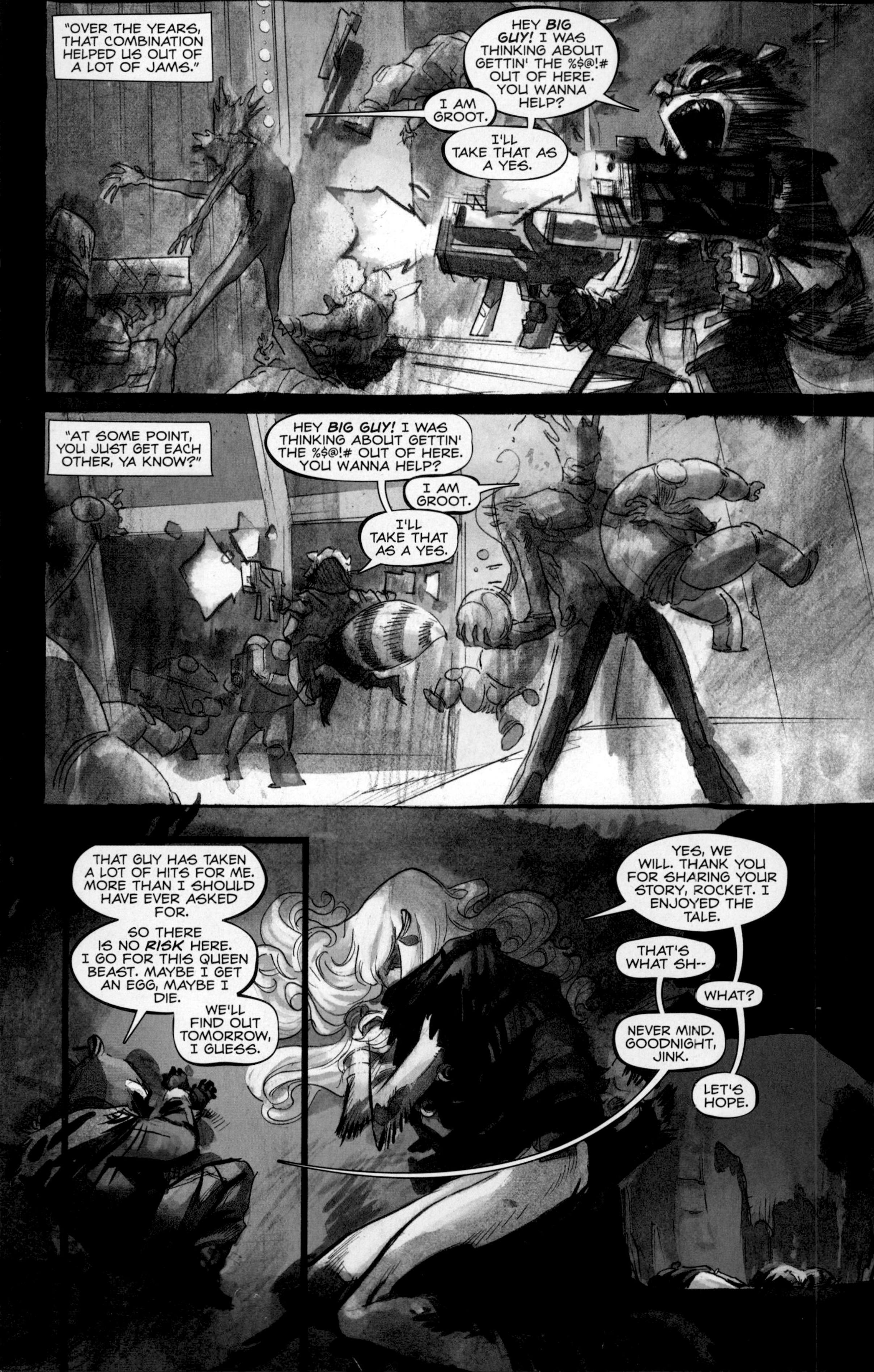

"OVER THE YEARS, THAT COMBINATION HELPED US OUT OF A LOT OF JAMS."
HEY BIG GUY! I WAS THINKING ABOUT GETTIN' THE %$@!# OUT OF HERE. YOU WANNA HELP?
I AM GROOT.
I'LL TAKE THAT AS A YES.
"AT SOME POINT, YOU JUST GET EACH OTHER, YA KNOW?"
HEY BIG GUY! I WAS THINKING ABOUT GETTIN' THE %$@!# OUT OF HERE. YOU WANNA HELP?
I AM GROOT.
I'LL TAKE THAT AS A YES.
THAT GUY HAS TAKEN A LOT OF HITS FOR ME. MORE THAN I SHOULD HAVE EVER ASKED FOR.
SO THERE IS NO RISK HERE. I GO FOR THIS QUEEN BEAST. MAYBE I GET AN EGG, MAYBE I DIE.
WE'LL FIND OUT TOMORROW, I GUESS.
YES, WE WILL. THANK YOU FOR SHARING YOUR STORY, ROCKET. I ENJOYED THE TALE.
THAT'S WHAT SH--
WHAT?
NEVER MIND. GOODNIGHT, JINK.
LET'S HOPE.

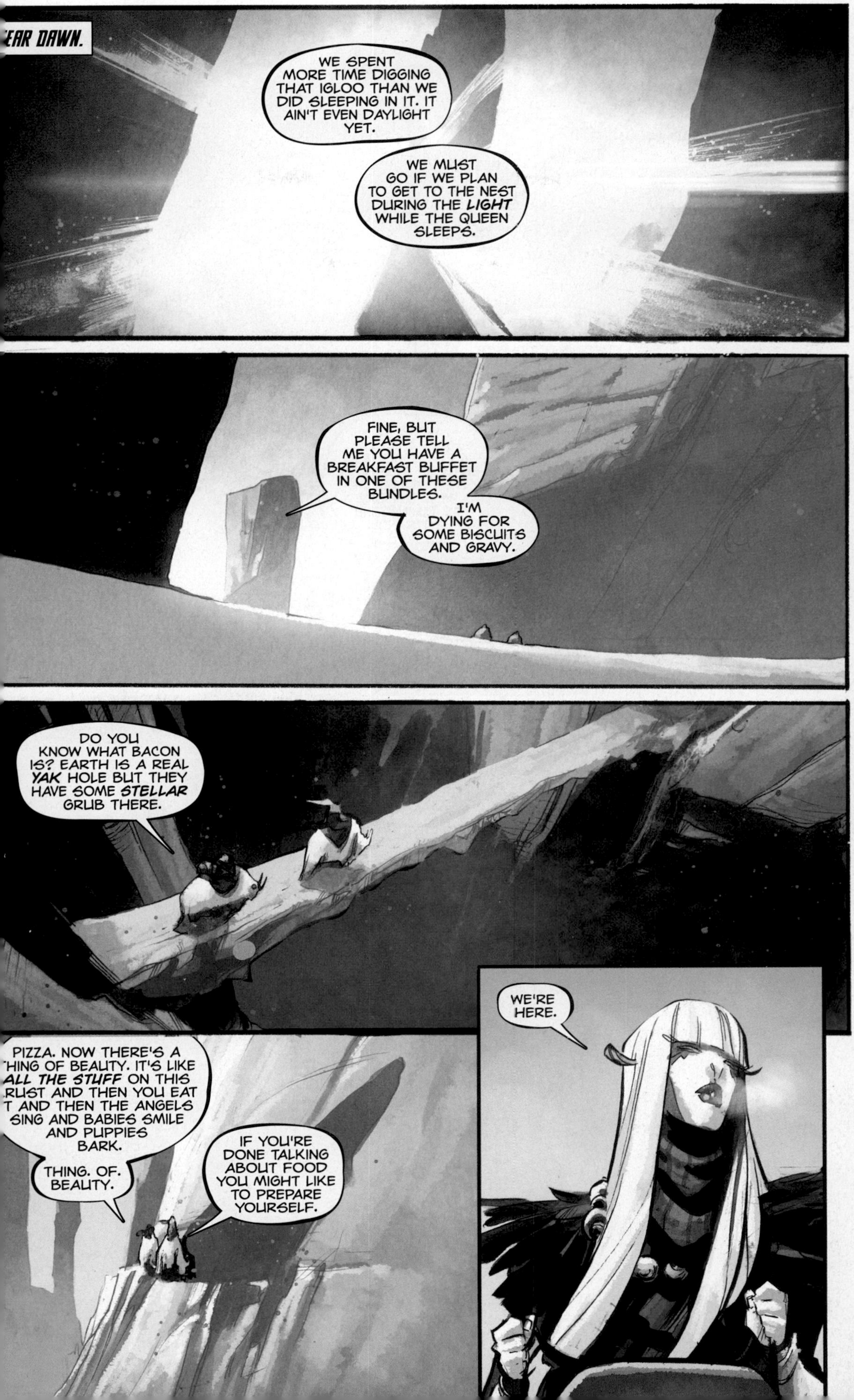

EAR DAWN.
WE SPENT MORE TIME DIGGING THAT IGLOO THAN WE DID SLEEPING IN IT. IT AIN'T EVEN DAYLIGHT YET.
WE MUST GO IF WE PLAN TO GET TO THE NEST DURING THE LIGHT WHILE THE QUEEN SLEEPS.
FINE, BUT PLEASE TELL ME YOU HAVE A BREAKFAST BUFFET IN ONE OF THESE BUNDLES.
I'M DYING FOR SOME BISCUITS AND GRAVY.
DO YOU KNOW WHAT BACON IS? EARTH IS A REAL YAK HOLE BUT THEY HAVE SOME STELLAR GRUB THERE.
PIZZA. NOW THERE'S A THING OF BEAUTY. IT'S LIKE ALL THE STUFF ON THIS CRUST AND THEN YOU EAT IT AND THEN THE ANGELS SING AND BABIES SMILE AND PUPPIES BARK.
THING. OF. BEAUTY.
IF YOU'RE DONE TALKING ABOUT FOOD YOU MIGHT LIKE TO PREPARE YOURSELF.
WE'RE HERE.

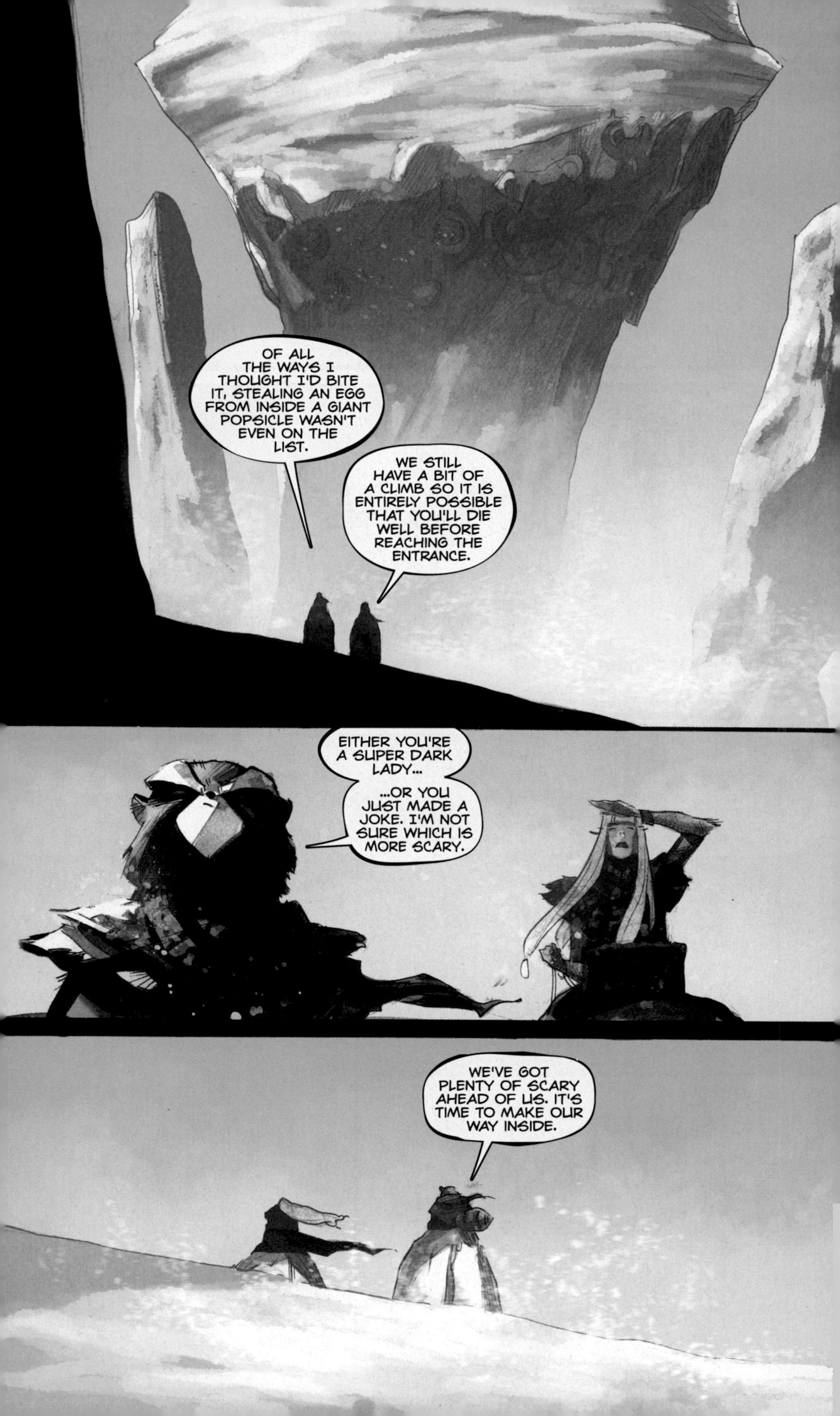
OF ALL THE WAYS I THOUGHT I'D BITE IT, STEALING AN EGG FROM INSIDE A GIANT POPSICLE WASN'T EVEN ON THE LIST.
WE STILL HAVE A BIT OF A CLIMB SO IT IS ENTIRELY POSSIBLE THAT YOU'LL DIE WELL BEFORE REACHING THE ENTRANCE.
EITHER YOU'RE A SUPER DARK LADY...
...OR YOU JUST MADE A JOKE. I'M NOT SURE WHICH IS MORE SCARY.
WE'VE GOT PLENTY OF SCARY AHEAD OF US. IT'S TIME TO MAKE OUR WAY INSIDE.

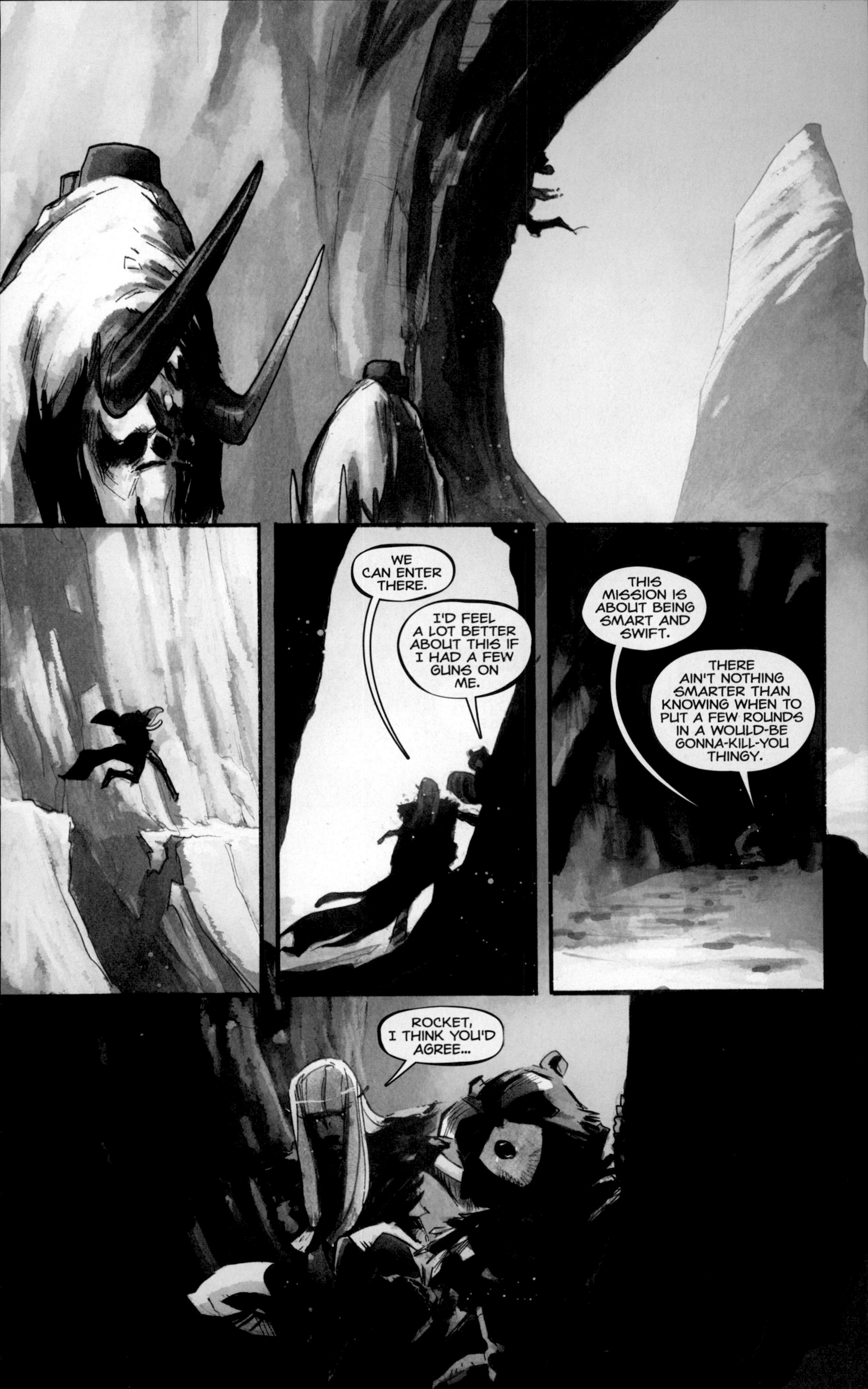
WE CAN ENTER THERE.
I'D FEEL A LOT BETTER ABOUT THIS IF I HAD A FEW GUNS ON ME.
THIS MISSION IS ABOUT BEING SMART AND SWIFT.
THERE AIN'T NOTHING SMARTER THAN KNOWING WHEN TO PUT A FEW ROUNDS IN A WOULD-BE GONNA-KILL-YOU THINGY.
ROCKET, I THINK YOU'D AGREE...

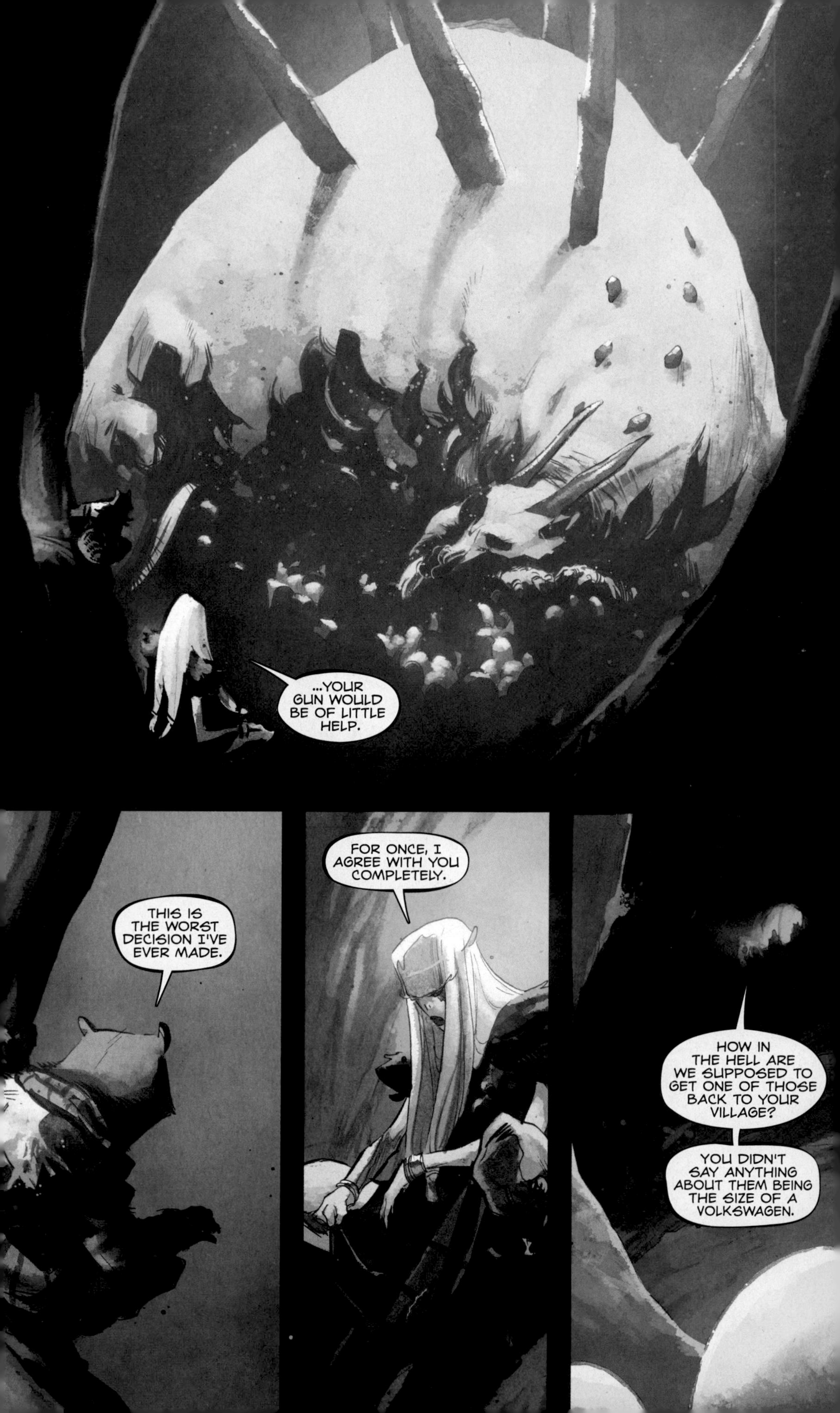
...YOUR GUN WOULD BE OF LITTLE HELP.
THIS IS THE WORST DECISION I'VE EVER MADE.
FOR ONCE, I AGREE WITH YOU COMPLETELY.
HOW IN THE HELL ARE WE SUPPOSED TO GET ONE OF THOSE BACK TO YOUR VILLAGE?
YOU DIDN'T SAY ANYTHING ABOUT THEM BEING THE SIZE OF A VOLKSWAGEN.

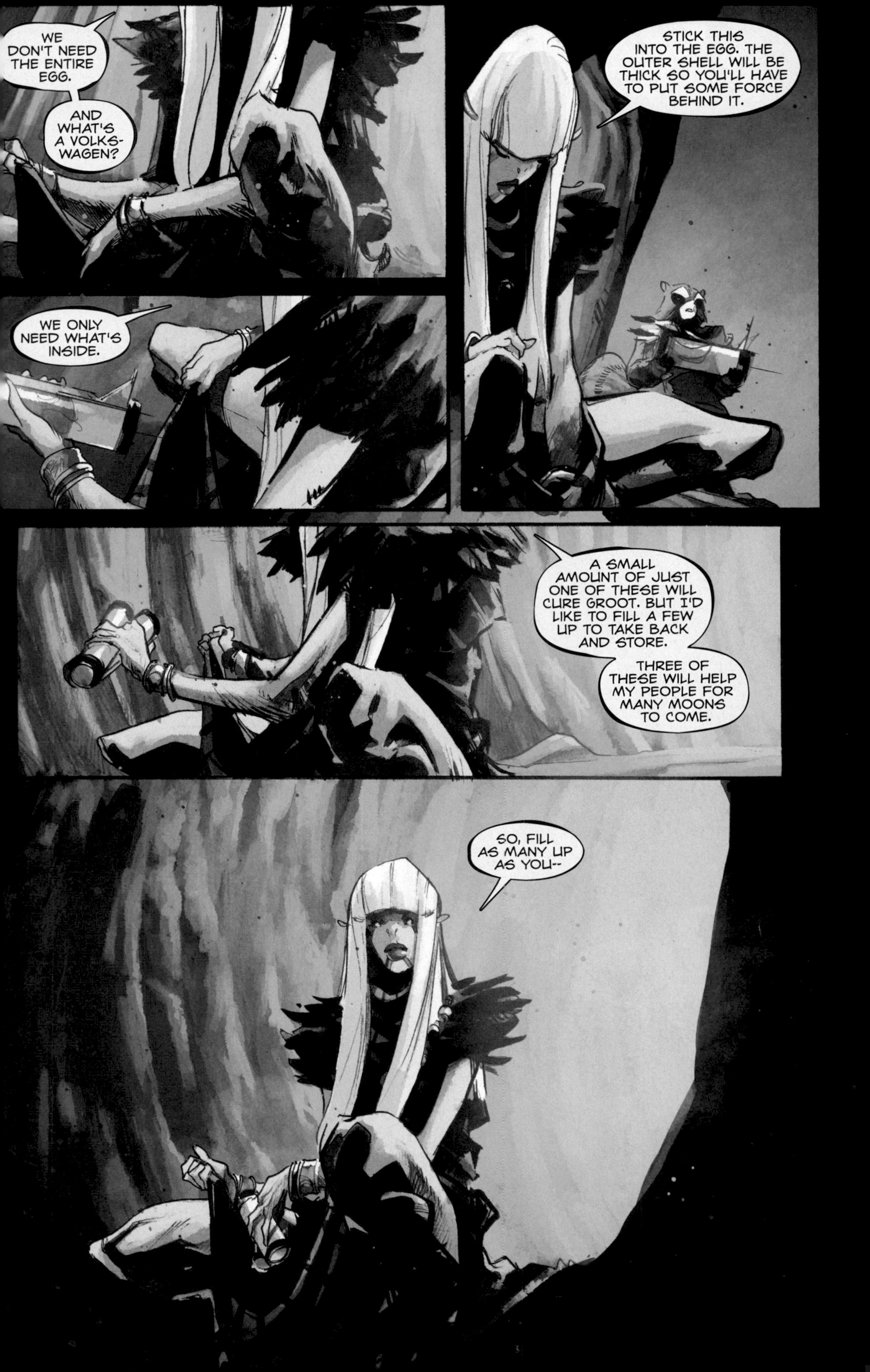
WE DON'T NEED THE ENTIRE EGG.
AND WHAT'S A VOLKS-WAGEN?
STICK THIS INTO THE EGG. THE OUTER SHELL WILL BE THICK SO YOU'LL HAVE TO PUT SOME FORCE BEHIND IT.
WE ONLY NEED WHAT'S INSIDE.
A SMALL AMOUNT OF JUST ONE OF THESE WILL CURE GROOT. BUT I'D LIKE TO FILL A FEW UP TO TAKE BACK AND STORE.
THREE OF THESE WILL HELP MY PEOPLE FOR MANY MOONS TO COME.
SO, FILL AS MANY UP AS YOU--

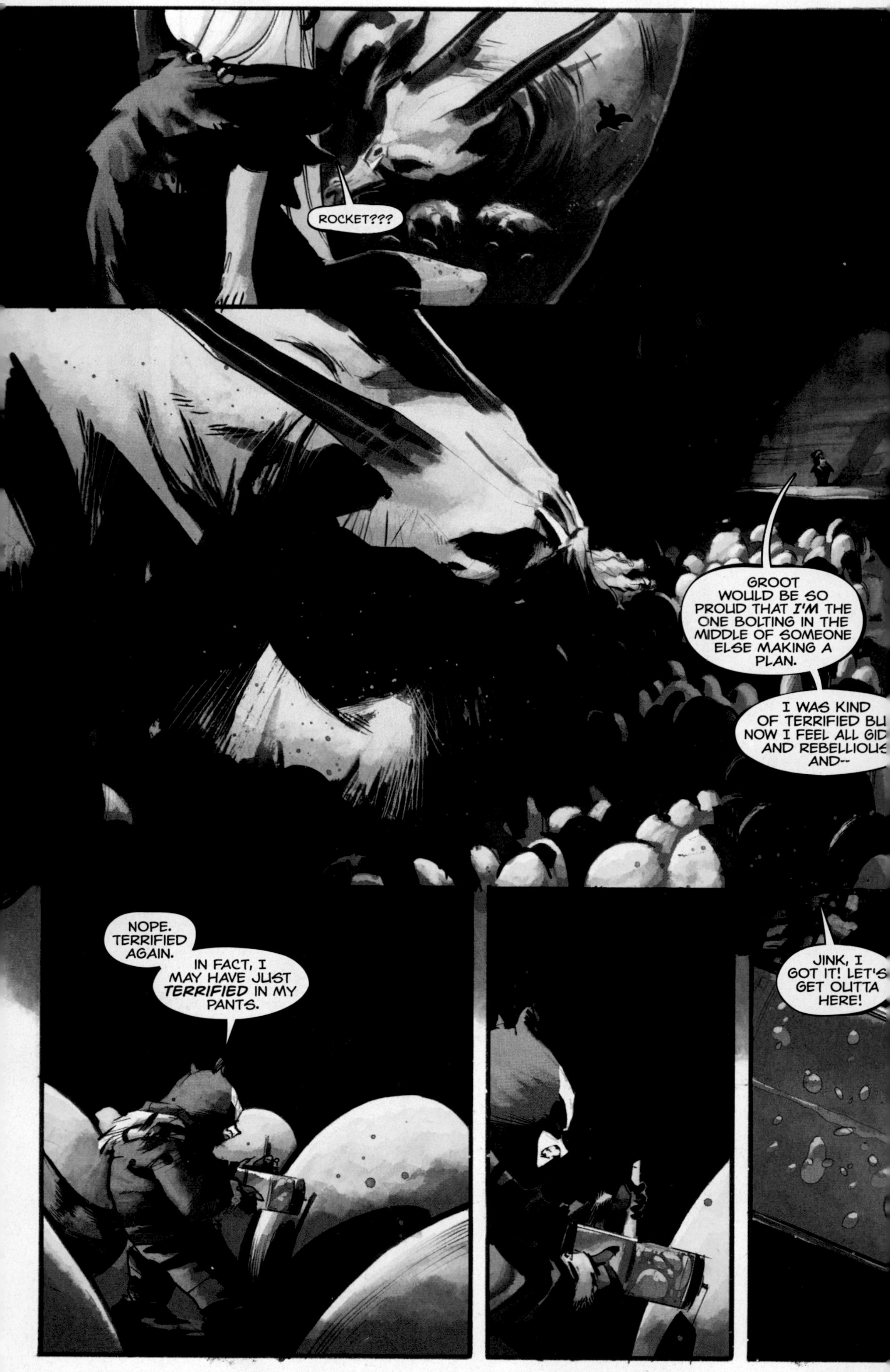
ROCKET???
GROOT WOULD BE SO PROUD THAT I'M THE ONE BOLTING IN THE MIDDLE OF SOMEONE ELSE MAKING A PLAN.
I WAS KIND OF TERRIFIED BU NOW I FEEL ALL GID AND REBELLIOU AND--
NOPE. TERRIFIED AGAIN.
IN FACT, I MAY HAVE JUST TERRIFIED IN MY PANTS.
JINK, I GOT IT! LET'S GET OUTTA HERE!

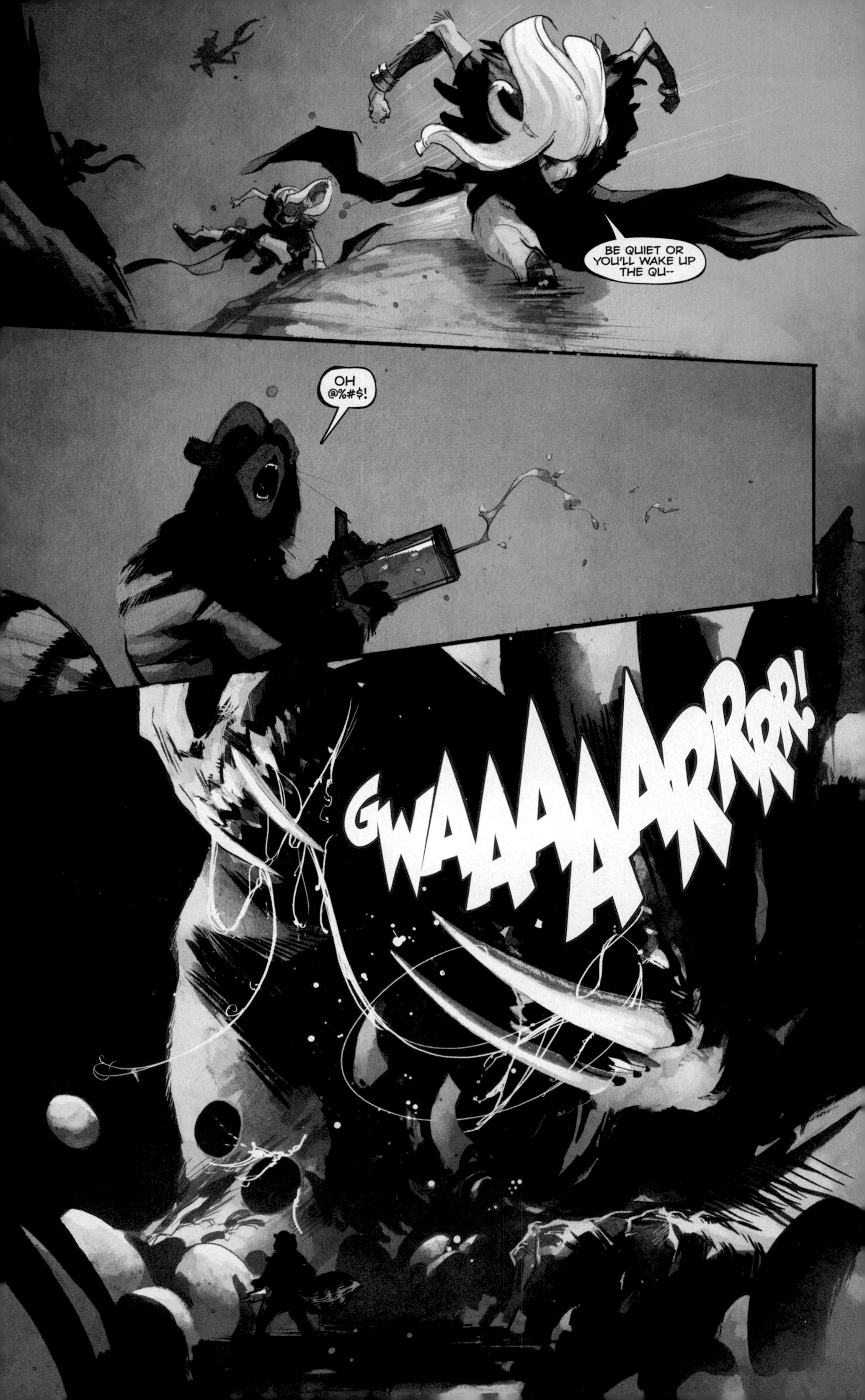
BE QUIET OR YOU'LL WAKE UP THE QU--
OH @%#$!
GWAAAAARRRR!

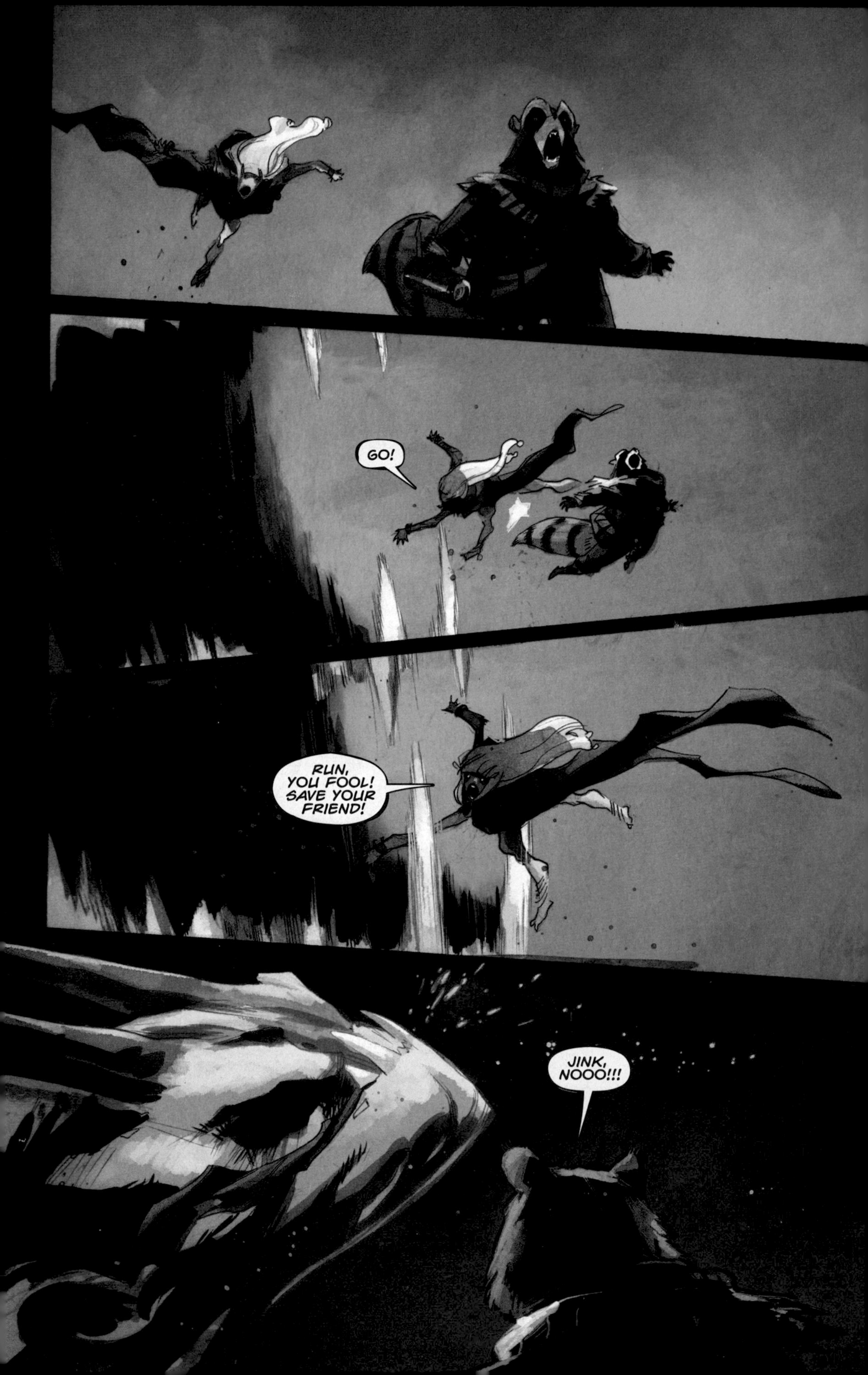
GO!
RUN, YOU FOOL! SAVE YOUR FRIEND!
JINK, NOOO!!!

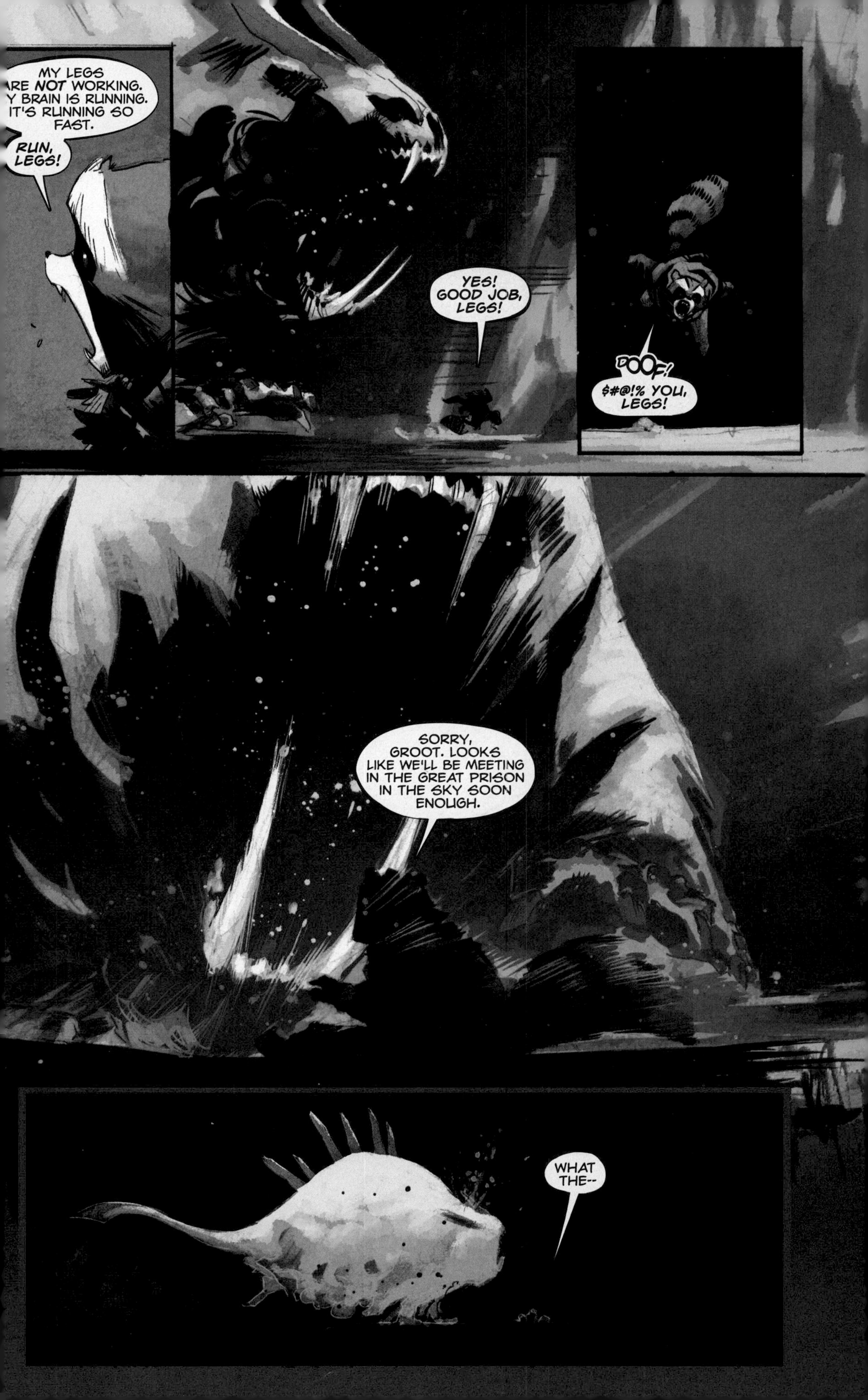
MY LEGS
ARE NOT WORKING.
Y BRAIN IS RUNNING.
IT'S RUNNING SO
FAST.
RUN,
LEGS!
YES!
GOOD JOB,
LEGS!
DOOF!
$#@!% YOU,
LEGS!
SORRY,
GROOT. LOOKS
LIKE WE'LL BE MEETING
IN THE GREAT PRISON
IN THE SKY SOON
ENOUGH.
WHAT
THE--

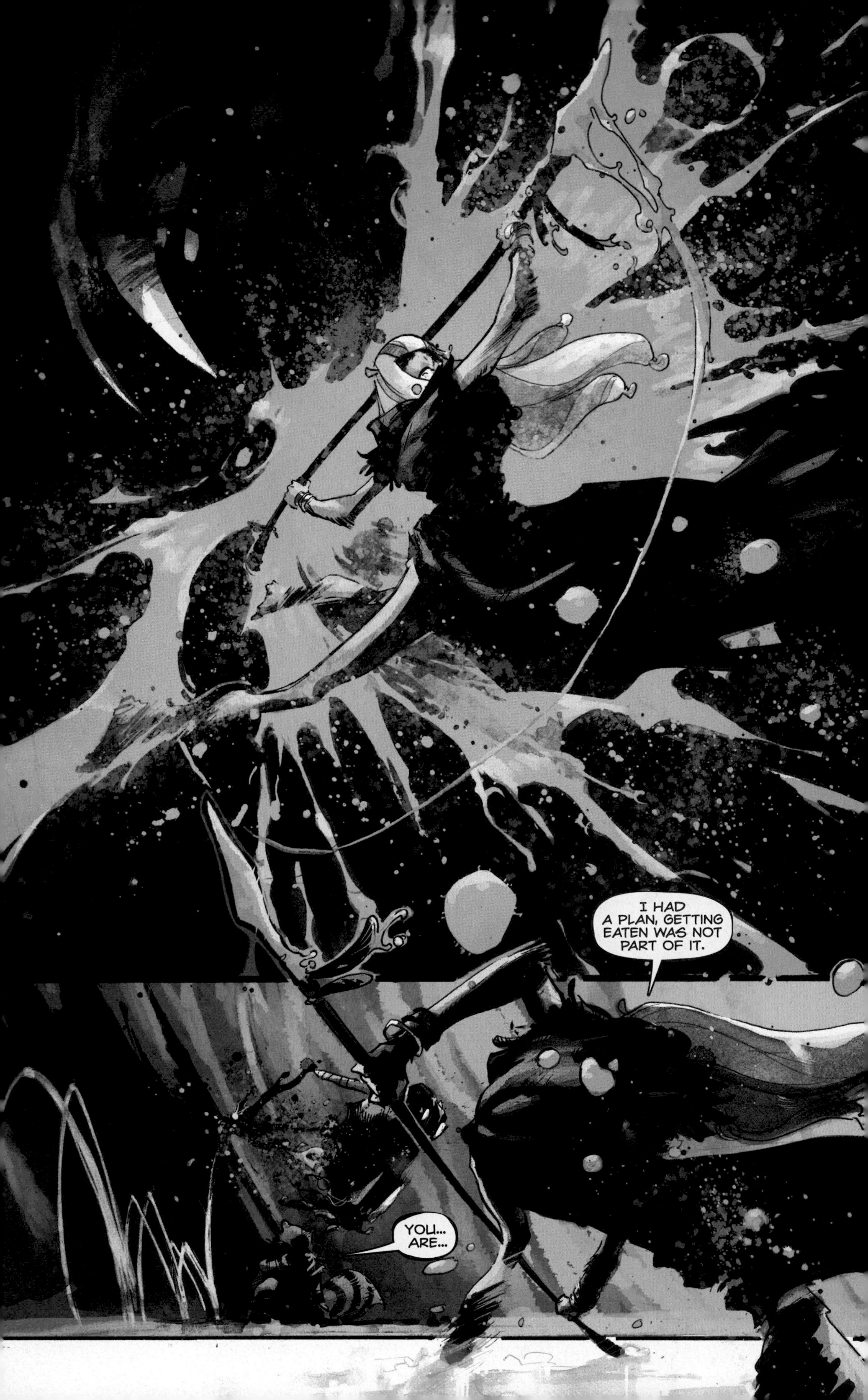
I HAD A PLAN, GETTING EATEN WAS NOT PART OF IT.
YOU... ARE...

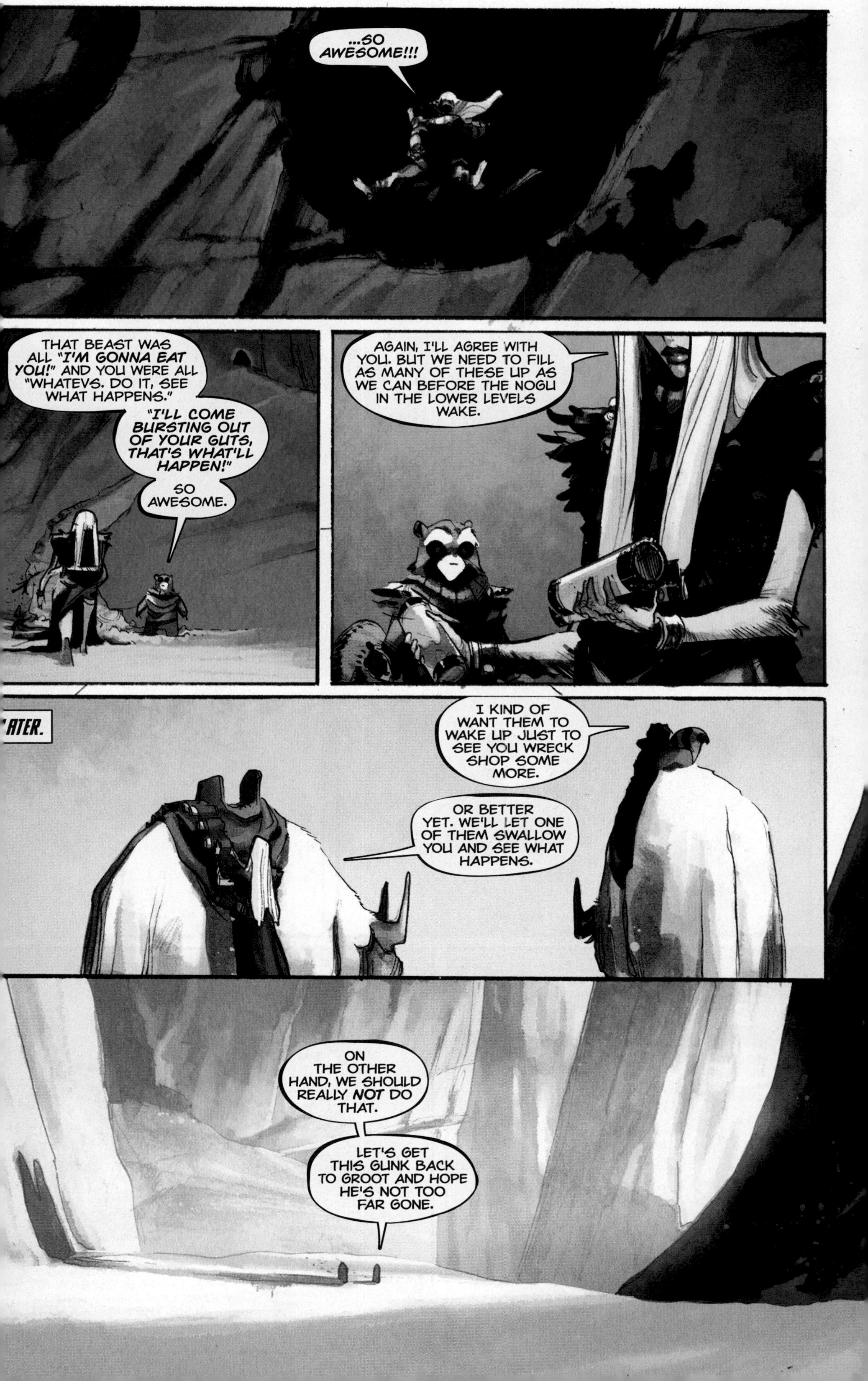
...SO AWESOME!!!
THAT BEAST WAS ALL "I'M GONNA EAT YOU!" AND YOU WERE ALL "WHATEVS. DO IT, SEE WHAT HAPPENS."
"I'LL COME BURSTING OUT OF YOUR GUTS, THAT'S WHAT'LL HAPPEN!"
SO AWESOME.
AGAIN, I'LL AGREE WITH YOU. BUT WE NEED TO FILL AS MANY OF THESE UP AS WE CAN BEFORE THE NOGU IN THE LOWER LEVELS WAKE.
ATER.
I KIND OF WANT THEM TO WAKE UP JUST TO SEE YOU WRECK SHOP SOME MORE.
OR BETTER YET. WE'LL LET ONE OF THEM SWALLOW YOU AND SEE WHAT HAPPENS.
ON THE OTHER HAND, WE SHOULD REALLY NOT DO THAT.
LET'S GET THIS GUNK BACK TO GROOT AND HOPE HE'S NOT TOO FAR GONE.

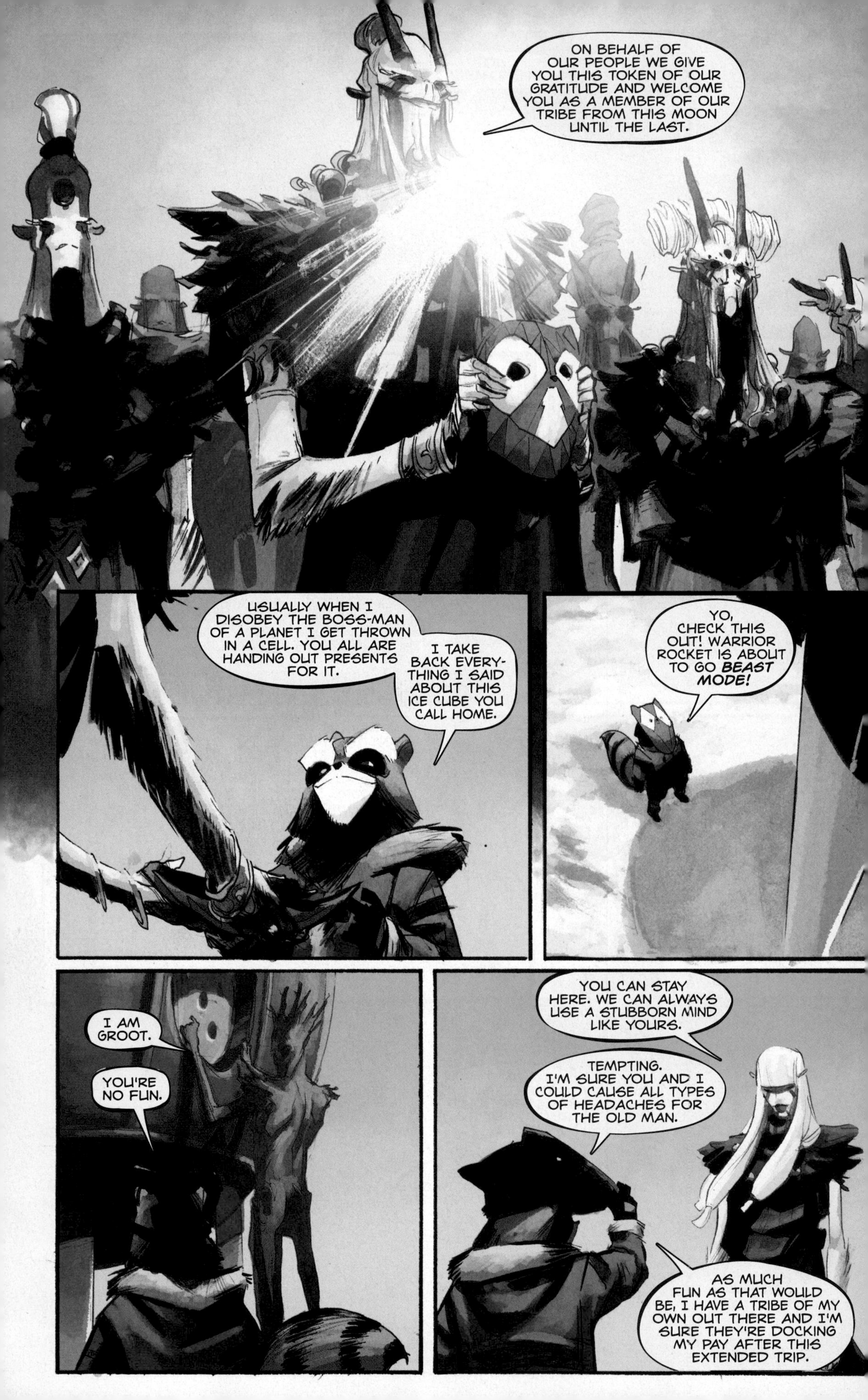
ON BEHALF OF OUR PEOPLE WE GIVE YOU THIS TOKEN OF OUR GRATITUDE AND WELCOME YOU AS A MEMBER OF OUR TRIBE FROM THIS MOON UNTIL THE LAST.
USUALLY WHEN I DISOBEY THE BOSS-MAN OF A PLANET I GET THROWN IN A CELL. YOU ALL ARE HANDING OUT PRESENTS FOR IT.
I TAKE BACK EVERY-THING I SAID ABOUT THIS ICE CUBE YOU CALL HOME.
YO, CHECK THIS OUT! WARRIOR ROCKET IS ABOUT TO GO **BEAST MODE!**
I AM GROOT.
YOU'RE NO FUN.
YOU CAN STAY HERE. WE CAN ALWAYS USE A STUBBORN MIND LIKE YOURS.
TEMPTING. I'M SURE YOU AND I COULD CAUSE ALL TYPES OF HEADACHES FOR THE OLD MAN.
AS MUCH FUN AS THAT WOULD BE, I HAVE A TRIBE OF MY OWN OUT THERE AND I'M SURE THEY'RE DOCKING MY PAY AFTER THIS EXTENDED TRIP.

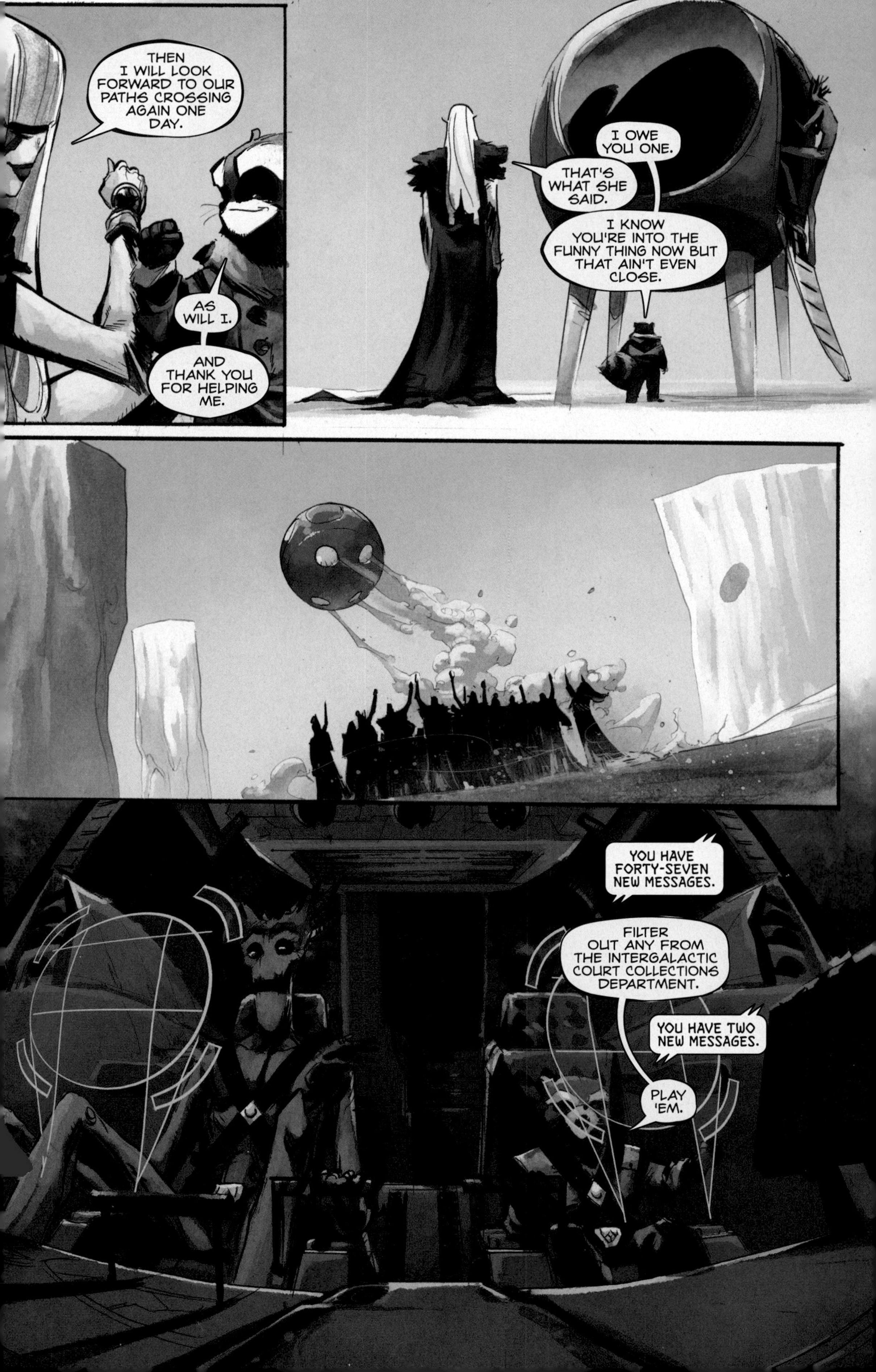
THEN I WILL LOOK FORWARD TO OUR PATHS CROSSING AGAIN ONE DAY.
AS WILL I.
AND THANK YOU FOR HELPING ME.
I OWE YOU ONE.
THAT'S WHAT SHE SAID.
I KNOW YOU'RE INTO THE FUNNY THING NOW BUT THAT AIN'T EVEN CLOSE.
YOU HAVE FORTY-SEVEN NEW MESSAGES.
FILTER OUT ANY FROM THE INTERGALACTIC COURT COLLECTIONS DEPARTMENT.
YOU HAVE TWO NEW MESSAGES.
PLAY 'EM.

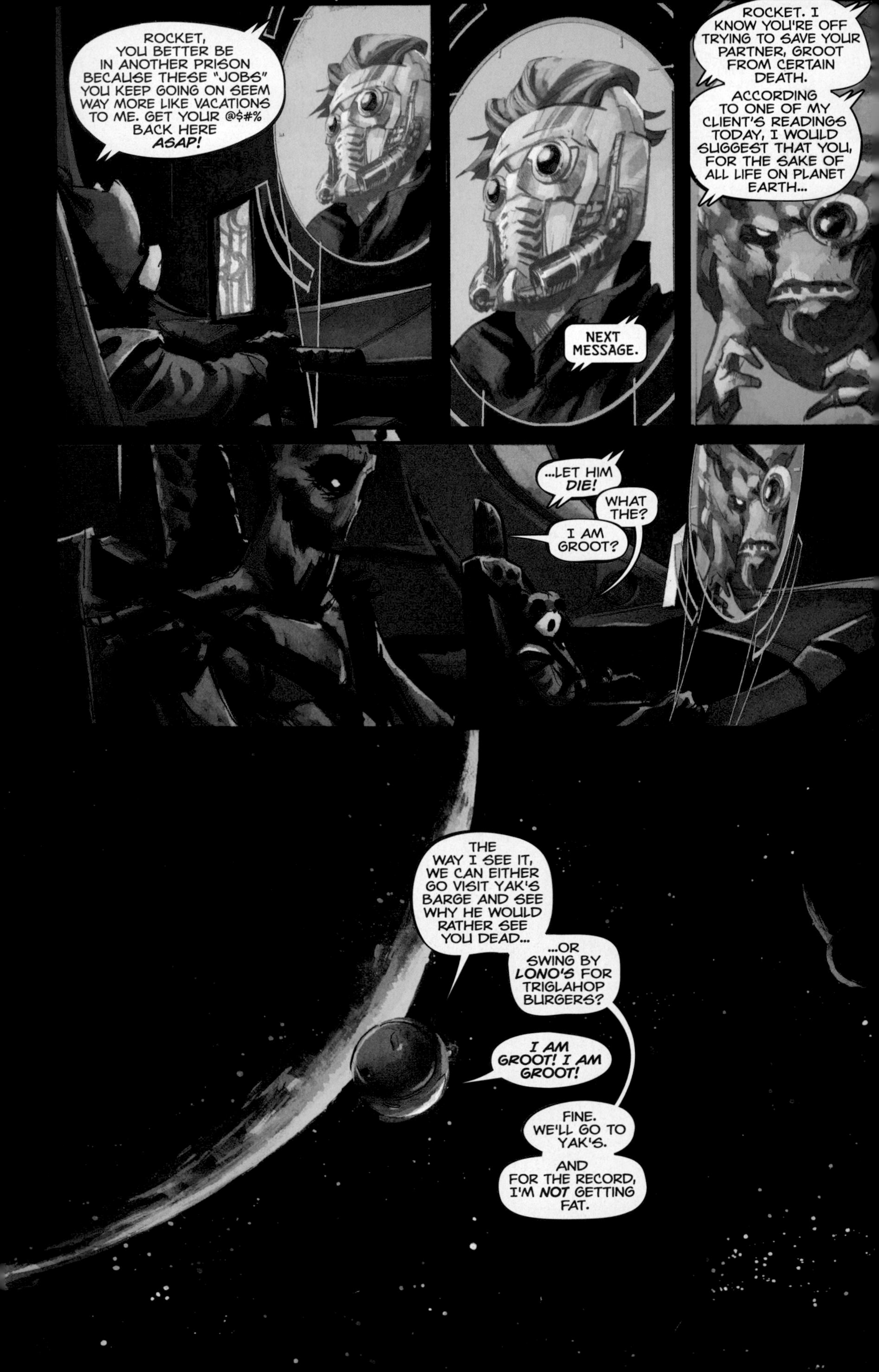
ROCKET, YOU BETTER BE IN ANOTHER PRISON BECAUSE THESE "JOBS" YOU KEEP GOING ON SEEM WAY MORE LIKE VACATIONS TO ME. GET YOUR @$#% BACK HERE ASAP!
NEXT MESSAGE.
ROCKET. I KNOW YOU'RE OFF TRYING TO SAVE YOUR PARTNER, GROOT FROM CERTAIN DEATH.
ACCORDING TO ONE OF MY CLIENT'S READINGS TODAY, I WOULD SUGGEST THAT YOU, FOR THE SAKE OF ALL LIFE ON PLANET EARTH...
...LET HIM DIE!
WHAT THE?
I AM GROOT?
THE WAY I SEE IT, WE CAN EITHER GO VISIT YAK'S BARGE AND SEE WHY HE WOULD RATHER SEE YOU DEAD...
...OR SWING BY LONO'S FOR TRIGLAHOP BURGERS?
I AM GROOT! I AM GROOT!
FINE. WE'LL GO TO YAK'S.
AND FOR THE RECORD, I'M NOT GETTING FAT.

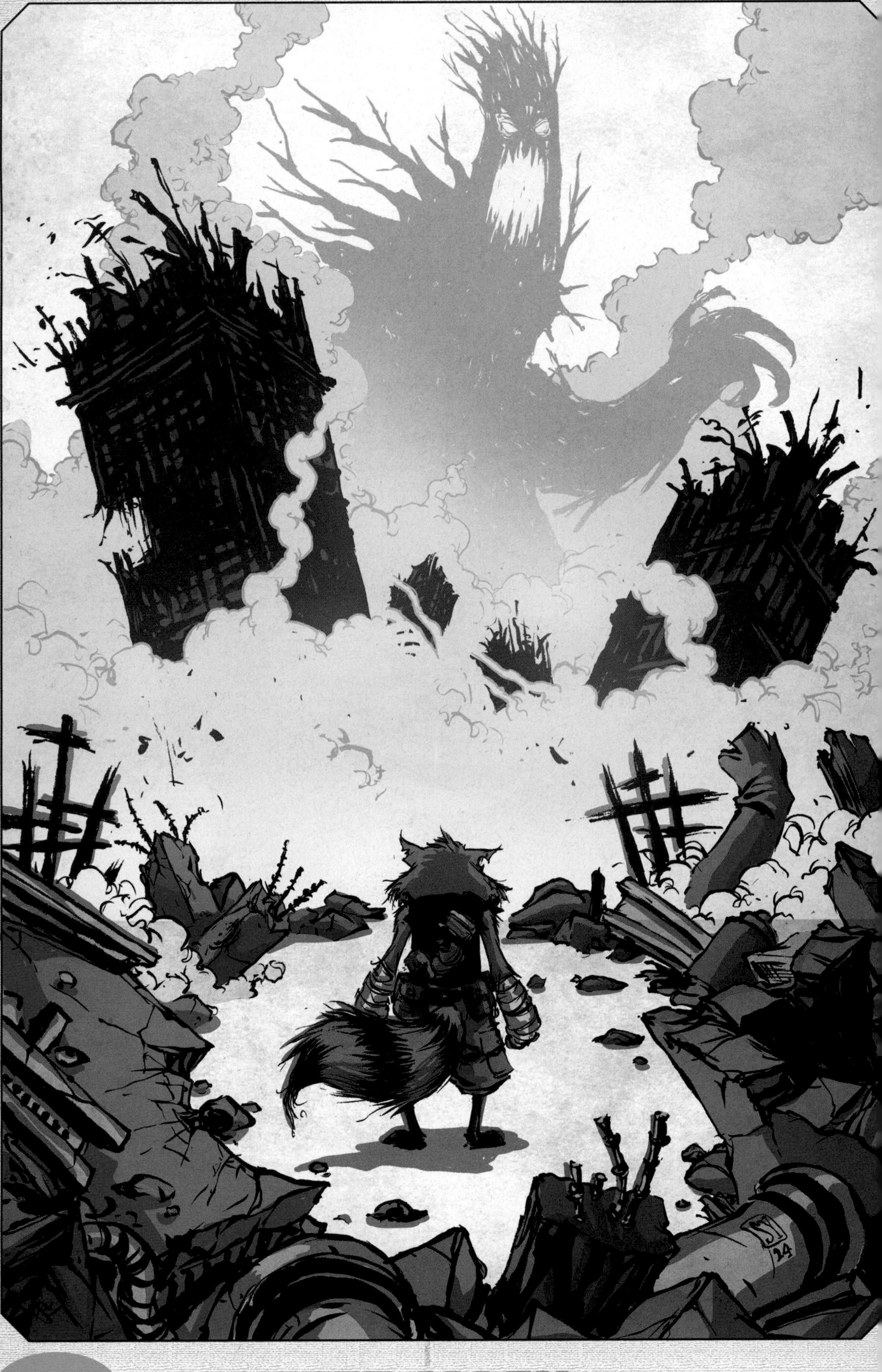

9 MONSTER MASH

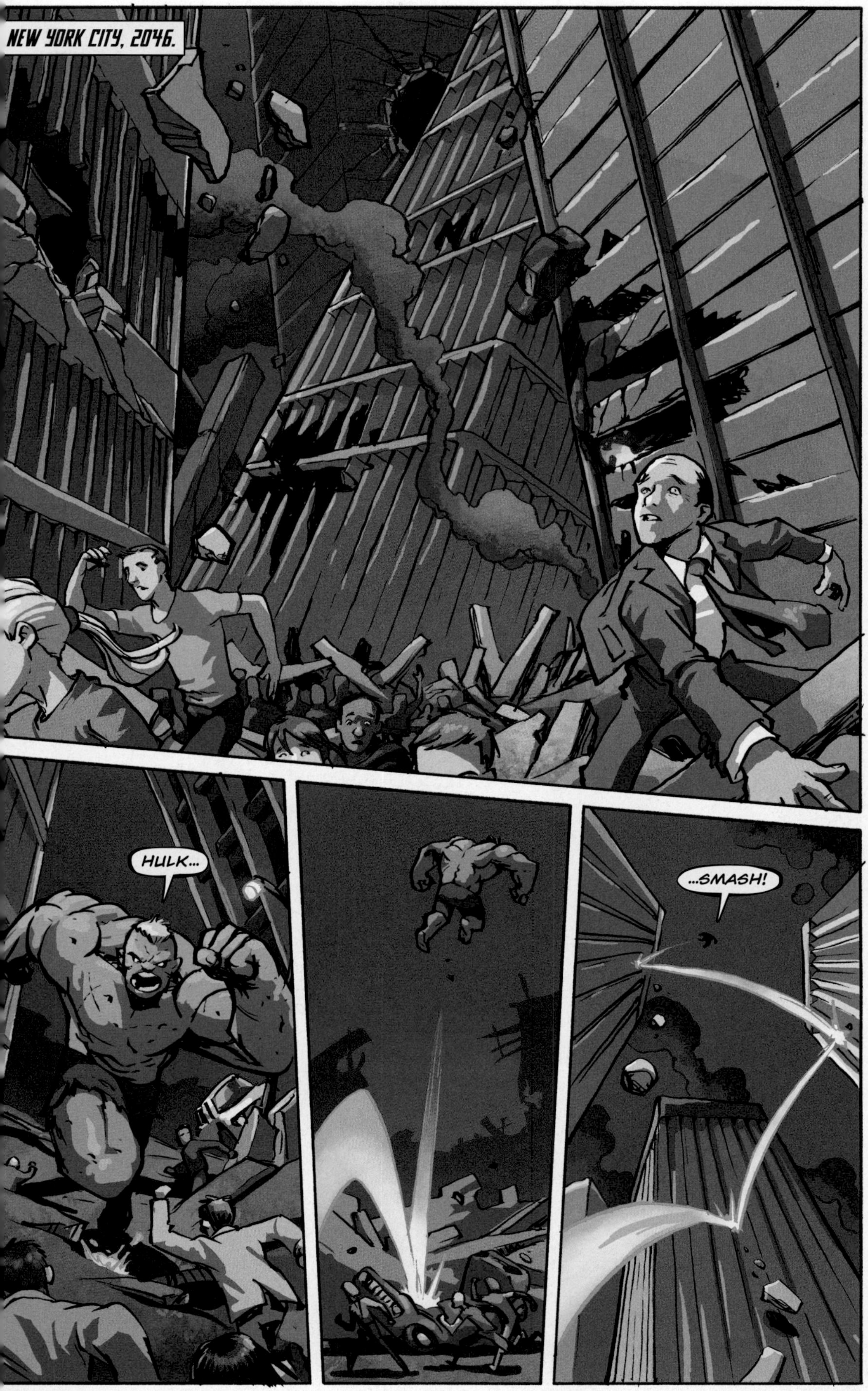
NEW YORK CITY, 2046.
HULK...
...SMASH!

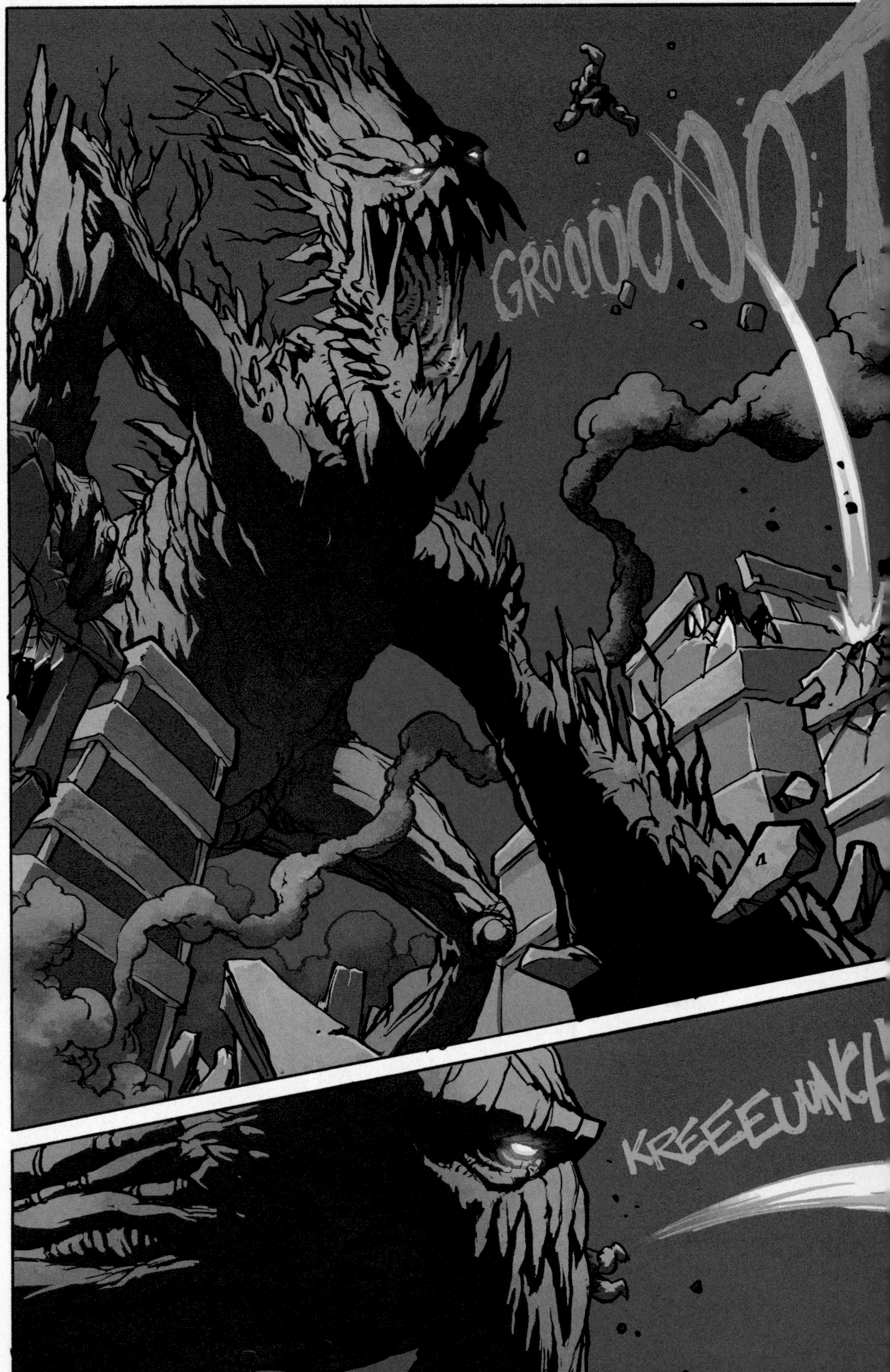
GROOOOOOT
KREEEUNCH

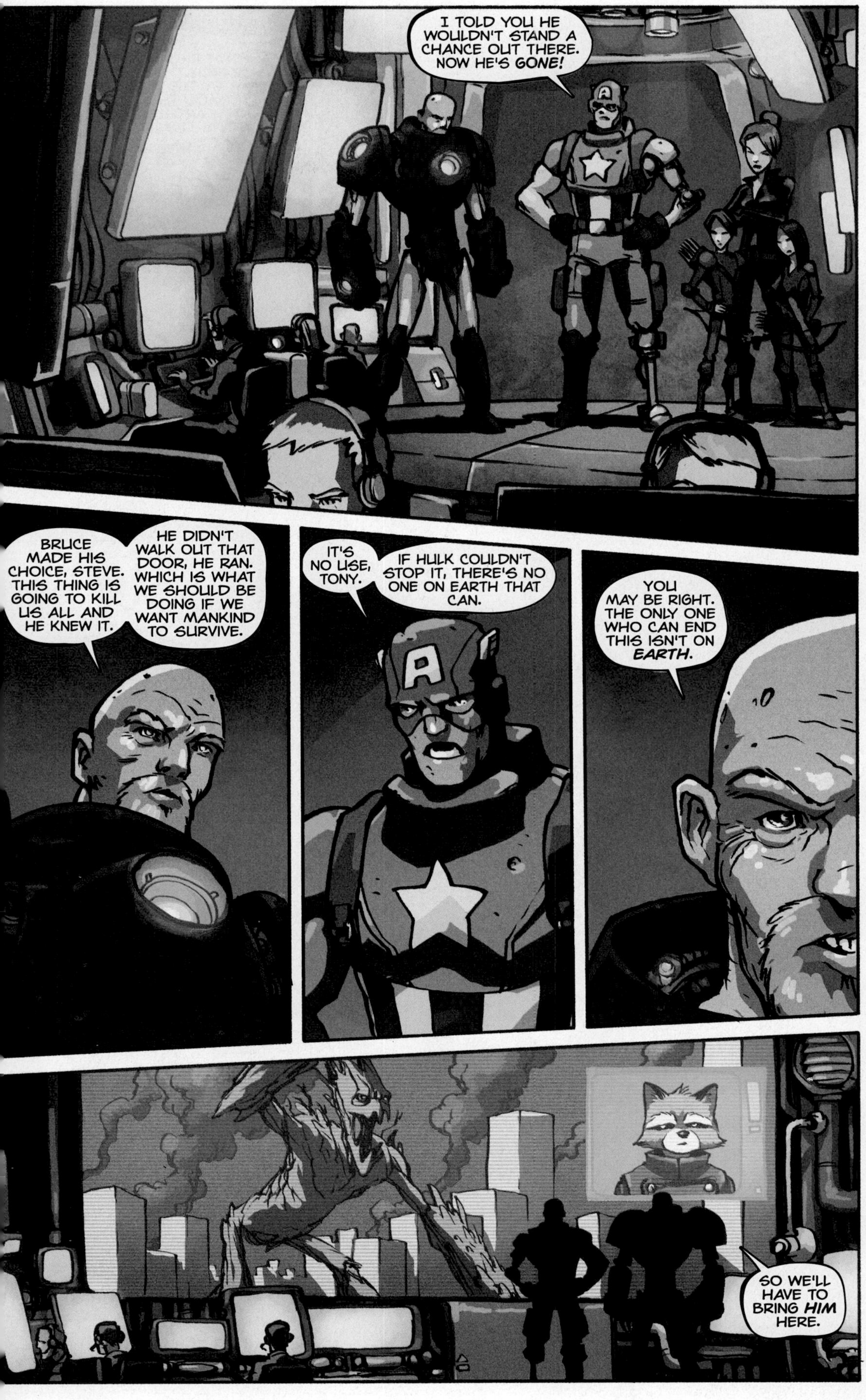
I TOLD YOU HE WOULDN'T STAND A CHANCE OUT THERE. NOW HE'S GONE!
BRUCE MADE HIS CHOICE, STEVE. THIS THING IS GOING TO KILL US ALL AND HE KNEW IT.
HE DIDN'T WALK OUT THAT DOOR, HE RAN. WHICH IS WHAT WE SHOULD BE DOING IF WE WANT MANKIND TO SURVIVE.
IT'S NO USE, TONY.
IF HULK COULDN'T STOP IT, THERE'S NO ONE ON EARTH THAT CAN.
YOU MAY BE RIGHT. THE ONLY ONE WHO CAN END THIS ISN'T ON EARTH.
SO WE'LL HAVE TO BRING HIM HERE.

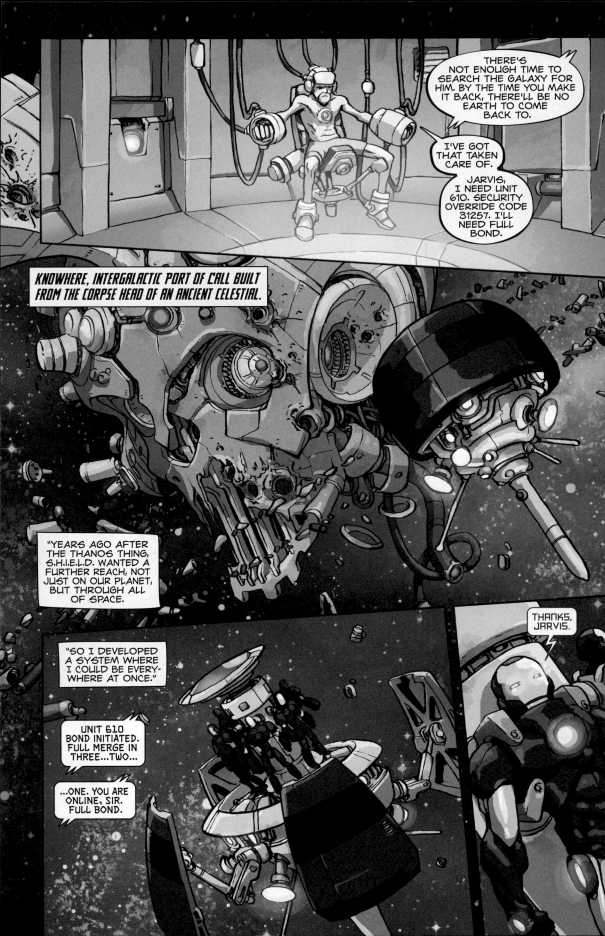

THERE'S NOT ENOUGH TIME TO SEARCH THE GALAXY FOR HIM. BY THE TIME YOU MAKE IT BACK, THERE'LL BE NO EARTH TO COME BACK TO.

I'VE GOT THAT TAKEN CARE OF.

JARVIS, I NEED UNIT 610. SECURITY OVERRIDE CODE 31257. I'LL NEED FULL BOND.

KNOWHERE, INTERGALACTIC PORT OF CALL BUILT FROM THE CORPSE HEAD OF AN ANCIENT CELESTIAL.

"YEARS AGO AFTER THE THANOS THING, S.H.I.E.L.D. WANTED A FURTHER REACH, NOT JUST ON OUR PLANET, BUT THROUGH ALL OF SPACE.

"SO I DEVELOPED A SYSTEM WHERE I COULD BE EVERY-WHERE AT ONCE."

UNIT 610 BOND INITIATED. FULL MERGE IN THREE...TWO...

...ONE. YOU ARE ONLINE, SIR. FULL BOND.

THANKS, JARVIS.

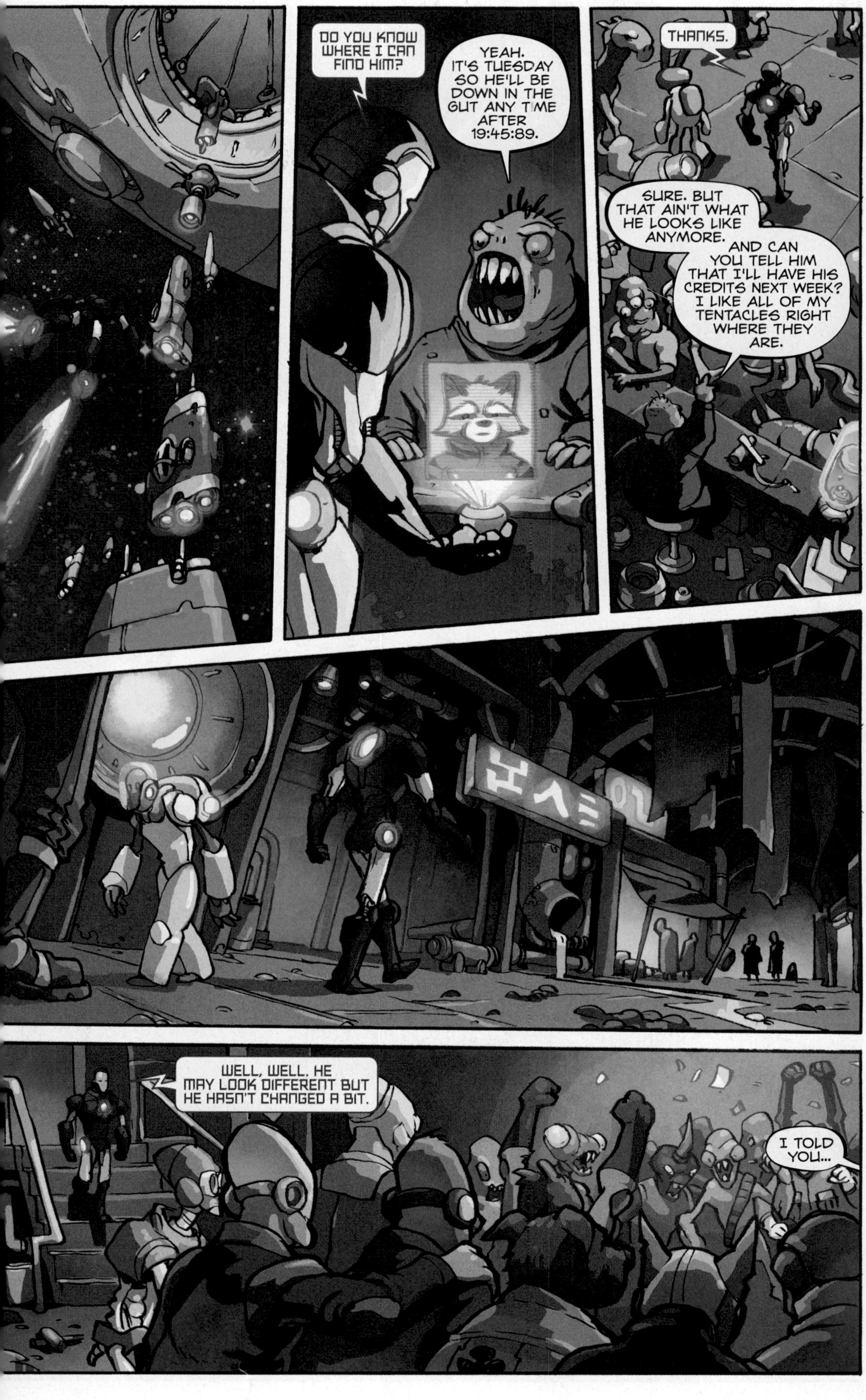
DO YOU KNOW WHERE I CAN FIND HIM?
YEAH. IT'S TUESDAY SO HE'LL BE DOWN IN THE GUT ANY TIME AFTER 19:45:89.
THANKS.
SURE. BUT THAT AIN'T WHAT HE LOOKS LIKE ANYMORE.
AND CAN YOU TELL HIM THAT I'LL HAVE HIS CREDITS NEXT WEEK? I LIKE ALL OF MY TENTACLES RIGHT WHERE THEY ARE.
WELL, WELL. HE MAY LOOK DIFFERENT BUT HE HASN'T CHANGED A BIT.
I TOLD YOU...

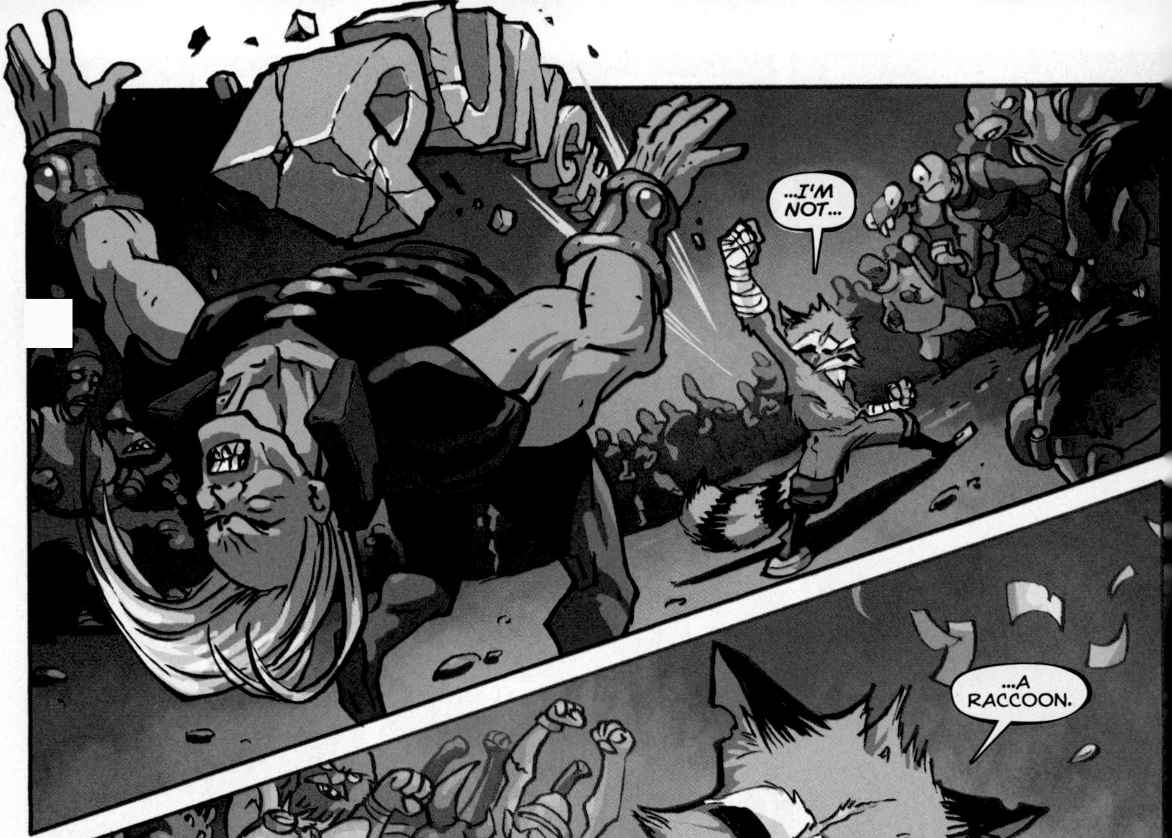
PLUNCH
...I'M NOT...

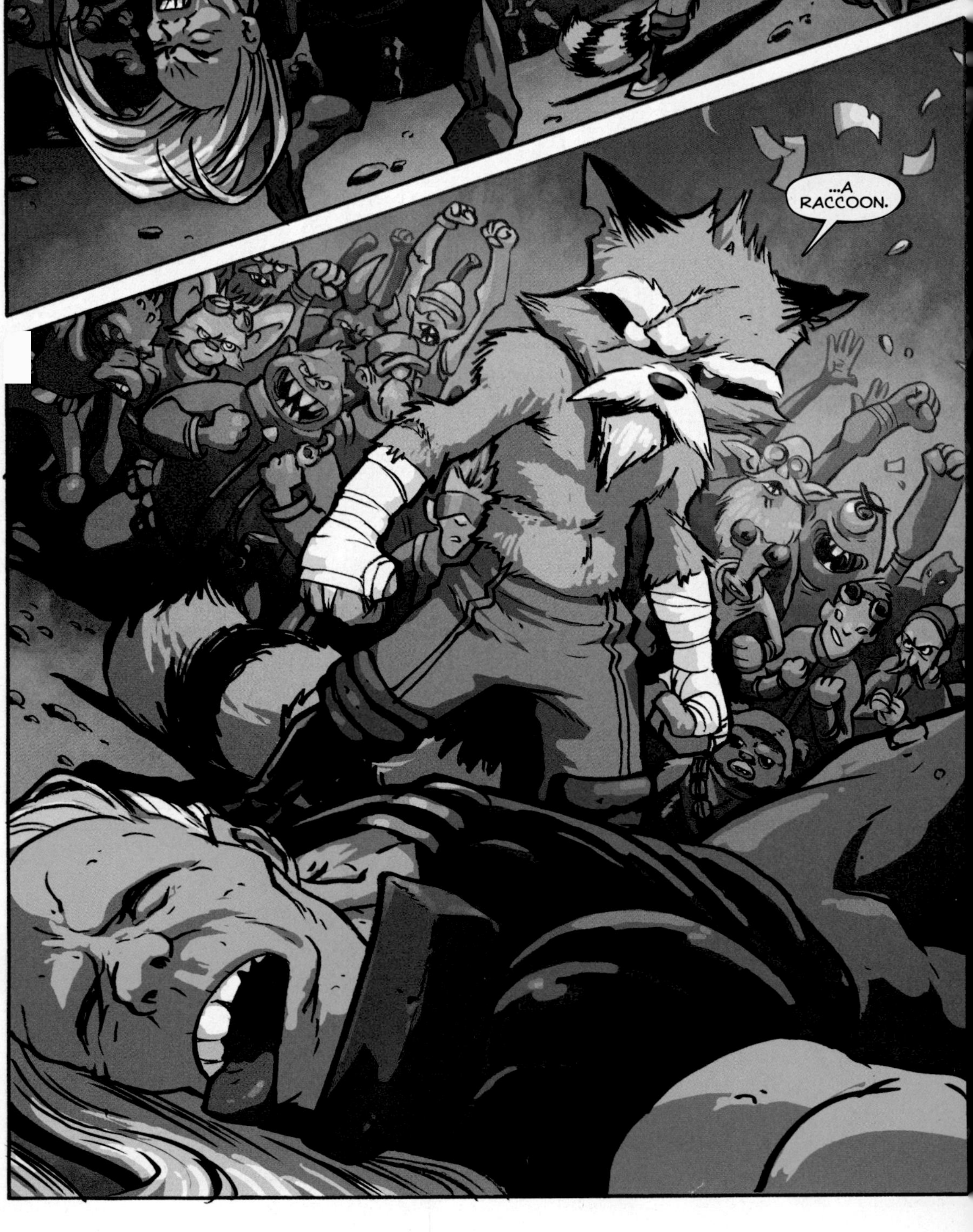
...A RACCOON.

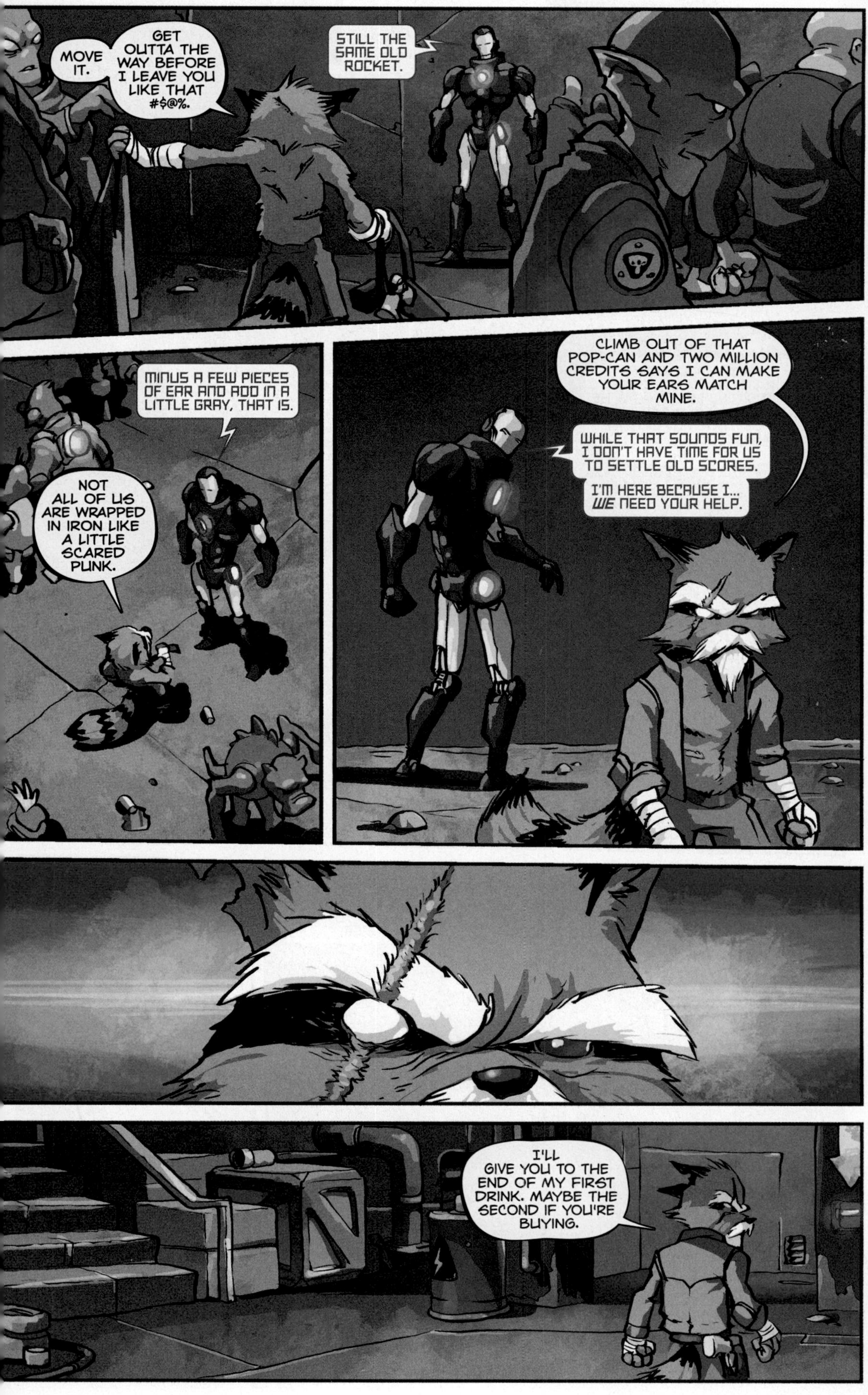
MOVE IT.
GET OUTTA THE WAY BEFORE I LEAVE YOU LIKE THAT #$@%.
STILL THE SAME OLD ROCKET.
MINUS A FEW PIECES OF EAR AND ADD IN A LITTLE GRAY, THAT IS.
NOT ALL OF US ARE WRAPPED IN IRON LIKE A LITTLE SCARED PUNK.
CLIMB OUT OF THAT POP-CAN AND TWO MILLION CREDITS SAYS I CAN MAKE YOUR EARS MATCH MINE.
WHILE THAT SOUNDS FUN, I DON'T HAVE TIME FOR US TO SETTLE OLD SCORES.
I'M HERE BECAUSE I... WE NEED YOUR HELP.
I'LL GIVE YOU TO THE END OF MY FIRST DRINK. MAYBE THE SECOND IF YOU'RE BUYING.

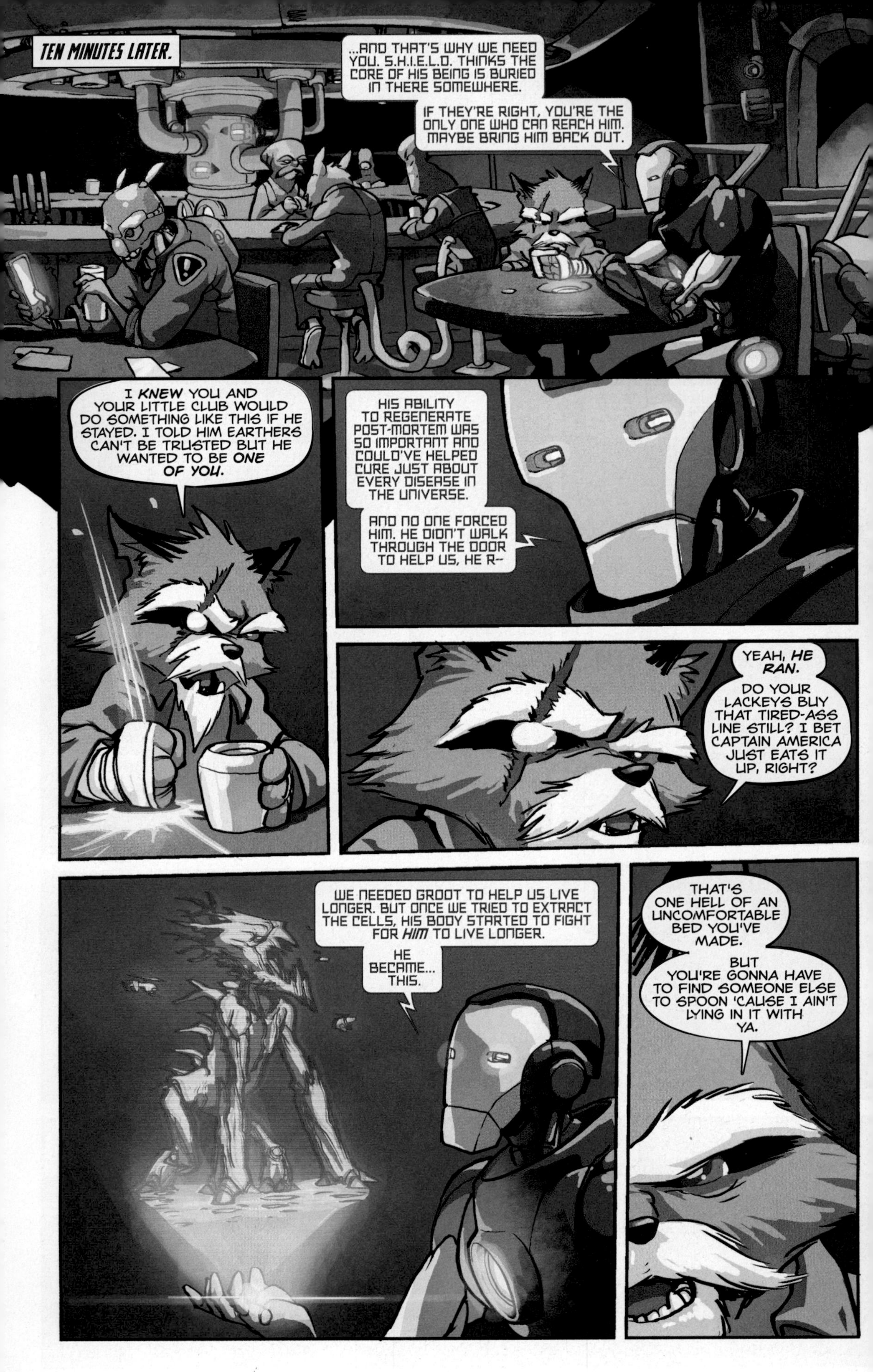
TEN MINUTES LATER.
...AND THAT'S WHY WE NEED YOU. S.H.I.E.L.D. THINKS THE CORE OF HIS BEING IS BURIED IN THERE SOMEWHERE.
IF THEY'RE RIGHT, YOU'RE THE ONLY ONE WHO CAN REACH HIM. MAYBE BRING HIM BACK OUT.
I KNEW YOU AND YOUR LITTLE CLUB WOULD DO SOMETHING LIKE THIS IF HE STAYED. I TOLD HIM EARTHERS CAN'T BE TRUSTED BUT HE WANTED TO BE ONE OF YOU.
HIS ABILITY TO REGENERATE POST-MORTEM WAS SO IMPORTANT AND COULD'VE HELPED CURE JUST ABOUT EVERY DISEASE IN THE UNIVERSE.
AND NO ONE FORCED HIM. HE DIDN'T WALK THROUGH THE DOOR TO HELP US, HE R--
YEAH, HE RAN.
DO YOUR LACKEYS BUY THAT TIRED-ASS LINE STILL? I BET CAPTAIN AMERICA JUST EATS IT UP, RIGHT?
WE NEEDED GROOT TO HELP US LIVE LONGER. BUT ONCE WE TRIED TO EXTRACT THE CELLS, HIS BODY STARTED TO FIGHT FOR HIM TO LIVE LONGER.
HE BECAME... THIS.
THAT'S ONE HELL OF AN UNCOMFORTABLE BED YOU'VE MADE.
BUT YOU'RE GONNA HAVE TO FIND SOMEONE ELSE TO SPOON 'CAUSE I AIN'T LYING IN IT WITH YA.

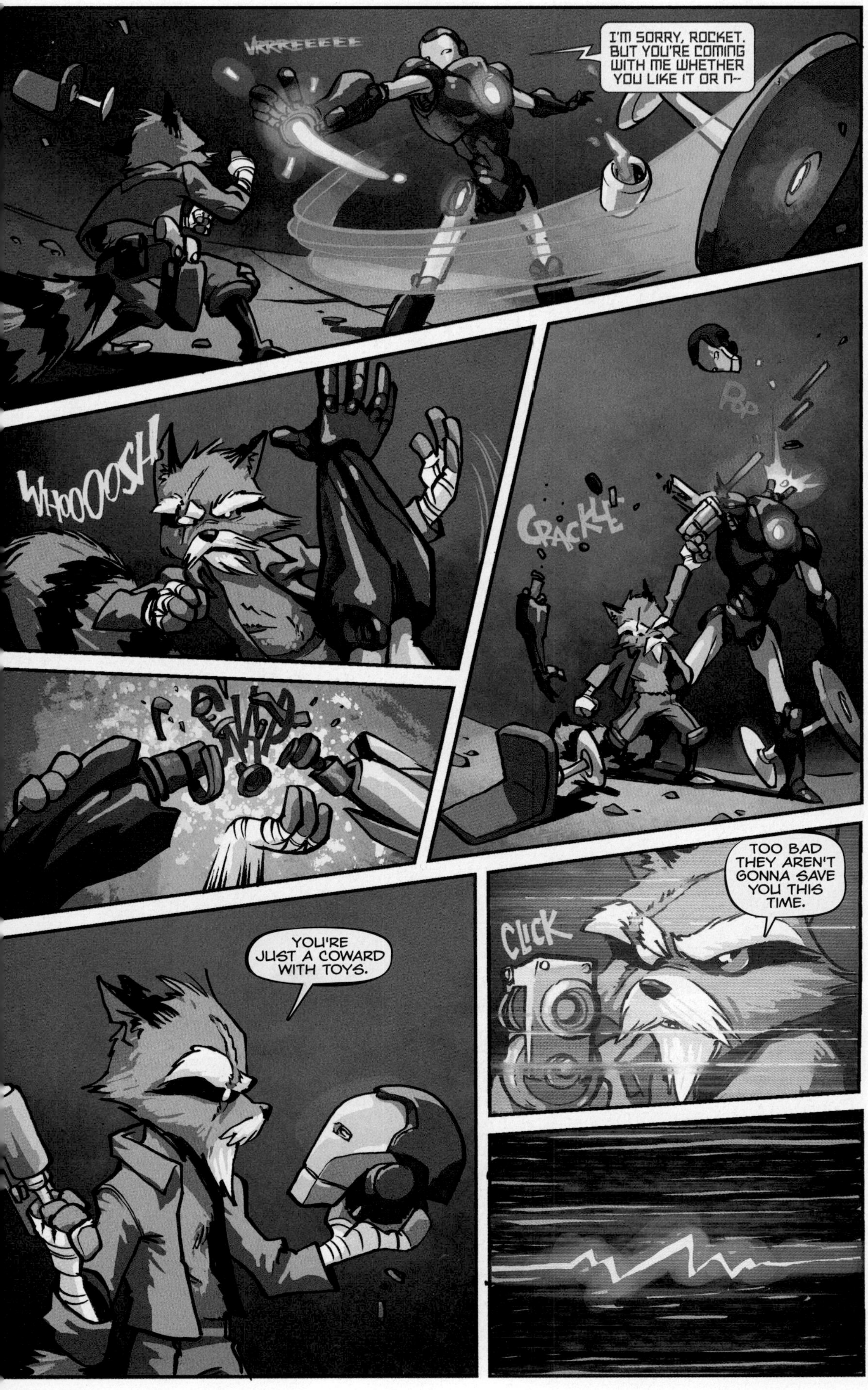

VRRREEEEE
I'M SORRY, ROCKET. BUT YOU'RE COMING WITH ME WHETHER YOU LIKE IT OR N--
WHOOOOSH
POP
CRACKLE
YOU'RE JUST A COWARD WITH TOYS.
CLICK
TOO BAD THEY AREN'T GONNA SAVE YOU THIS TIME.

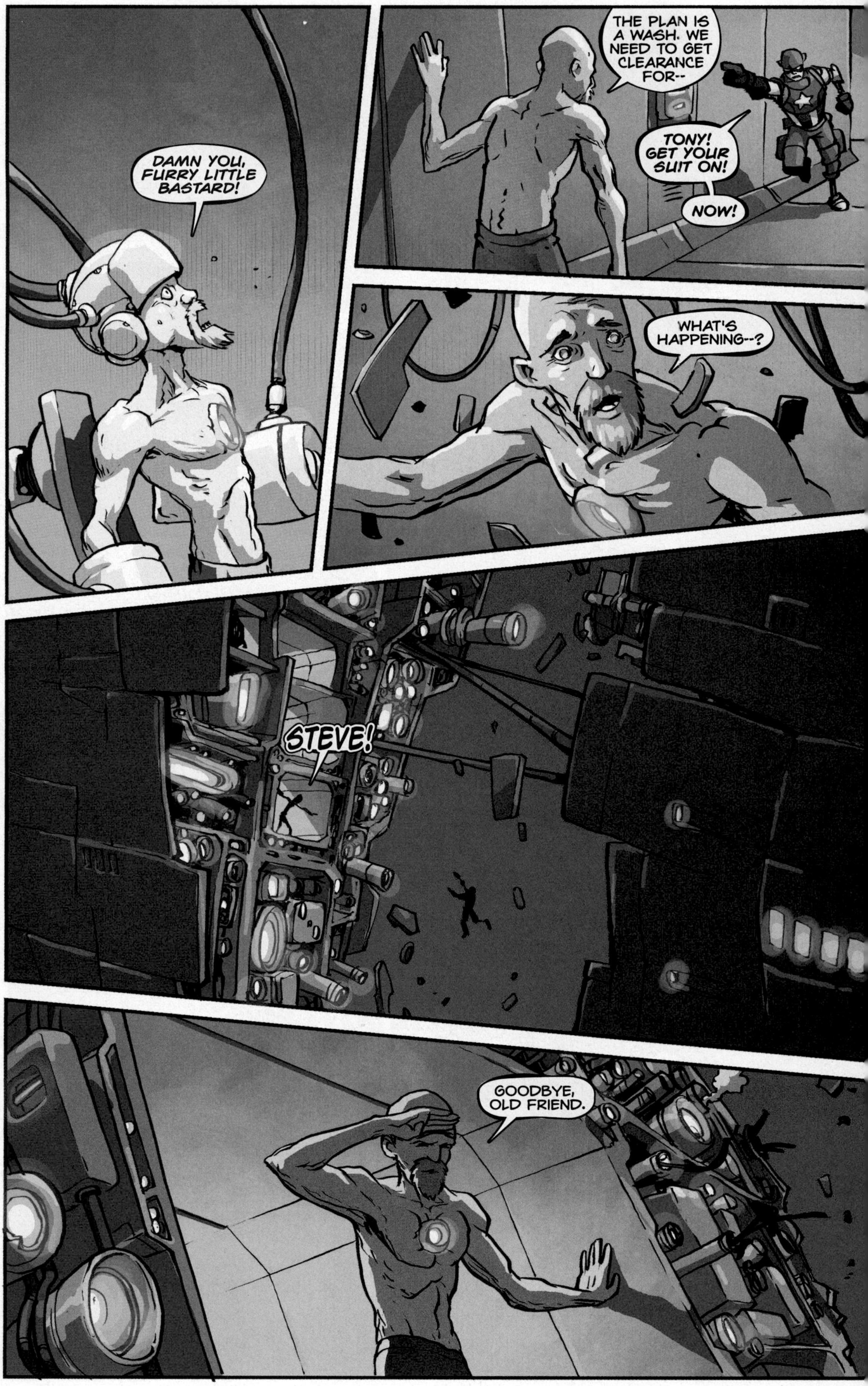
DAMN YOU, FURRY LITTLE BASTARD!
THE PLAN IS A WASH. WE NEED TO GET CLEARANCE FOR--
TONY! GET YOUR SUIT ON!
NOW!
WHAT'S HAPPENING--?
STEVE!
GOODBYE, OLD FRIEND.

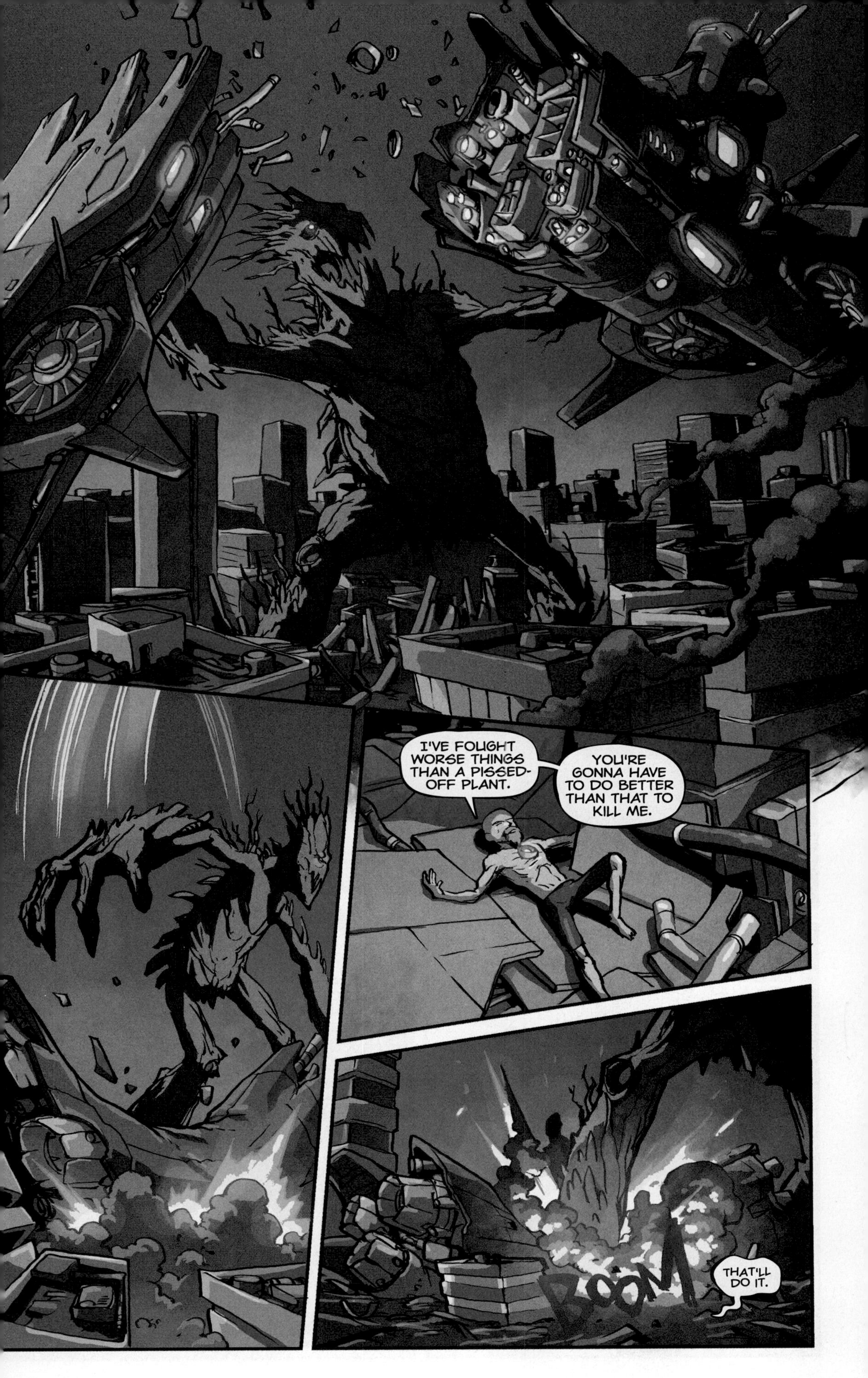
I'VE FOUGHT WORSE THINGS THAN A PISSED-OFF PLANT.
YOU'RE GONNA HAVE TO DO BETTER THAN THAT TO KILL ME.
BOOM
THAT'LL DO IT.

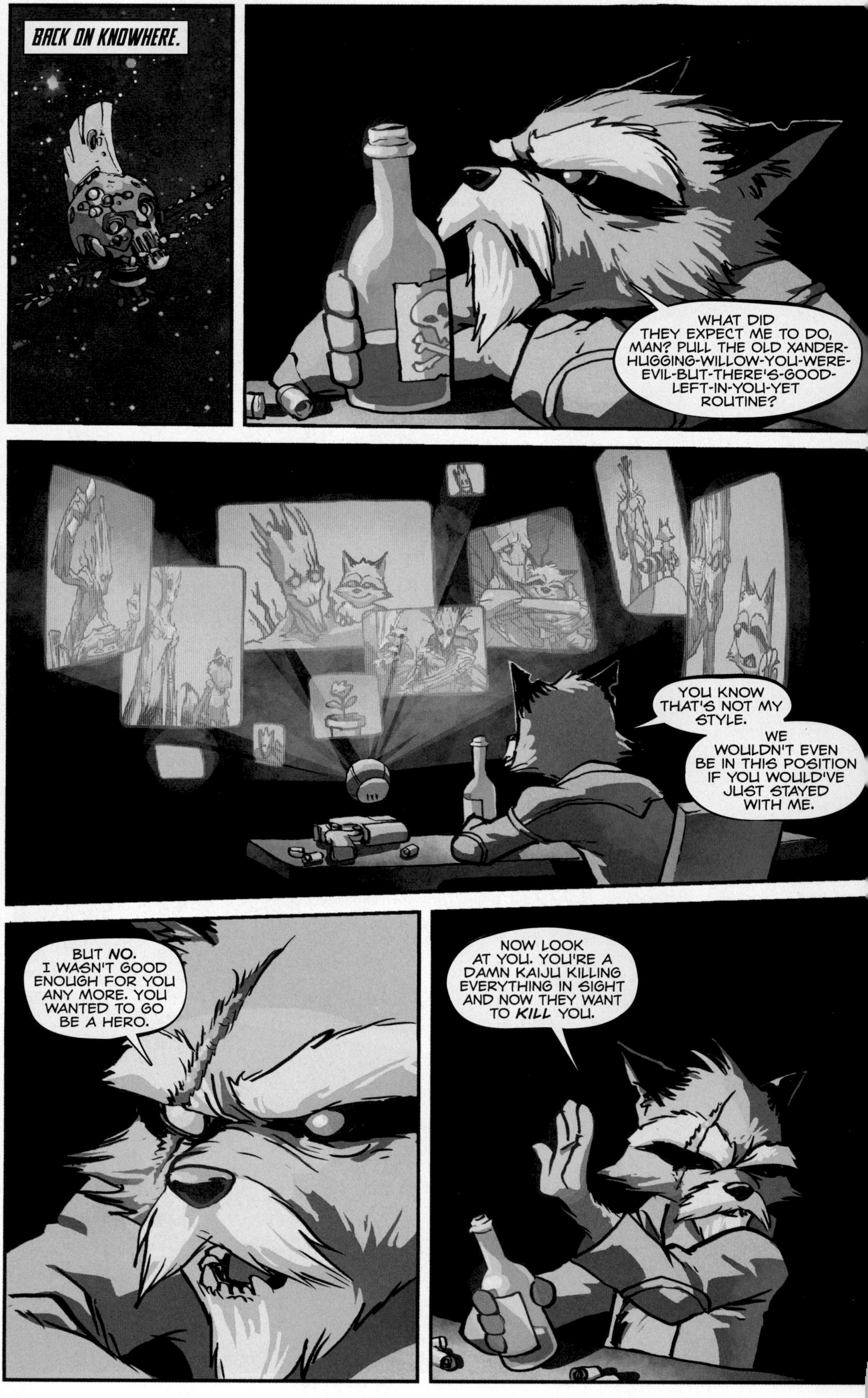
BACK ON KNOWHERE.
WHAT DID THEY EXPECT ME TO DO, MAN? PULL THE OLD XANDER-HUGGING-WILLOW-YOU-WERE-EVIL-BUT-THERE'S-GOOD-LEFT-IN-YOU-YET ROUTINE?
YOU KNOW THAT'S NOT MY STYLE.
WE WOULDN'T EVEN BE IN THIS POSITION IF YOU WOULD'VE JUST STAYED WITH ME.
BUT NO. I WASN'T GOOD ENOUGH FOR YOU ANY MORE. YOU WANTED TO GO BE A HERO.
NOW LOOK AT YOU. YOU'RE A DAMN KAIJU KILLING EVERYTHING IN SIGHT AND NOW THEY WANT TO KILL YOU.

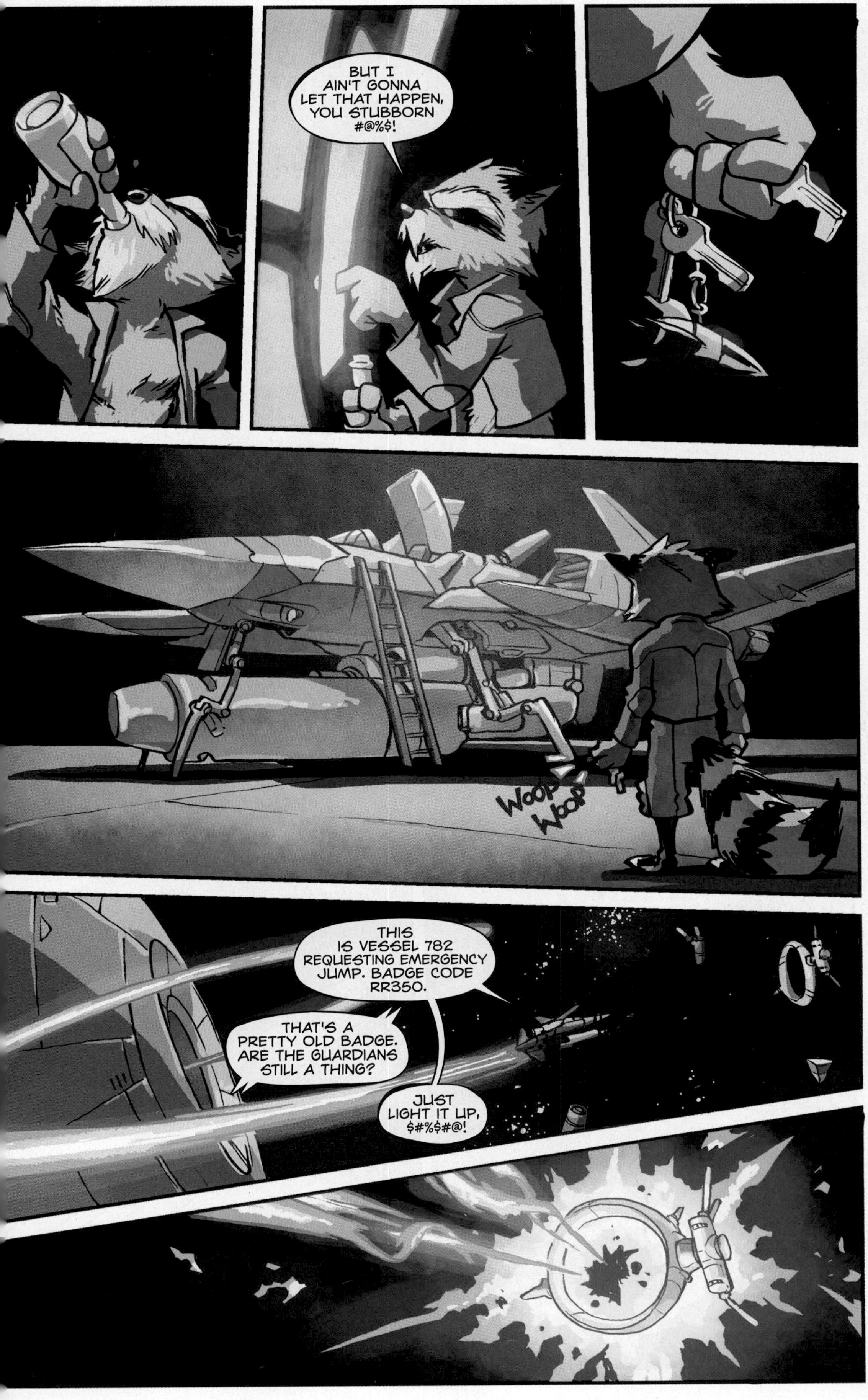
BUT I AIN'T GONNA LET THAT HAPPEN, YOU STUBBORN #@%$!
WOOP WOOP
THIS IS VESSEL 782 REQUESTING EMERGENCY JUMP. BADGE CODE RR350.
THAT'S A PRETTY OLD BADGE. ARE THE GUARDIANS STILL A THING?
JUST LIGHT IT UP, $#%$#@!

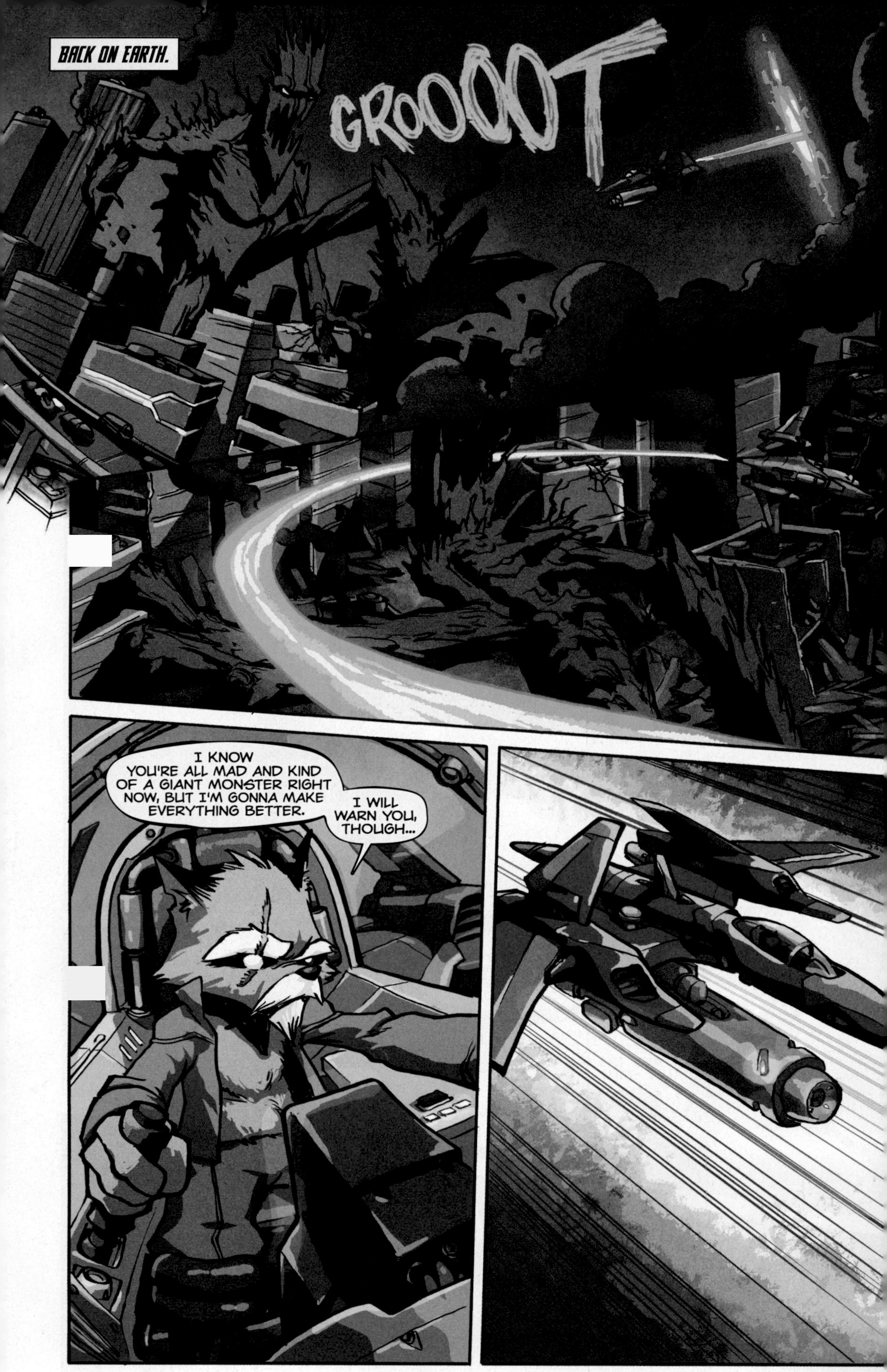
BACK ON EARTH.
GROOOOT
I KNOW YOU'RE ALL MAD AND KIND OF A GIANT MONSTER RIGHT NOW, BUT I'M GONNA MAKE EVERYTHING BETTER.
I WILL WARN YOU, THOUGH...

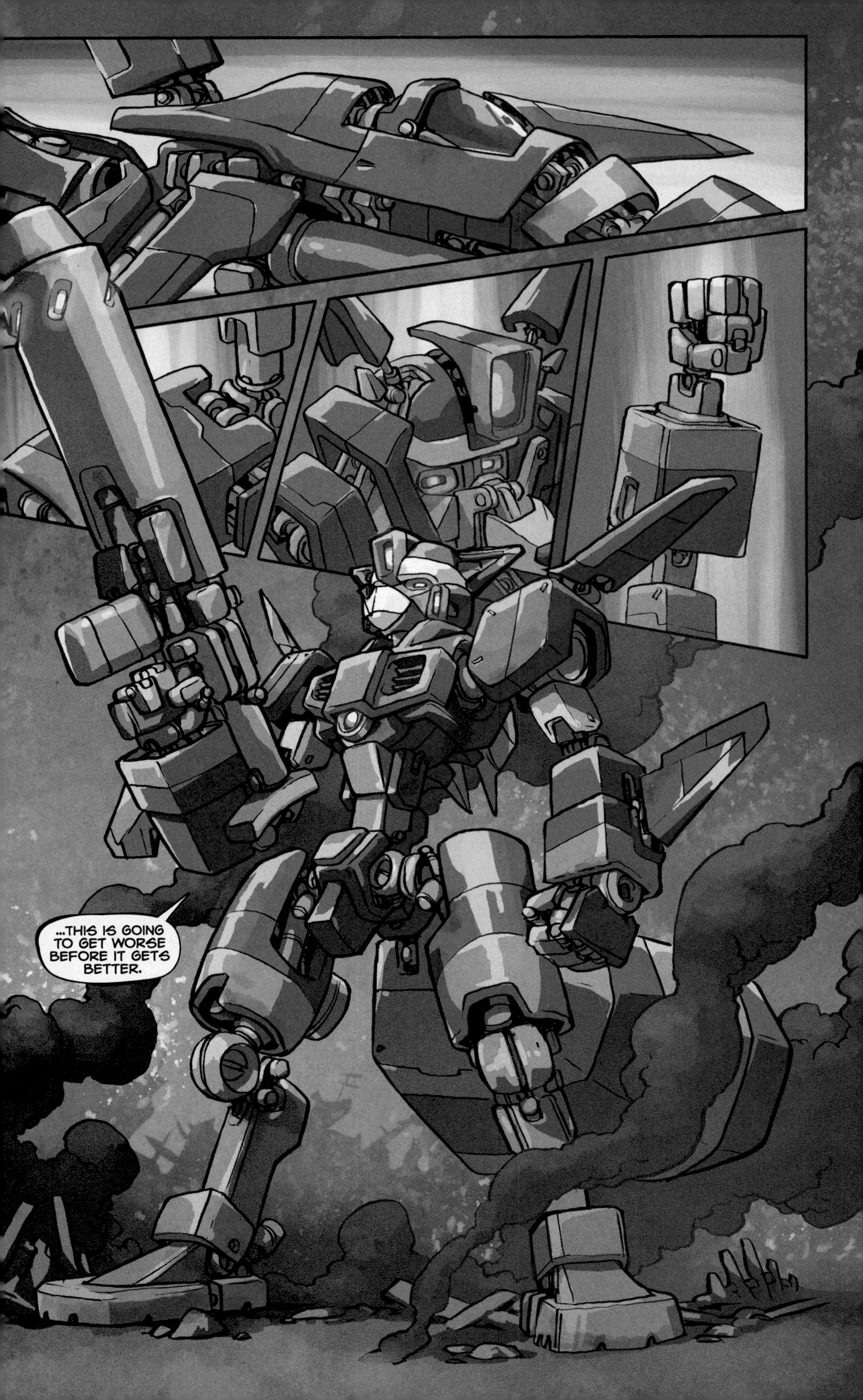
...THIS IS GOING TO GET WORSE BEFORE IT GETS BETTER.

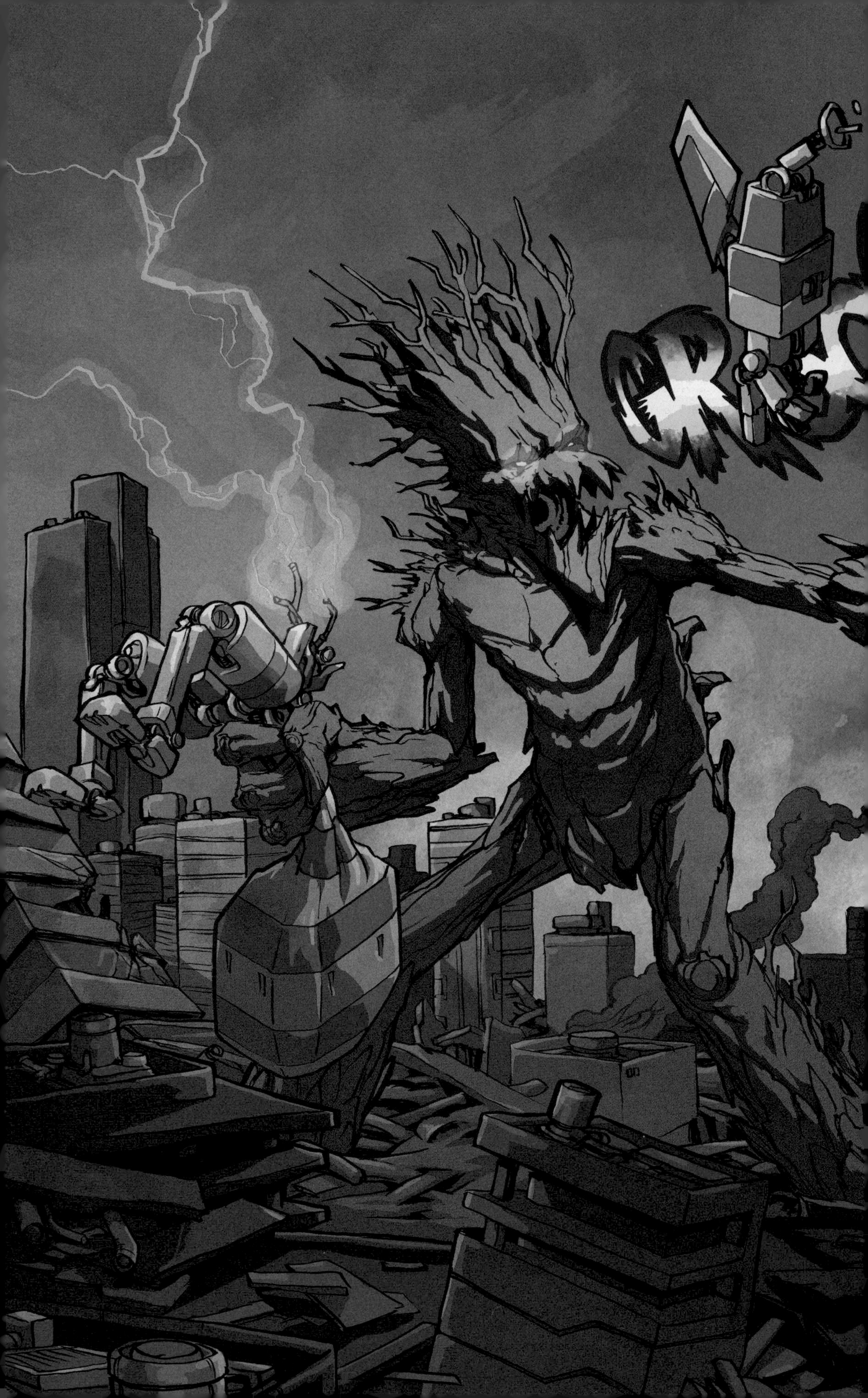

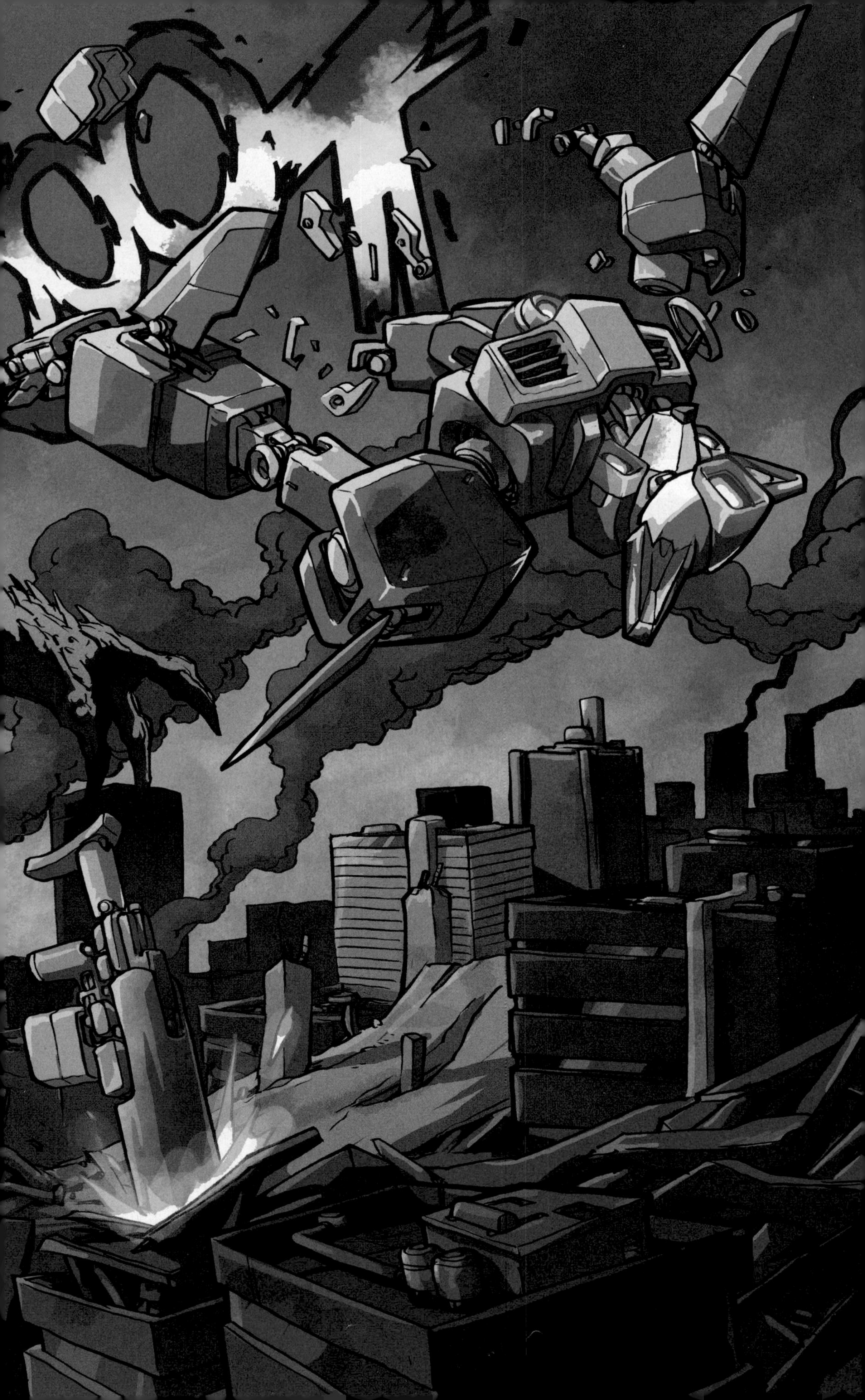
OOM

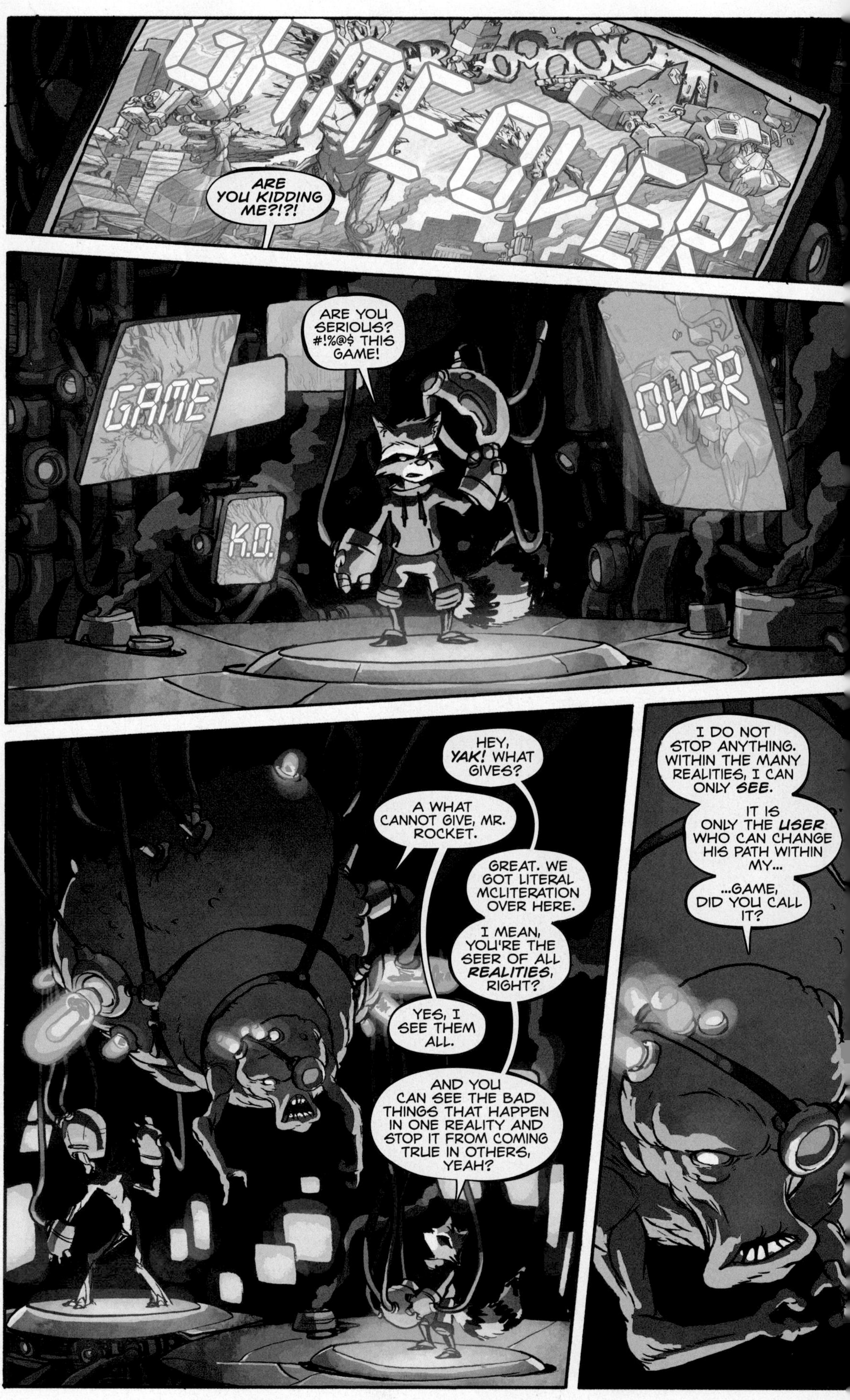
GAME OVER
ARE YOU KIDDING ME?!?!
GAME
OVER
K.O.
ARE YOU SERIOUS? #!%@$ THIS GAME!
HEY, YAK! WHAT GIVES?
A WHAT CANNOT GIVE, MR. ROCKET.
GREAT. WE GOT LITERAL MCLITERATION OVER HERE.
I MEAN, YOU'RE THE SEER OF ALL REALITIES, RIGHT?
YES, I SEE THEM ALL.
AND YOU CAN SEE THE BAD THINGS THAT HAPPEN IN ONE REALITY AND STOP IT FROM COMING TRUE IN OTHERS, YEAH?
I DO NOT STOP ANYTHING. WITHIN THE MANY REALITIES, I CAN ONLY SEE.
IT IS ONLY THE USER WHO CAN CHANGE HIS PATH WITHIN MY...
...GAME, DID YOU CALL IT?

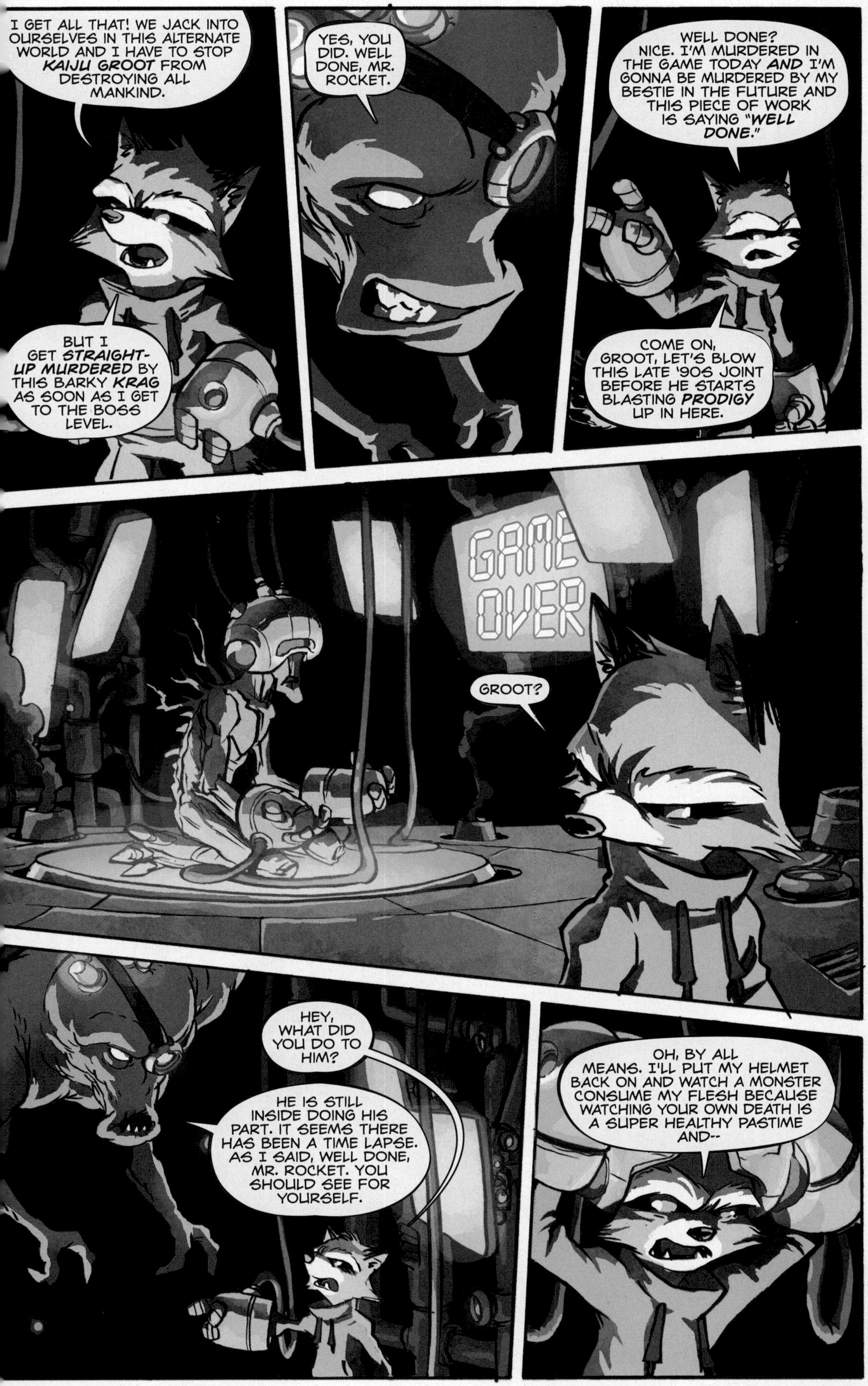
I GET ALL THAT! WE JACK INTO OURSELVES IN THIS ALTERNATE WORLD AND I HAVE TO STOP KAIJU GROOT FROM DESTROYING ALL MANKIND.
BUT I GET STRAIGHT-UP MURDERED BY THIS BARKY KRAG AS SOON AS I GET TO THE BOSS LEVEL.
YES, YOU DID. WELL DONE, MR. ROCKET.
WELL DONE? NICE. I'M MURDERED IN THE GAME TODAY AND I'M GONNA BE MURDERED BY MY BESTIE IN THE FUTURE AND THIS PIECE OF WORK IS SAYING "WELL DONE."
COME ON, GROOT, LET'S BLOW THIS LATE '90S JOINT BEFORE HE STARTS BLASTING PRODIGY UP IN HERE.
GAME OVER
GROOT?
HEY, WHAT DID YOU DO TO HIM?
HE IS STILL INSIDE DOING HIS PART. IT SEEMS THERE HAS BEEN A TIME LAPSE. AS I SAID, WELL DONE, MR. ROCKET. YOU SHOULD SEE FOR YOURSELF.
OH, BY ALL MEANS. I'LL PUT MY HELMET BACK ON AND WATCH A MONSTER CONSUME MY FLESH BECAUSE WATCHING YOUR OWN DEATH IS A SUPER HEALTHY PASTIME AND--

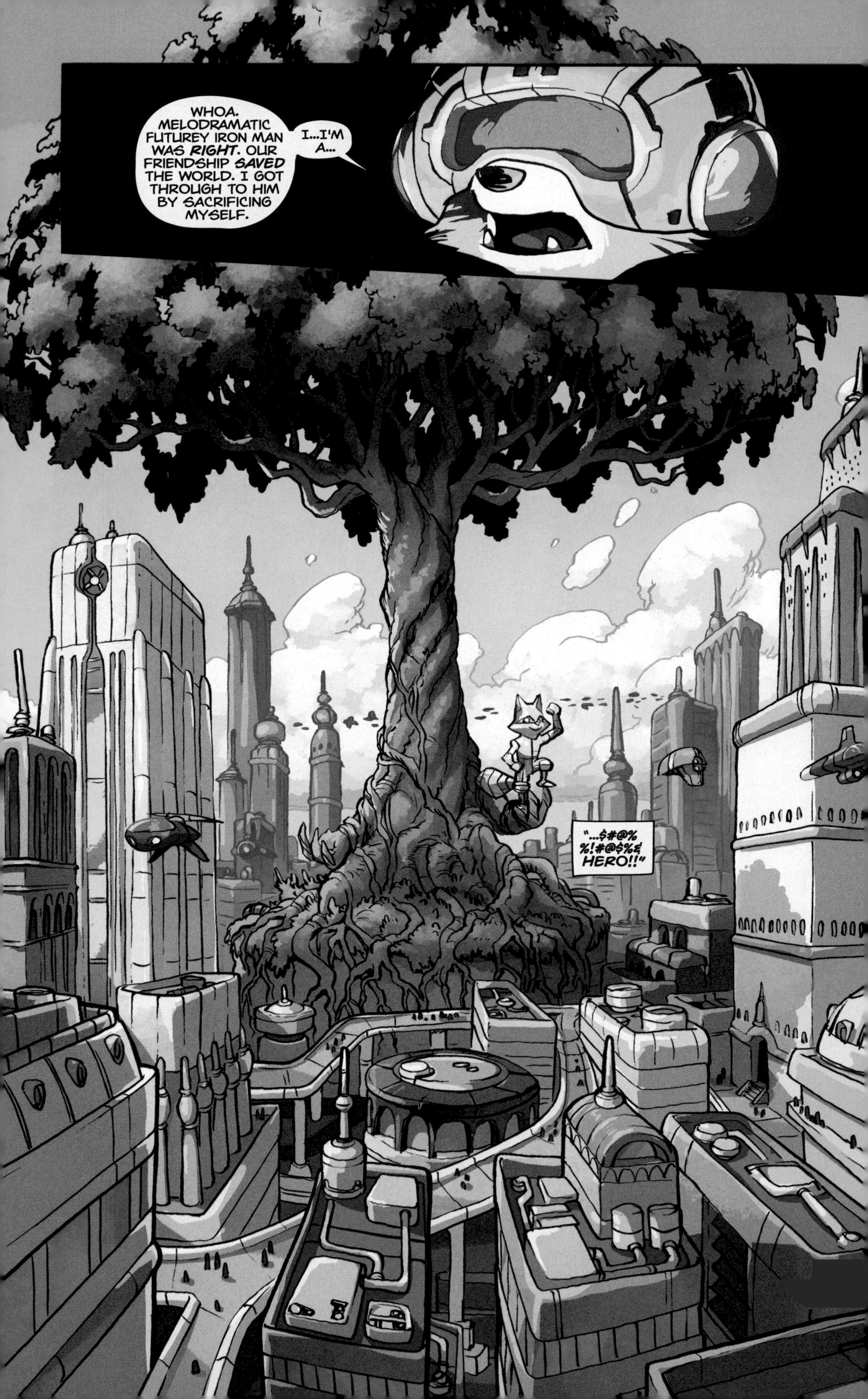
WHOA. MELODRAMATIC FUTUREY IRON MAN WAS RIGHT. OUR FRIENDSHIP SAVED THE WORLD. I GOT THROUGH TO HIM BY SACRIFICING MYSELF.
I...I'M A...
"...$#@% %!#@$%& HERO!!"

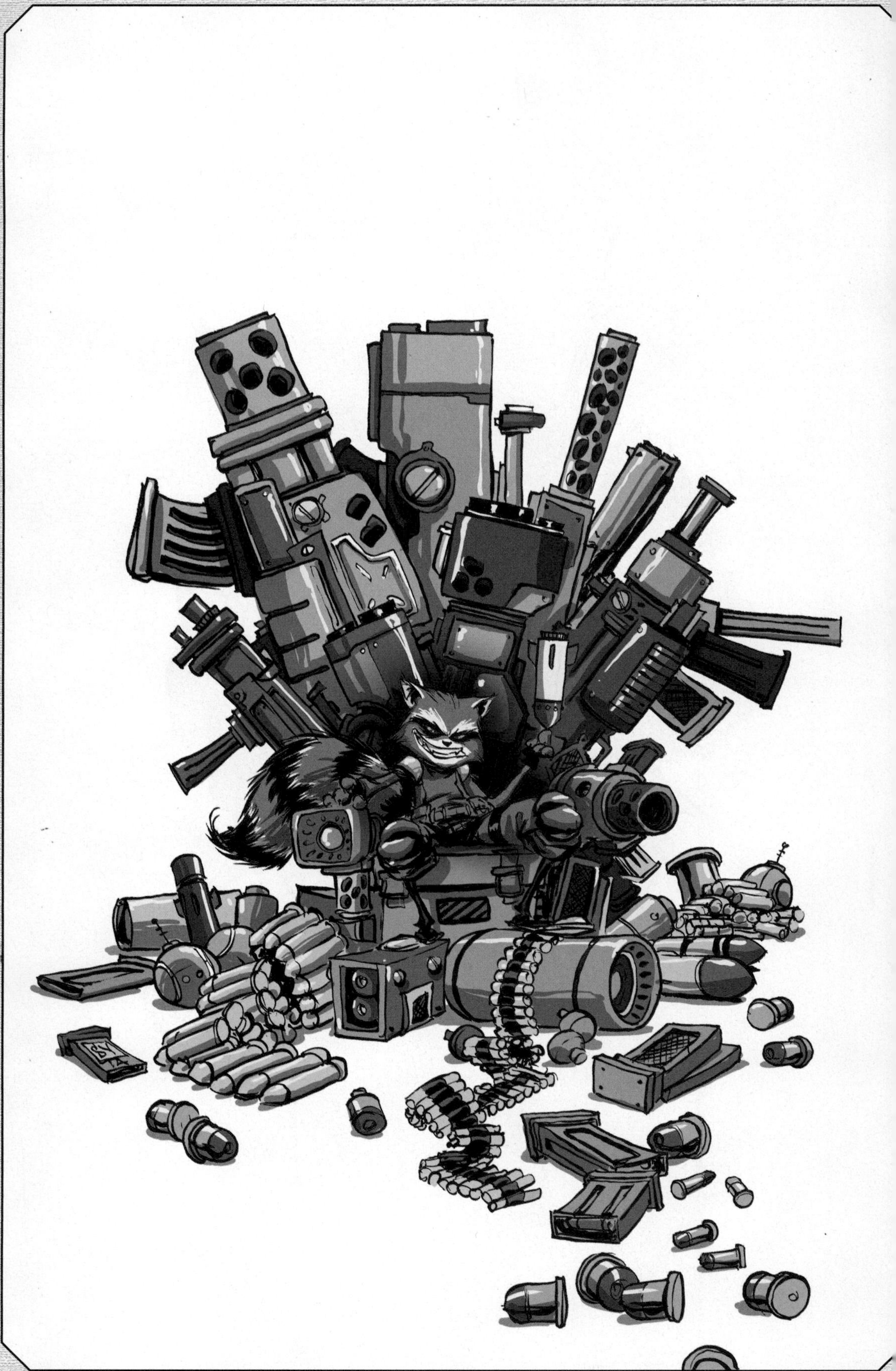

10 BOOKENDS part 1

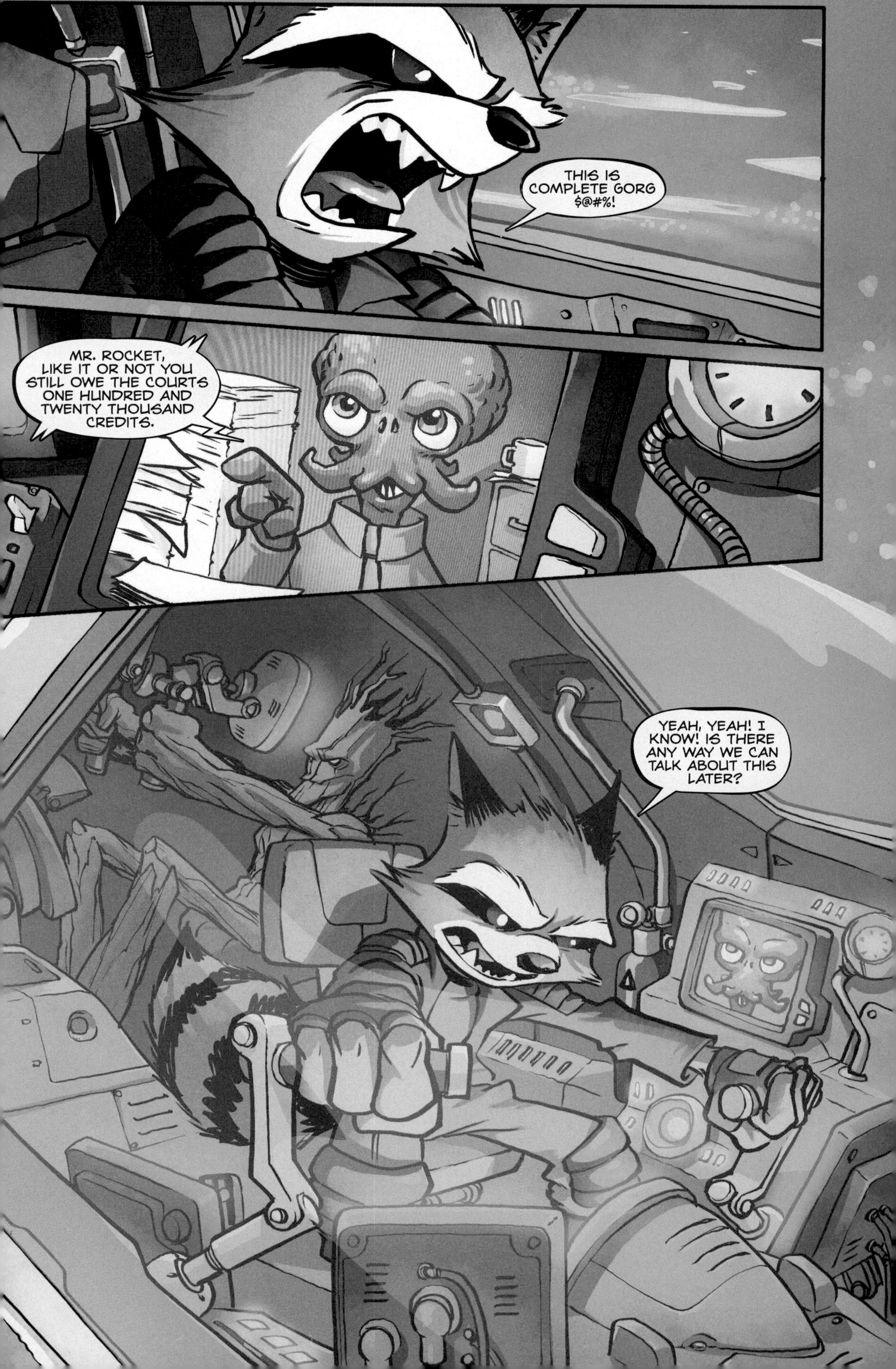
THIS IS COMPLETE GORG $@#%!
MR. ROCKET, LIKE IT OR NOT YOU STILL OWE THE COURTS ONE HUNDRED AND TWENTY THOUSAND CREDITS.
YEAH, YEAH! I KNOW! IS THERE ANY WAY WE CAN TALK ABOUT THIS LATER?

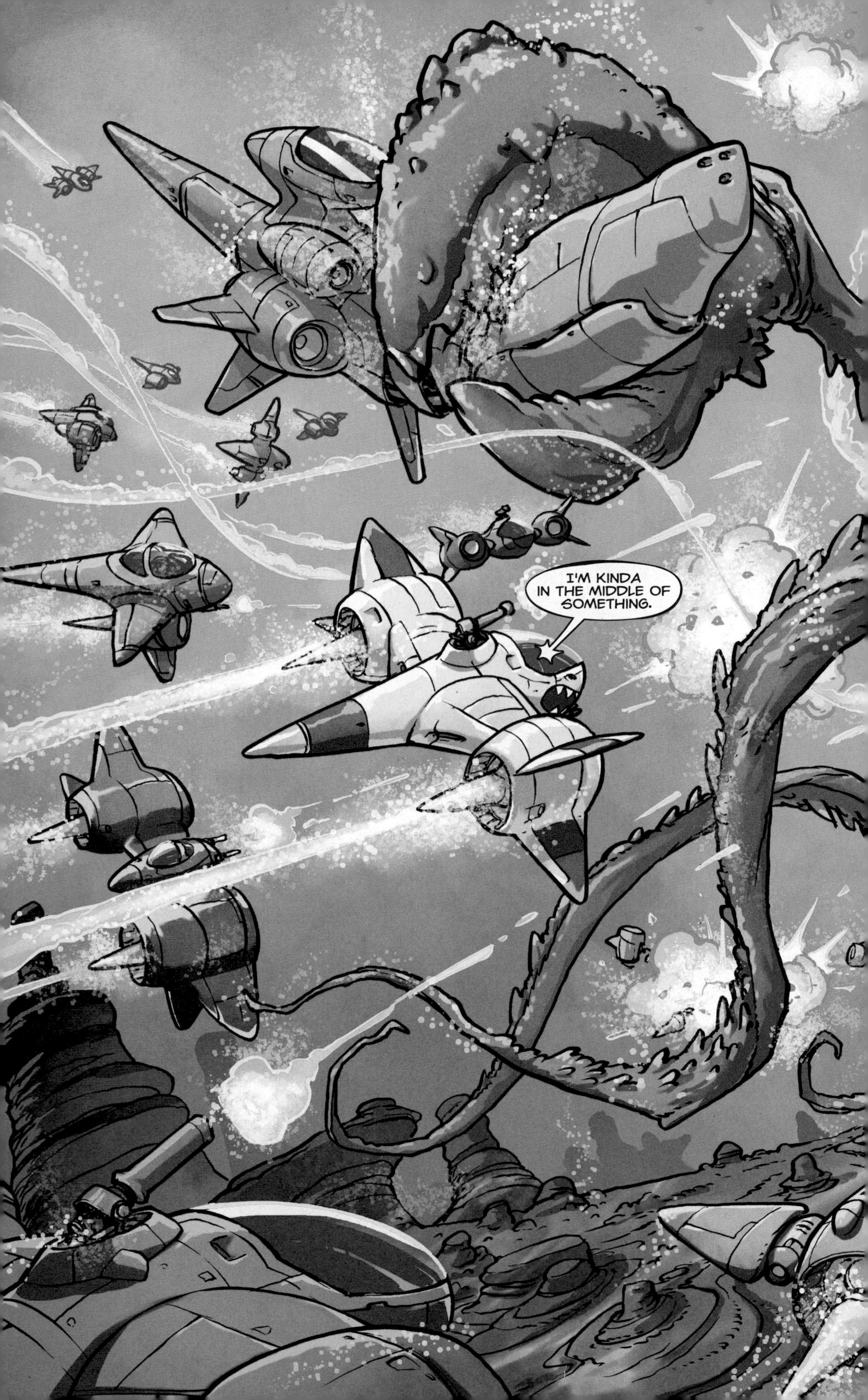
I'M KINDA IN THE MIDDLE OF SOMETHING.

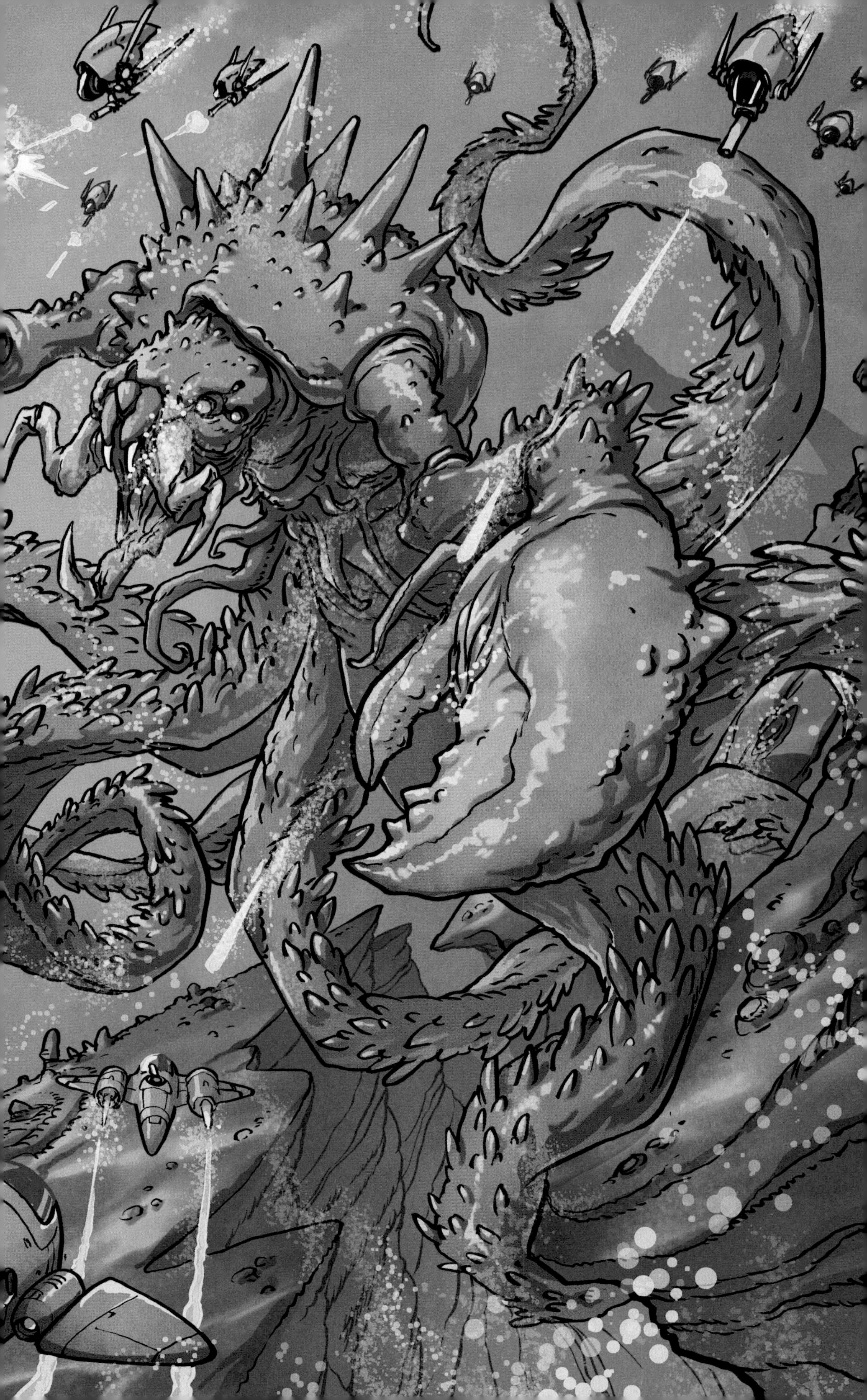

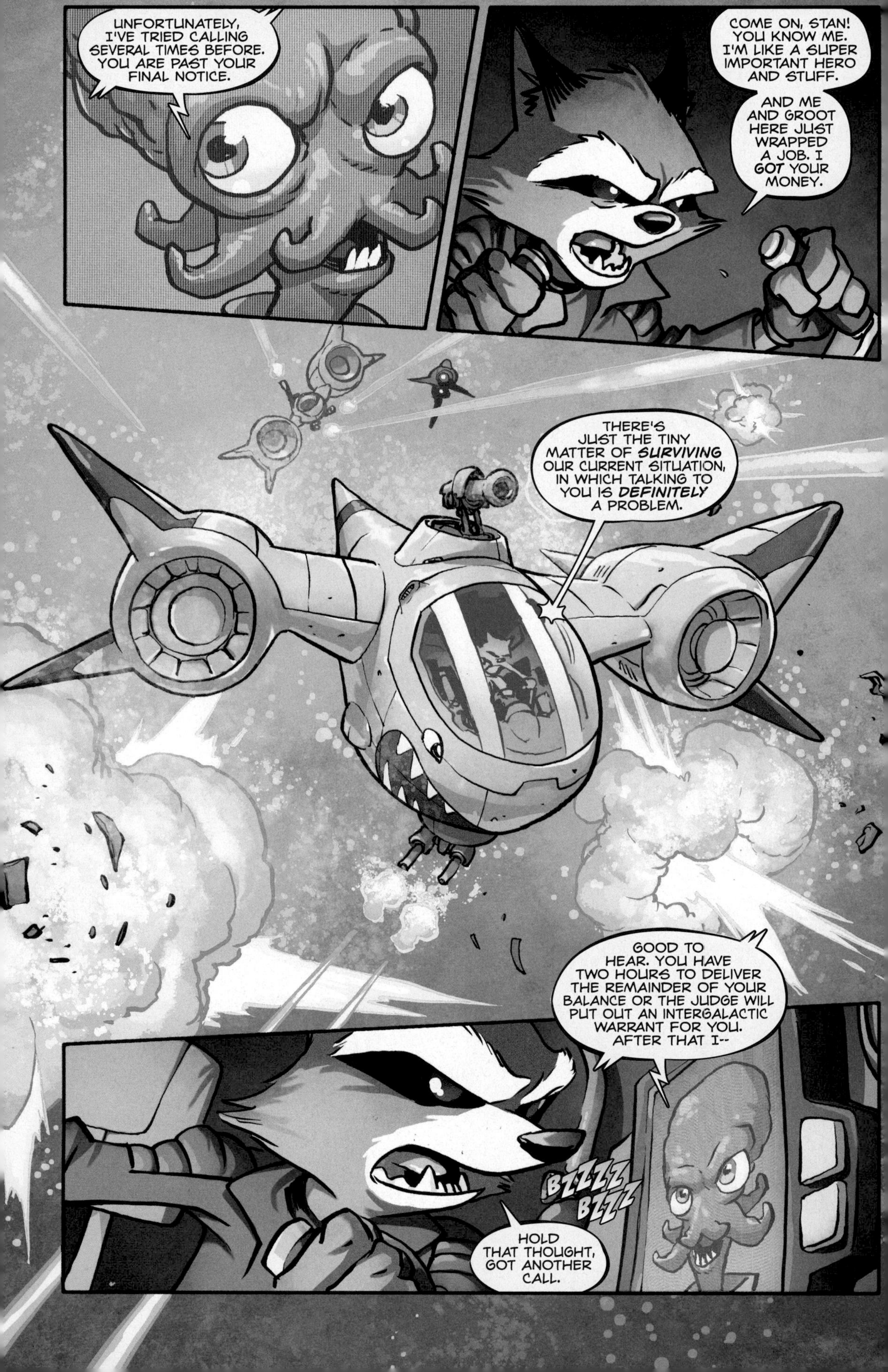
UNFORTUNATELY, I'VE TRIED CALLING SEVERAL TIMES BEFORE. YOU ARE PAST YOUR FINAL NOTICE.
COME ON, STAN! YOU KNOW ME. I'M LIKE A SUPER IMPORTANT HERO AND STUFF.
AND ME AND GROOT HERE JUST WRAPPED A JOB. I GOT YOUR MONEY.
THERE'S JUST THE TINY MATTER OF SURVIVING OUR CURRENT SITUATION, IN WHICH TALKING TO YOU IS DEFINITELY A PROBLEM.
GOOD TO HEAR. YOU HAVE TWO HOURS TO DELIVER THE REMAINDER OF YOUR BALANCE OR THE JUDGE WILL PUT OUT AN INTERGALACTIC WARRANT FOR YOU. AFTER THAT I--
BZZZZ BZZZ
HOLD THAT THOUGHT, GOT ANOTHER CALL.

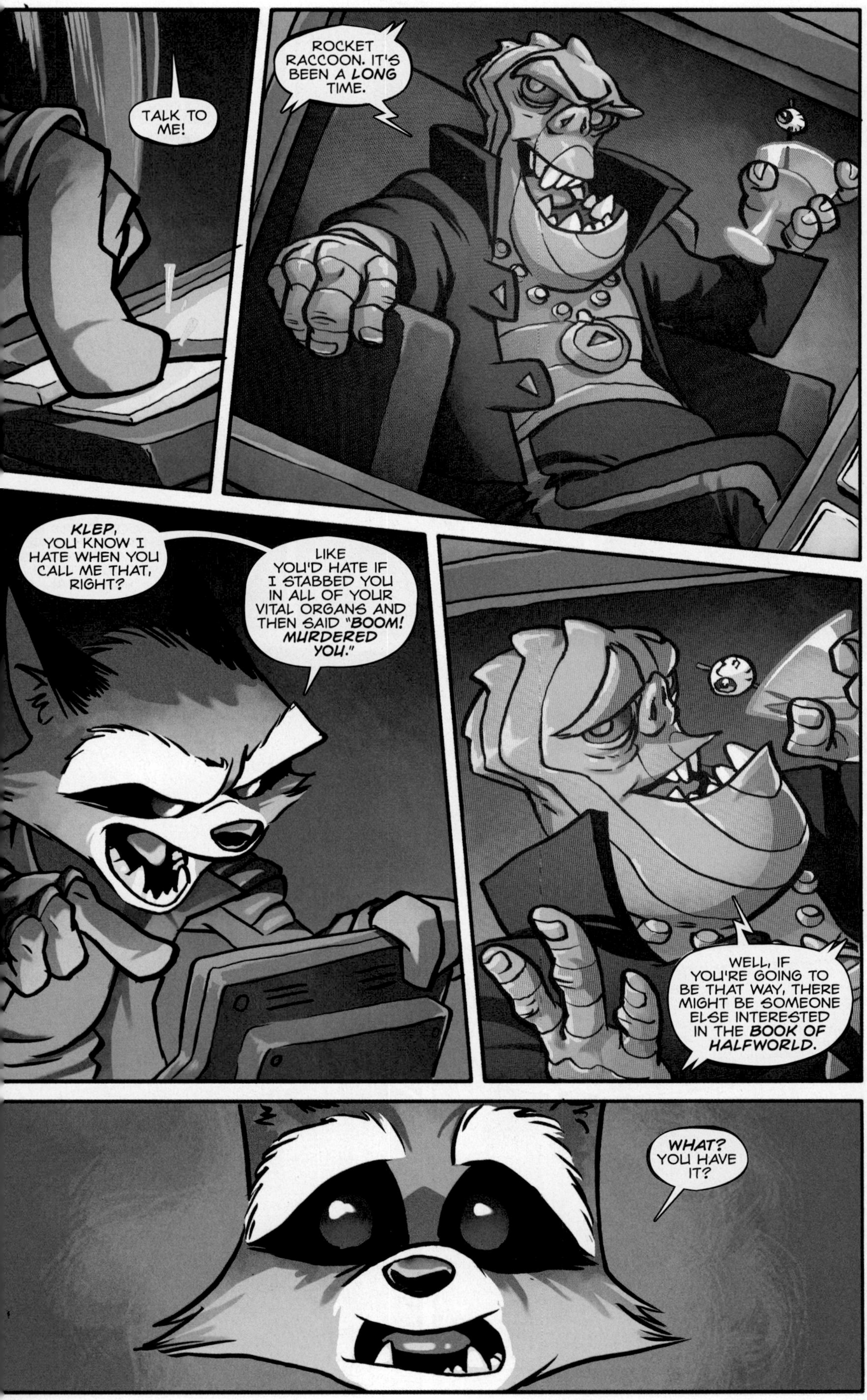
TALK TO ME!
ROCKET RACCOON. IT'S BEEN A LONG TIME.
KLEP, YOU KNOW I HATE WHEN YOU CALL ME THAT, RIGHT?
LIKE YOU'D HATE IF I STABBED YOU IN ALL OF YOUR VITAL ORGANS AND THEN SAID "BOOM! MURDERED YOU."
WELL, IF YOU'RE GOING TO BE THAT WAY, THERE MIGHT BE SOMEONE ELSE INTERESTED IN THE BOOK OF HALFWORLD.
WHAT? YOU HAVE IT?

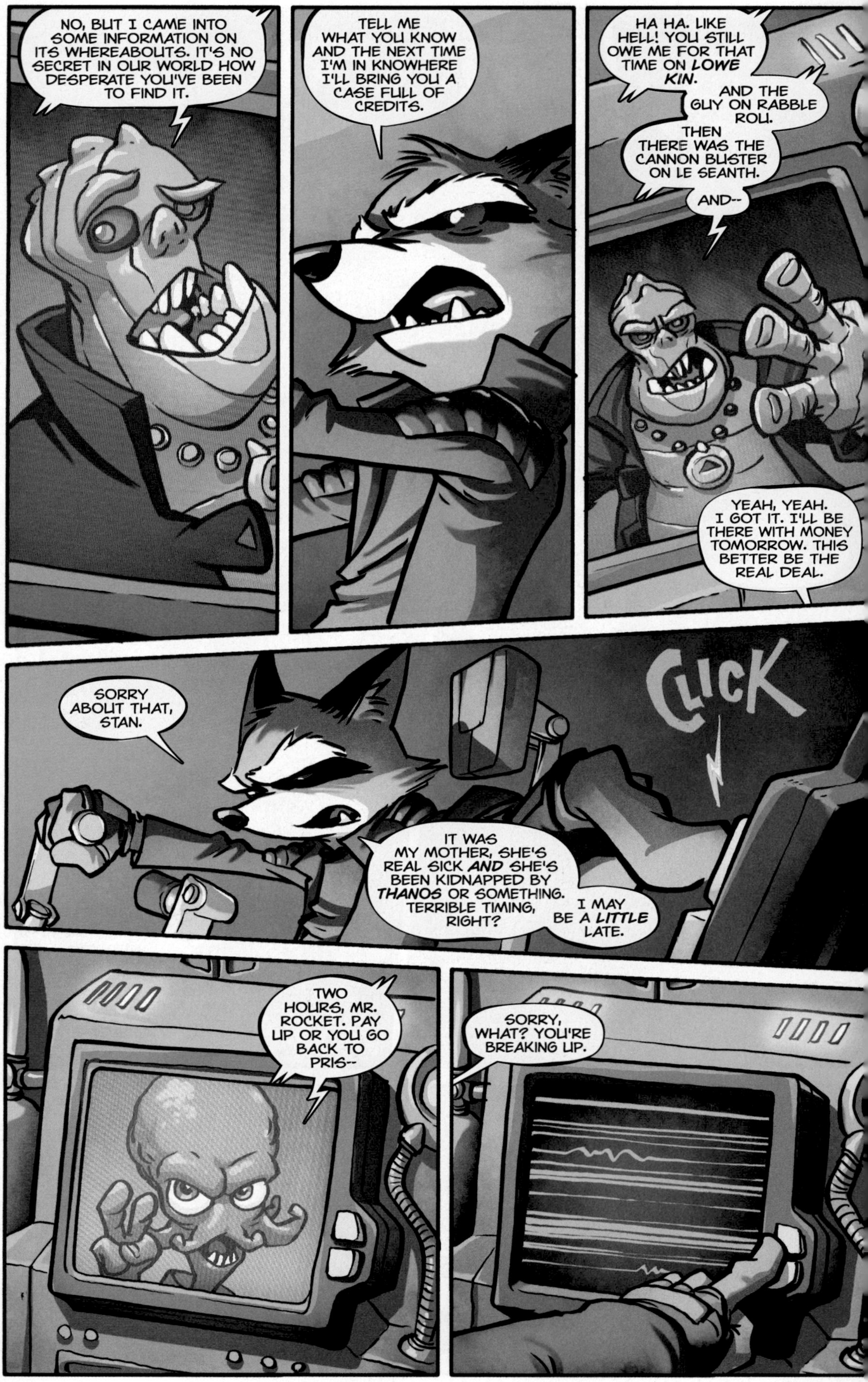
NO, BUT I CAME INTO SOME INFORMATION ON ITS WHEREABOUTS. IT'S NO SECRET IN OUR WORLD HOW DESPERATE YOU'VE BEEN TO FIND IT.
TELL ME WHAT YOU KNOW AND THE NEXT TIME I'M IN KNOWHERE I'LL BRING YOU A CASE FULL OF CREDITS.
HA HA. LIKE HELL! YOU STILL OWE ME FOR THAT TIME ON *LOWE KIN*.
AND THE GUY ON RABBLE ROU.
THEN THERE WAS THE CANNON BUSTER ON LE SEANTH.
AND--
YEAH, YEAH. I GOT IT. I'LL BE THERE WITH MONEY TOMORROW. THIS BETTER BE THE REAL DEAL.
CLICK
SORRY ABOUT THAT, STAN.
IT WAS MY MOTHER, SHE'S REAL SICK *AND* SHE'S BEEN KIDNAPPED BY *THANOS* OR SOMETHING. TERRIBLE TIMING, RIGHT?
I MAY BE A *LITTLE* LATE.
TWO HOURS, MR. ROCKET. PAY UP OR YOU GO BACK TO PRIS--
SORRY, WHAT? YOU'RE BREAKING UP.

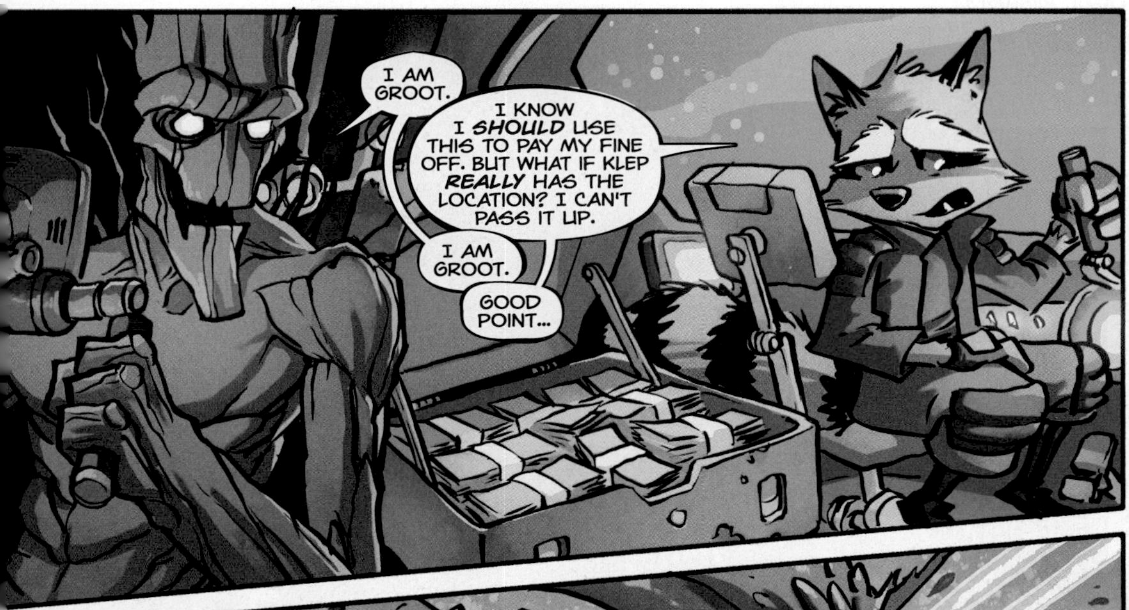
I AM GROOT.
I KNOW I SHOULD USE THIS TO PAY MY FINE OFF. BUT WHAT IF KLEP REALLY HAS THE LOCATION? I CAN'T PASS IT UP.
I AM GROOT.
GOOD POINT...

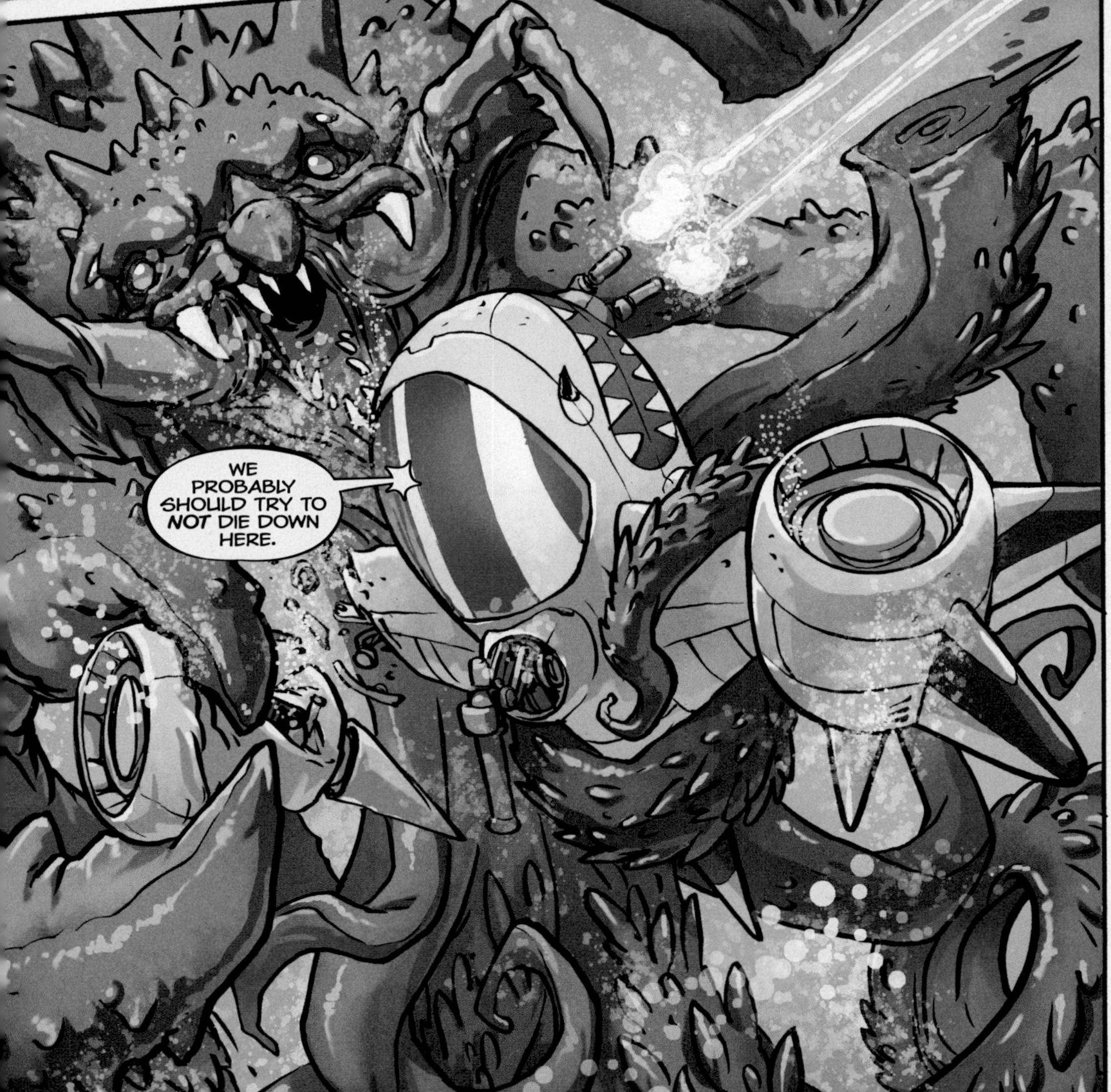
WE PROBABLY SHOULD TRY TO NOT DIE DOWN HERE.

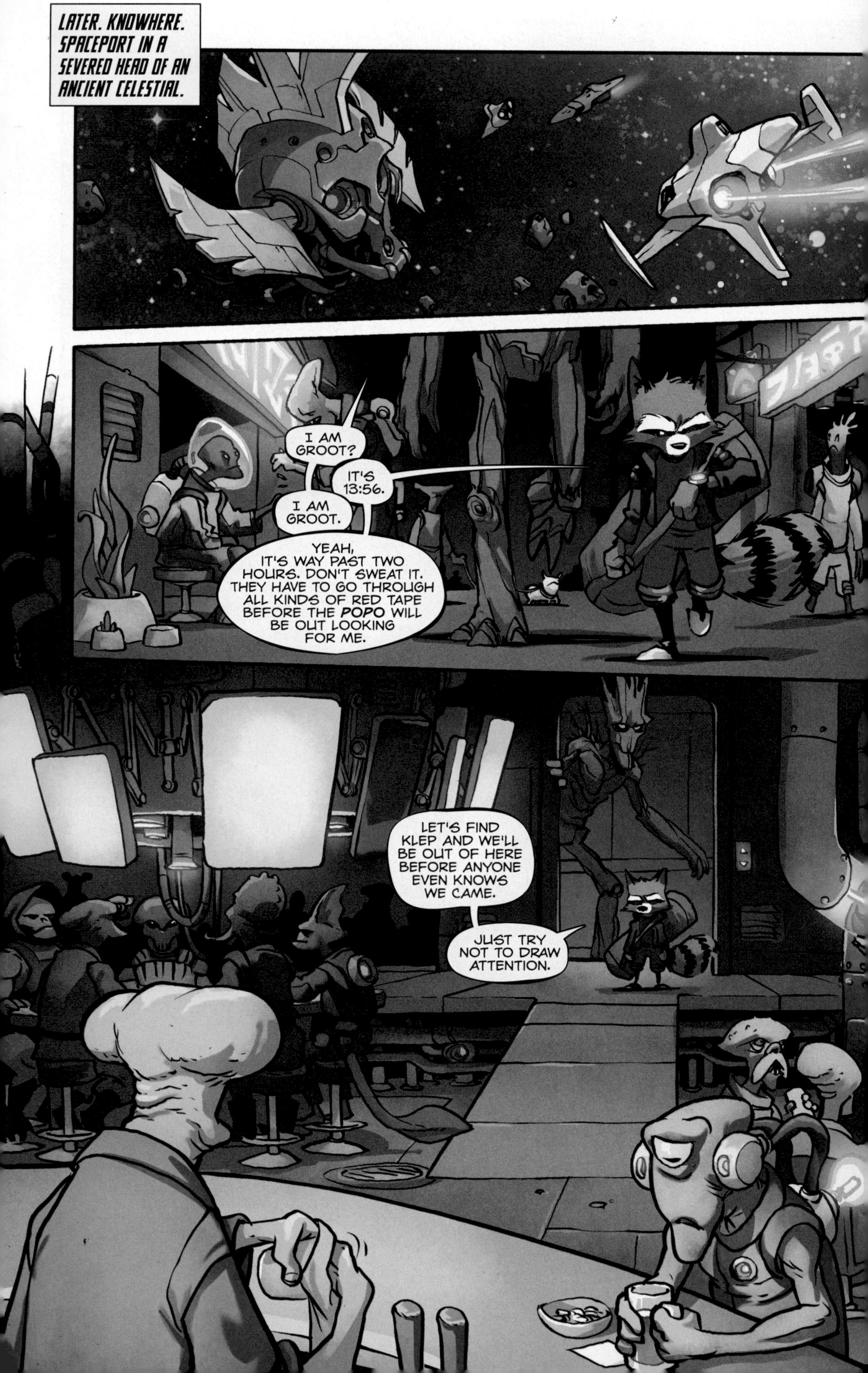
LATER. KNOWHERE. SPACEPORT IN A SEVERED HEAD OF AN ANCIENT CELESTIAL.
I AM GROOT?
IT'S 13:56.
I AM GROOT.
YEAH, IT'S WAY PAST TWO HOURS. DON'T SWEAT IT. THEY HAVE TO GO THROUGH ALL KINDS OF RED TAPE BEFORE THE *POPO* WILL BE OUT LOOKING FOR ME.
LET'S FIND KLEP AND WE'LL BE OUT OF HERE BEFORE ANYONE EVEN KNOWS WE CAME.
JUST TRY NOT TO DRAW ATTENTION.

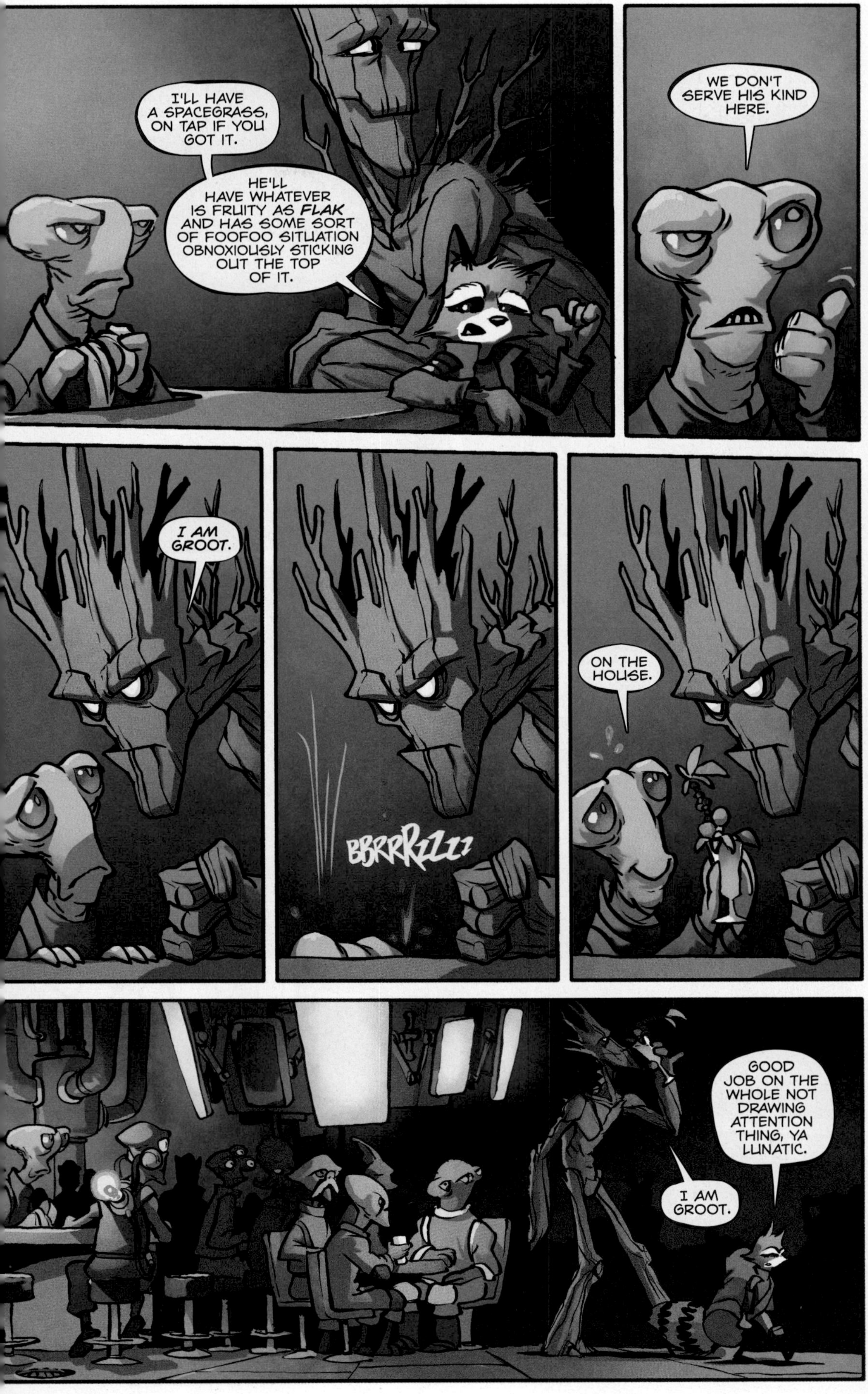
I'LL HAVE A SPACEGRASS, ON TAP IF YOU GOT IT.
HE'LL HAVE WHATEVER IS FRUITY AS FLAK AND HAS SOME SORT OF FOOFOO SITUATION OBNOXIOUSLY STICKING OUT THE TOP OF IT.
WE DON'T SERVE HIS KIND HERE.
I AM GROOT.
BBRRRZZZZ
ON THE HOUSE.
GOOD JOB ON THE WHOLE NOT DRAWING ATTENTION THING, YA LUNATIC.
I AM GROOT.

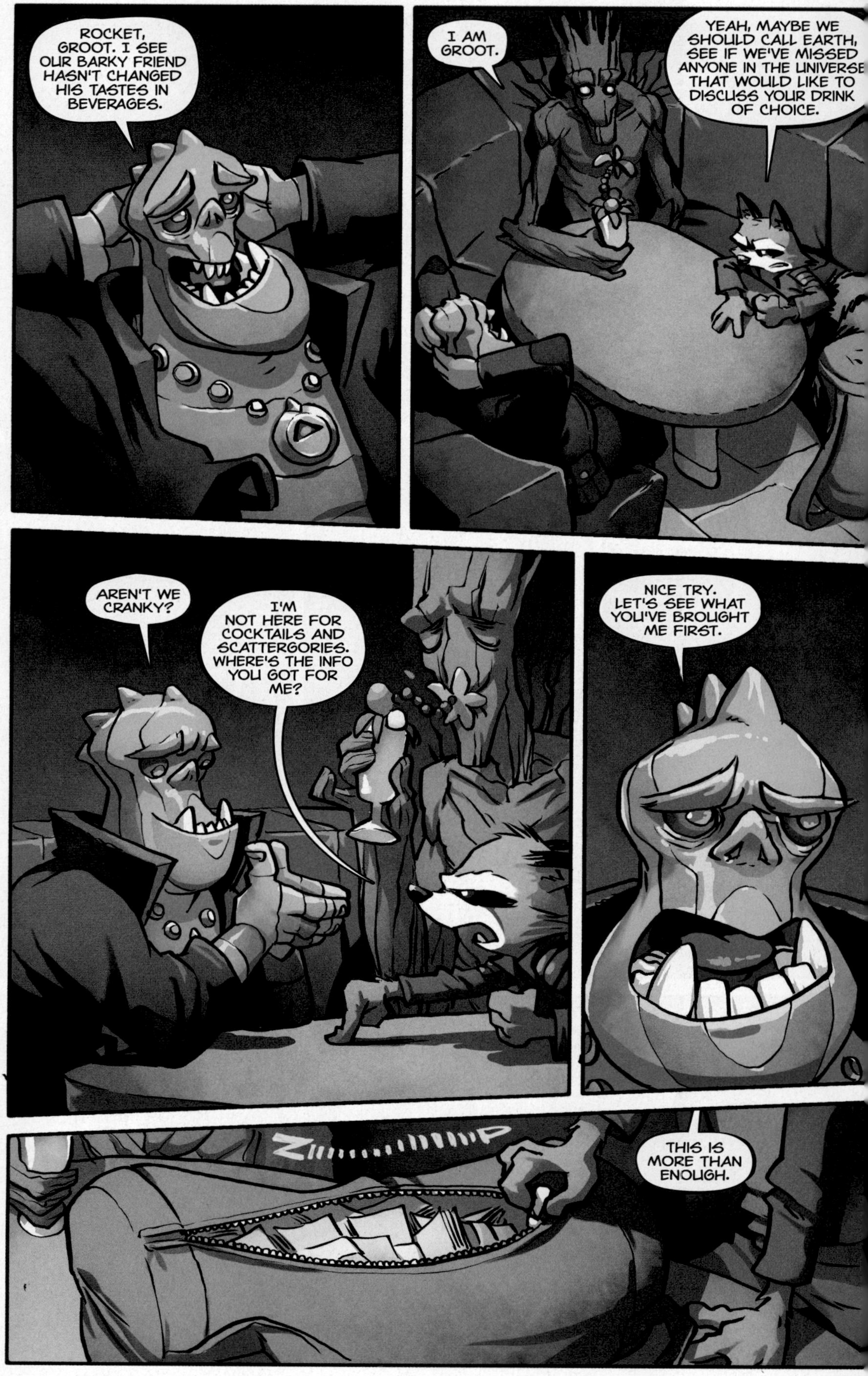
ROCKET, GROOT. I SEE OUR BARKY FRIEND HASN'T CHANGED HIS TASTES IN BEVERAGES.
I AM GROOT.
YEAH, MAYBE WE SHOULD CALL EARTH, SEE IF WE'VE MISSED ANYONE IN THE UNIVERSE THAT WOULD LIKE TO DISCUSS YOUR DRINK OF CHOICE.
AREN'T WE CRANKY?
I'M NOT HERE FOR COCKTAILS AND SCATTERGORIES. WHERE'S THE INFO YOU GOT FOR ME?
NICE TRY. LET'S SEE WHAT YOU'VE BROUGHT ME FIRST.
ZIIIIIIIIIIIIIP
THIS IS MORE THAN ENOUGH.

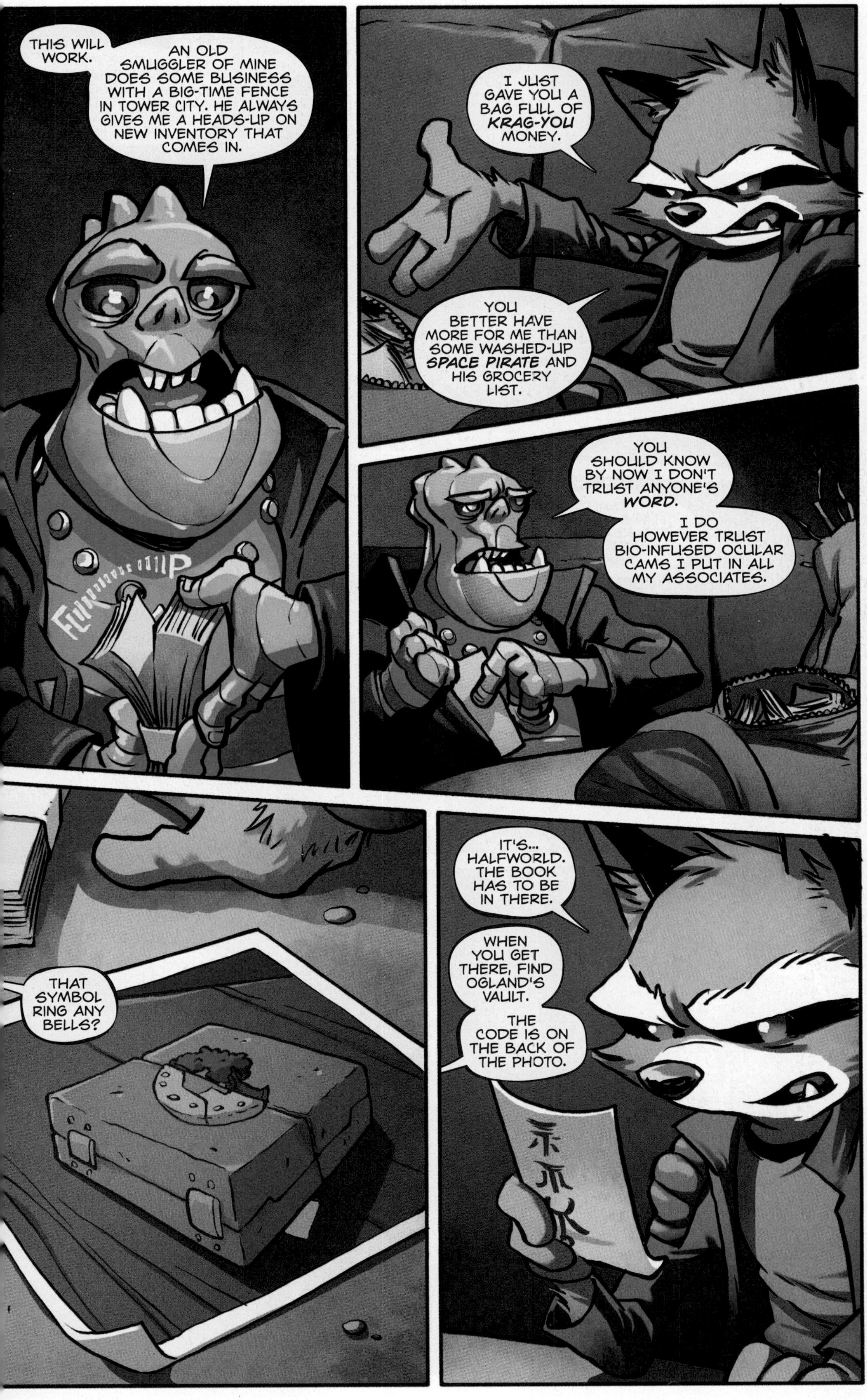
THIS WILL WORK.
AN OLD SMUGGLER OF MINE DOES SOME BUSINESS WITH A BIG-TIME FENCE IN TOWER CITY. HE ALWAYS GIVES ME A HEADS-UP ON NEW INVENTORY THAT COMES IN.
I JUST GAVE YOU A BAG FULL OF KRAG-YOU MONEY.
YOU BETTER HAVE MORE FOR ME THAN SOME WASHED-UP SPACE PIRATE AND HIS GROCERY LIST.
YOU SHOULD KNOW BY NOW I DON'T TRUST ANYONE'S WORD.
I DO HOWEVER TRUST BIO-INFUSED OCULAR CAMS I PUT IN ALL MY ASSOCIATES.
THAT SYMBOL RING ANY BELLS?
IT'S... HALFWORLD. THE BOOK HAS TO BE IN THERE.
WHEN YOU GET THERE, FIND OGLAND'S VAULT.
THE CODE IS ON THE BACK OF THE PHOTO.

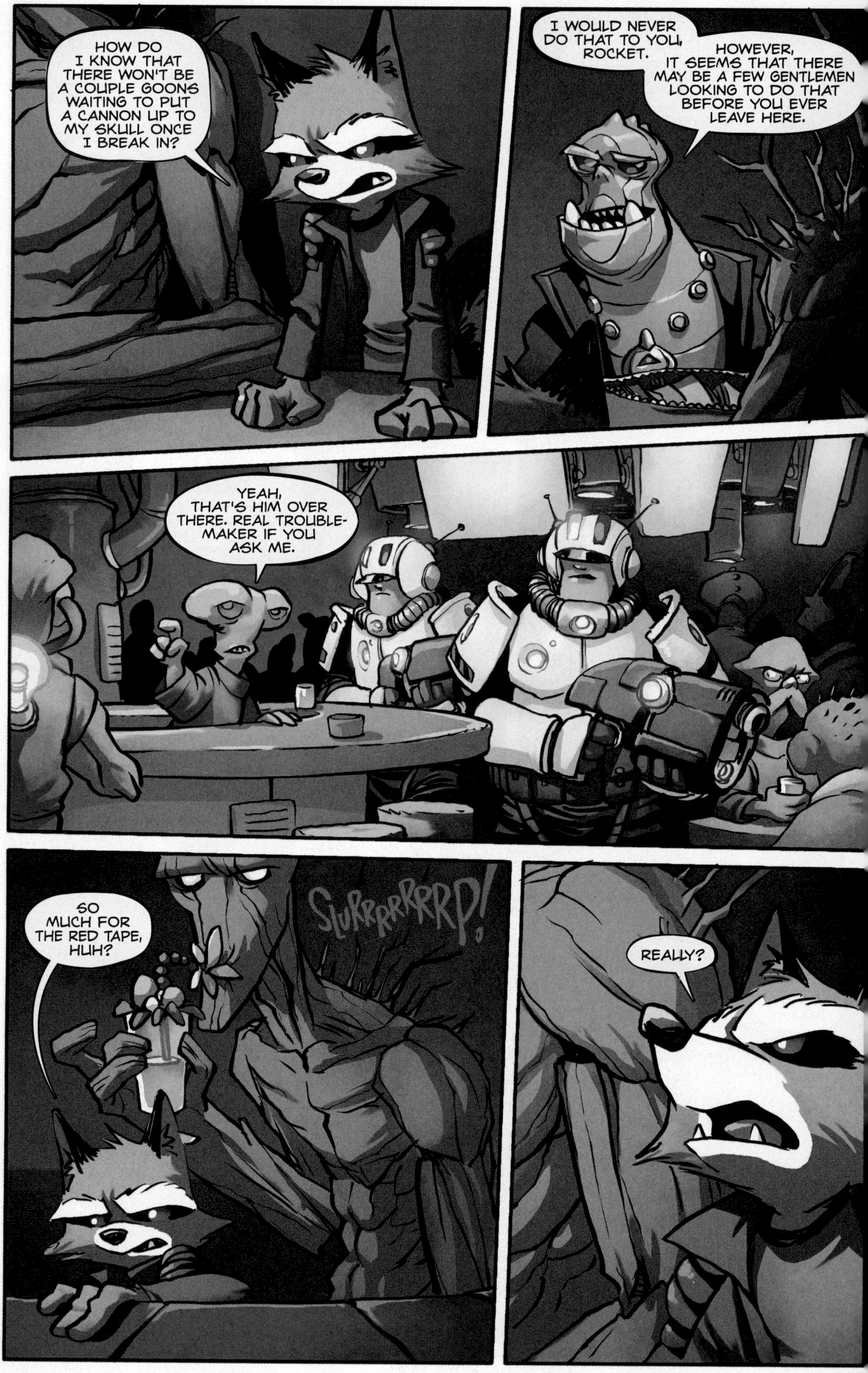
HOW DO I KNOW THAT THERE WON'T BE A COUPLE GOONS WAITING TO PUT A CANNON UP TO MY SKULL ONCE I BREAK IN?
I WOULD NEVER DO THAT TO YOU, ROCKET.
HOWEVER, IT SEEMS THAT THERE MAY BE A FEW GENTLEMEN LOOKING TO DO THAT BEFORE YOU EVER LEAVE HERE.
YEAH, THAT'S HIM OVER THERE. REAL TROUBLE-MAKER IF YOU ASK ME.
SLURRRRRRP!
SO MUCH FOR THE RED TAPE, HUH?
REALLY?

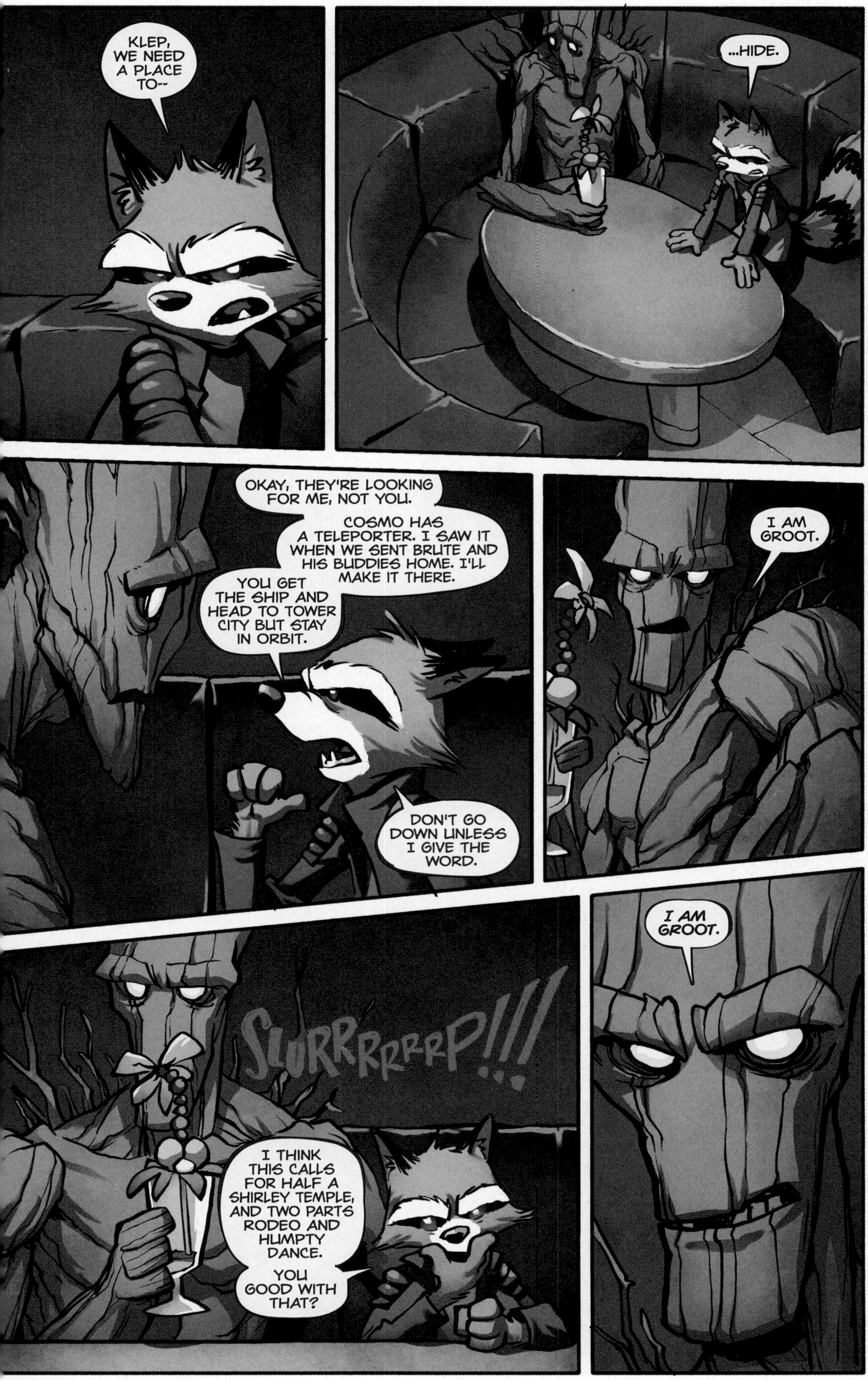
KLEP, WE NEED A PLACE TO--
...HIDE.
OKAY, THEY'RE LOOKING FOR ME, NOT YOU.
COSMO HAS A TELEPORTER. I SAW IT WHEN WE SENT BRUTE AND HIS BUDDIES HOME. I'LL MAKE IT THERE.
YOU GET THE SHIP AND HEAD TO TOWER CITY BUT STAY IN ORBIT.
DON'T GO DOWN UNLESS I GIVE THE WORD.
I AM GROOT.
SLURRRRRRP!!!
I THINK THIS CALLS FOR HALF A SHIRLEY TEMPLE, AND TWO PARTS RODEO AND HUMPTY DANCE.
YOU GOOD WITH THAT?
I AM GROOT.

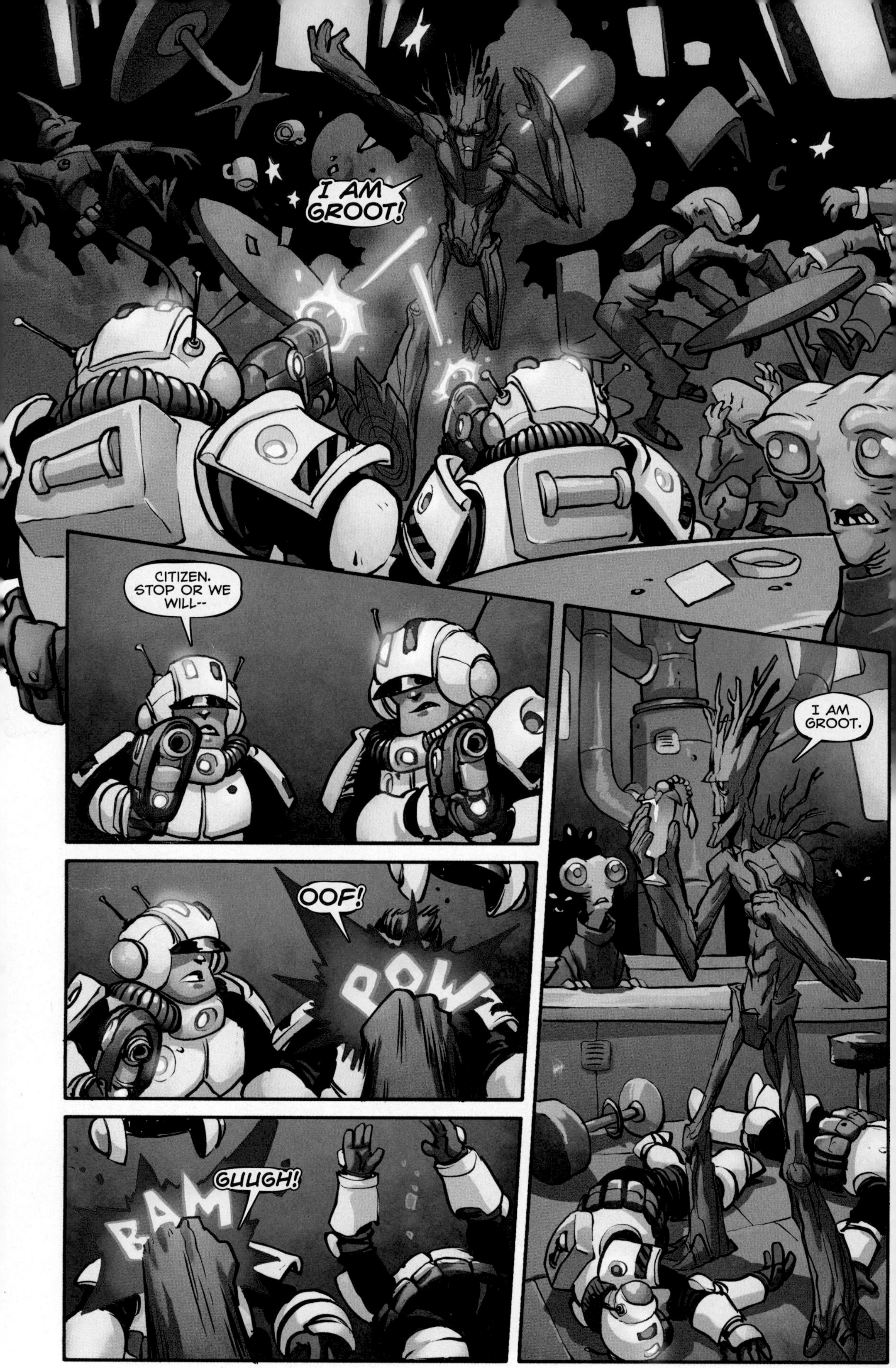
I AM GROOT!
CITIZEN. STOP OR WE WILL--
OOF!
POW
GULUGH!
BAM
I AM GROOT.

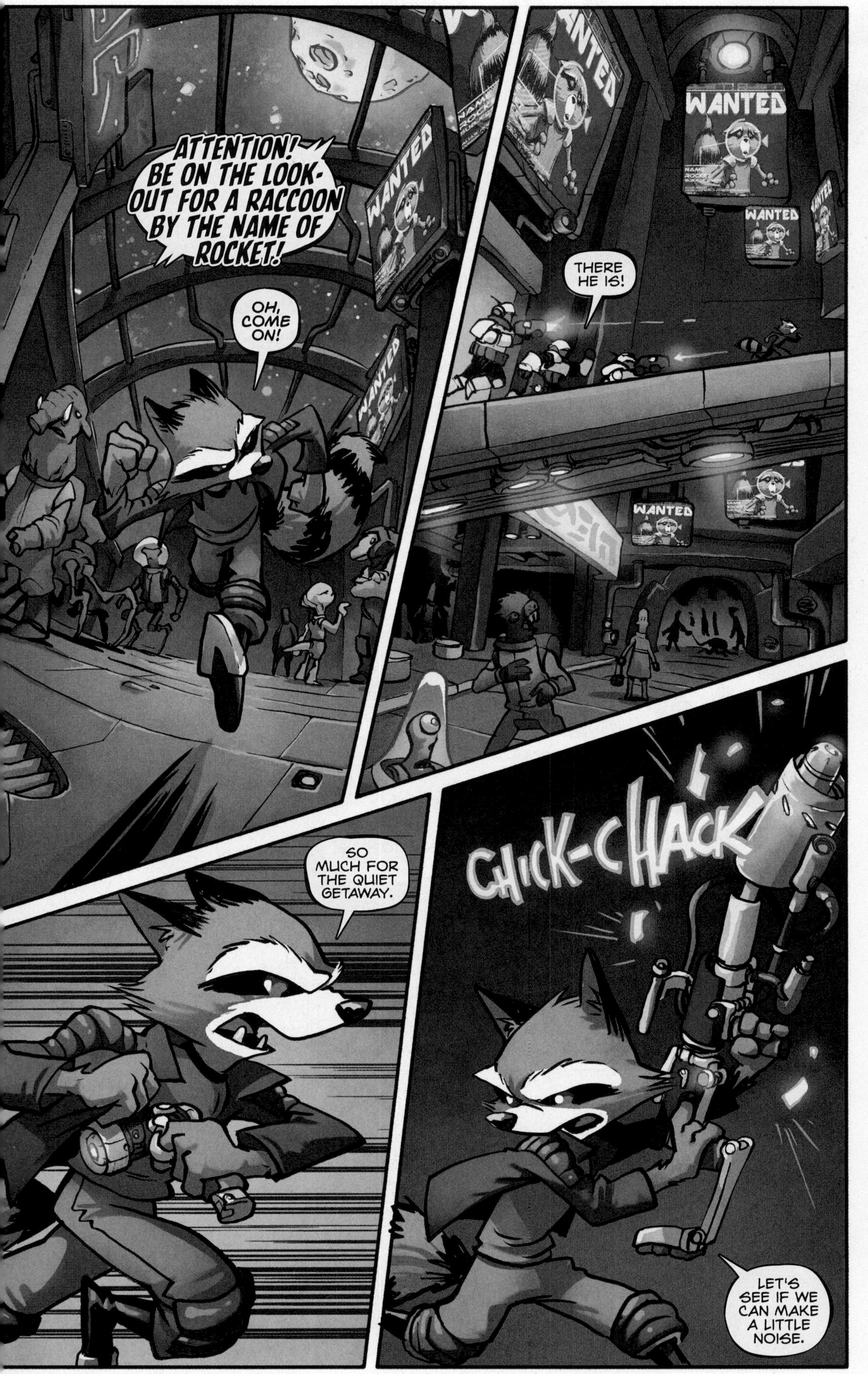
ATTENTION! BE ON THE LOOK-OUT FOR A RACCOON BY THE NAME OF ROCKET!
OH, COME ON!
WANTED
THERE HE IS!
SO MUCH FOR THE QUIET GETAWAY.
CHICK-CHACK
LET'S SEE IF WE CAN MAKE A LITTLE NOISE.

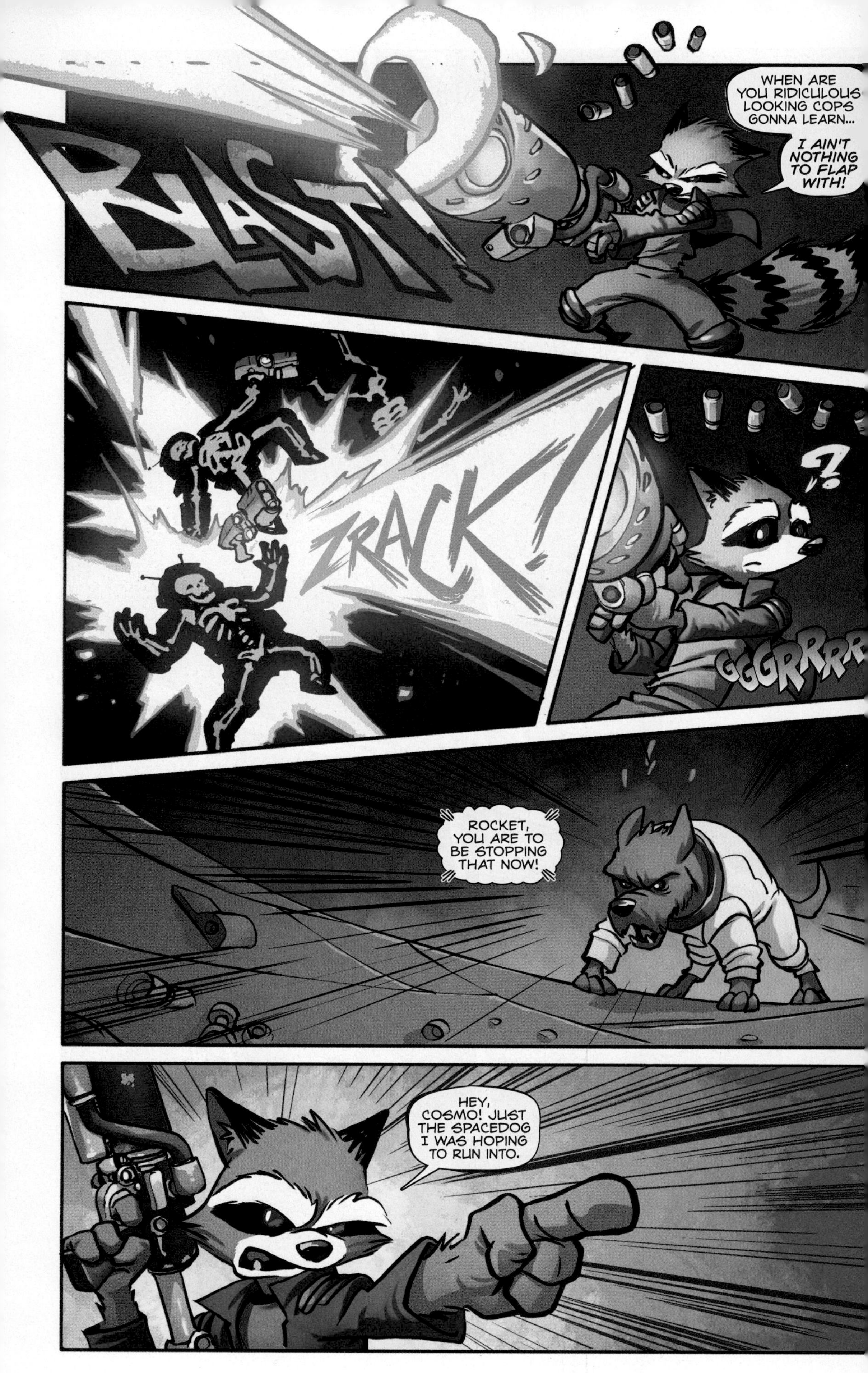
BLAST!
WHEN ARE YOU RIDICULOUS LOOKING COPS GONNA LEARN...
I AIN'T NOTHING TO FLAP WITH!
ZRACK!
GGGRRRR
ROCKET, YOU ARE TO BE STOPPING THAT NOW!
HEY, COSMO! JUST THE SPACEDOG I WAS HOPING TO RUN INTO.

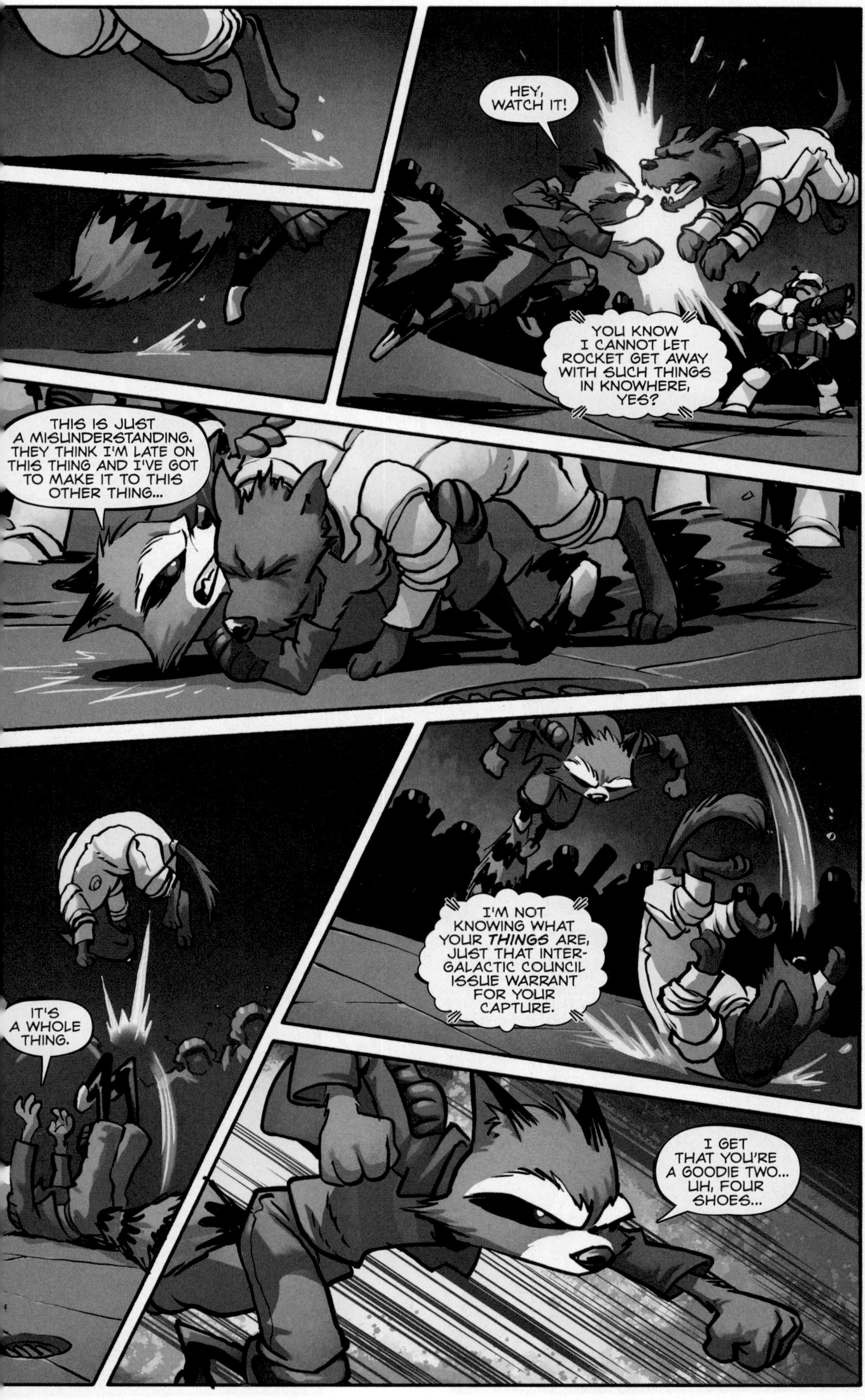

HEY, WATCH IT!
YOU KNOW I CANNOT LET ROCKET GET AWAY WITH SUCH THINGS IN KNOWHERE, YES?
THIS IS JUST A MISUNDERSTANDING. THEY THINK I'M LATE ON THIS THING AND I'VE GOT TO MAKE IT TO THIS OTHER THING...
I'M NOT KNOWING WHAT YOUR *THINGS* ARE, JUST THAT INTER-GALACTIC COUNCIL ISSUE WARRANT FOR YOUR CAPTURE.
IT'S A WHOLE THING.
I GET THAT YOU'RE A GOODIE TWO... UH, FOUR SHOES...

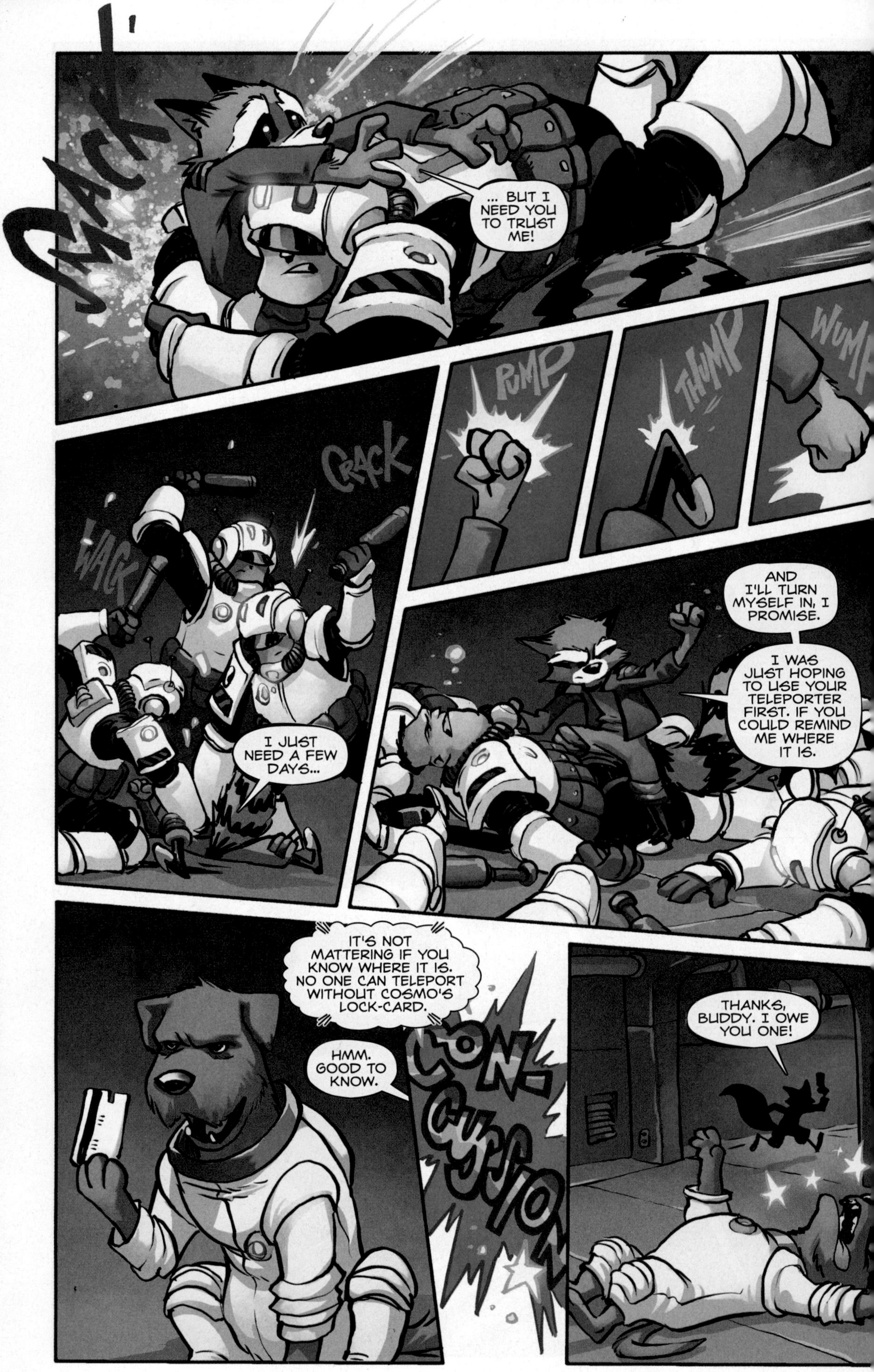
SMACK!
... BUT I NEED YOU TO TRUST ME!
PUMP
THUMP
WUMP
CRACK
WACK
I JUST NEED A FEW DAYS...
AND I'LL TURN MYSELF IN, I PROMISE.
I WAS JUST HOPING TO USE YOUR TELEPORTER FIRST. IF YOU COULD REMIND ME WHERE IT IS.
IT'S NOT MATTERING IF YOU KNOW WHERE IT IS. NO ONE CAN TELEPORT WITHOUT COSMO'S LOCK-CARD.
HMM. GOOD TO KNOW.
CONCUSSION
THANKS, BUDDY. I OWE YOU ONE!

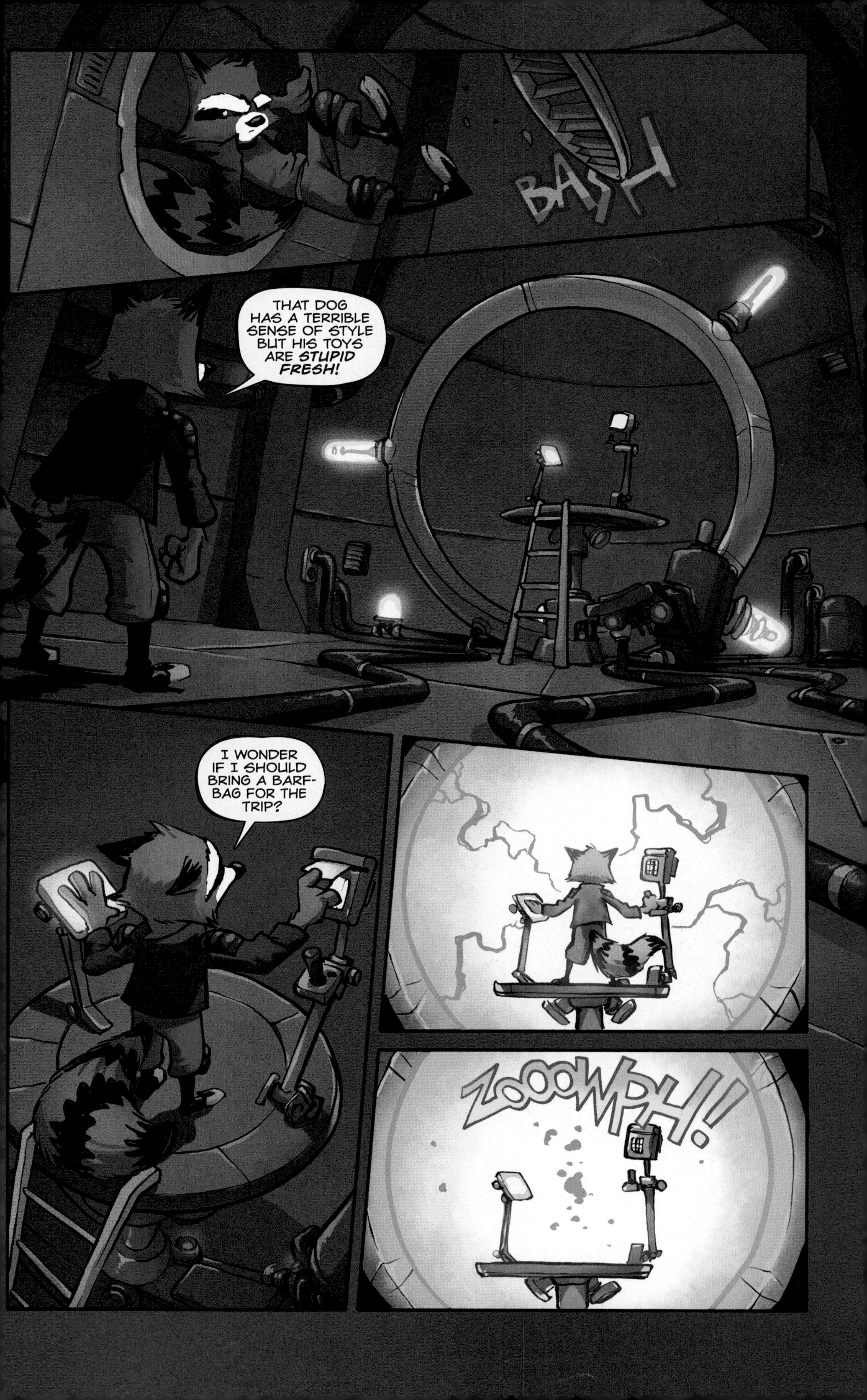
BASH
THAT DOG HAS A TERRIBLE SENSE OF STYLE BUT HIS TOYS ARE STUPID FRESH!
I WONDER IF I SHOULD BRING A BARF-BAG FOR THE TRIP?
ZOOOWPH!!

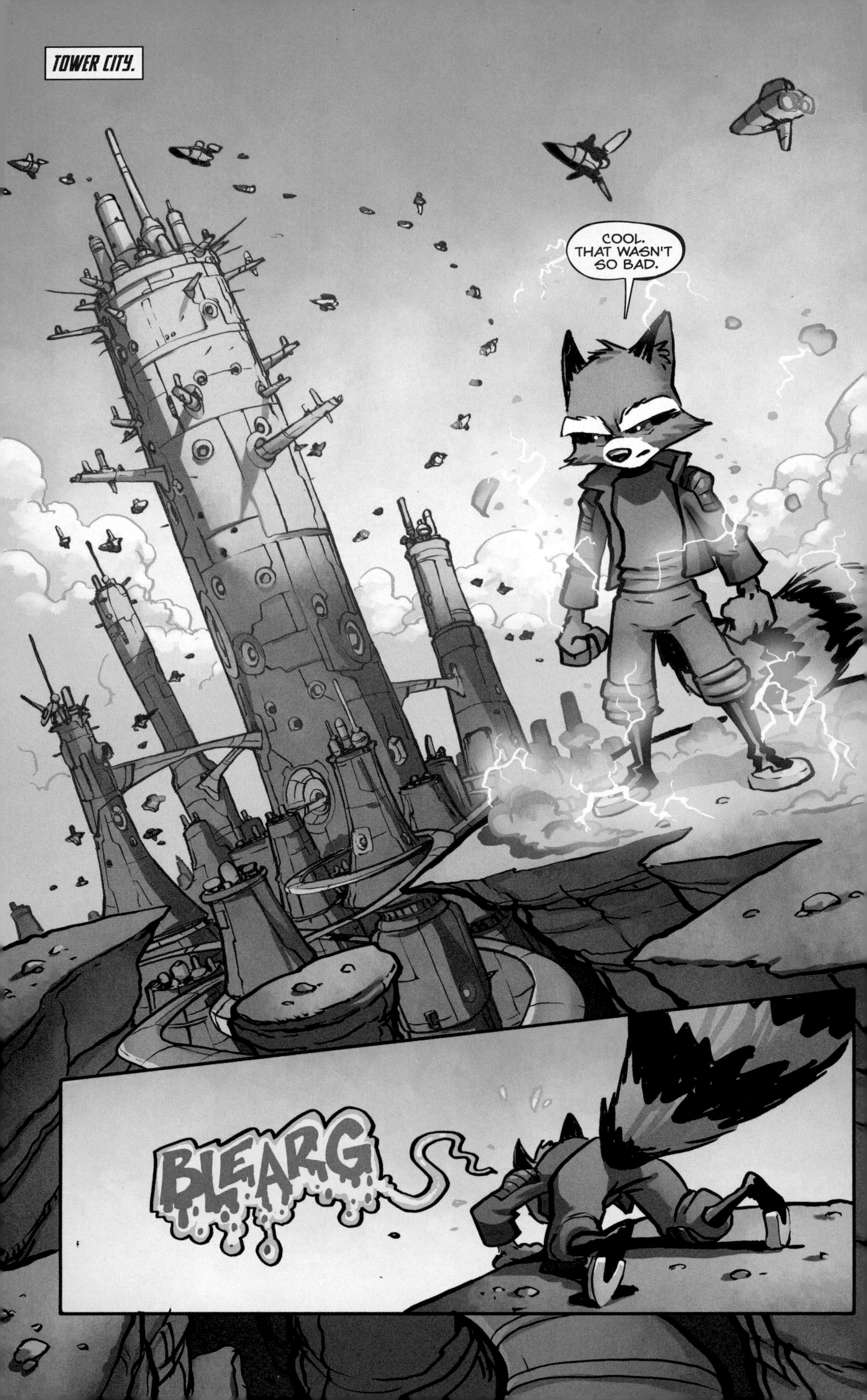
TOWER CITY.
COOL. THAT WASN'T SO BAD.
BLEARG

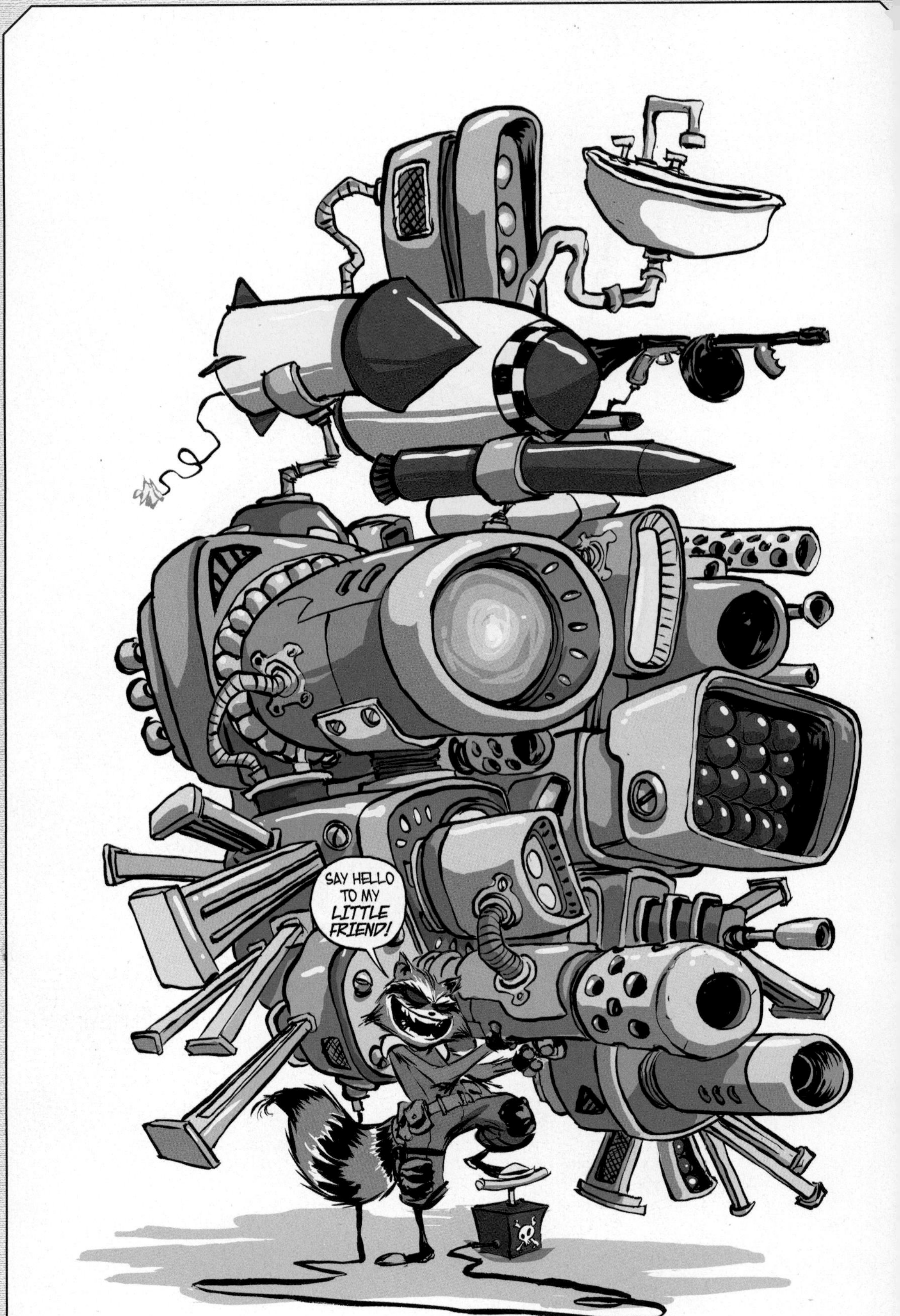
SAY HELLO
TO MY
LITTLE
FRIEND!

11 BOOKENDS part 2

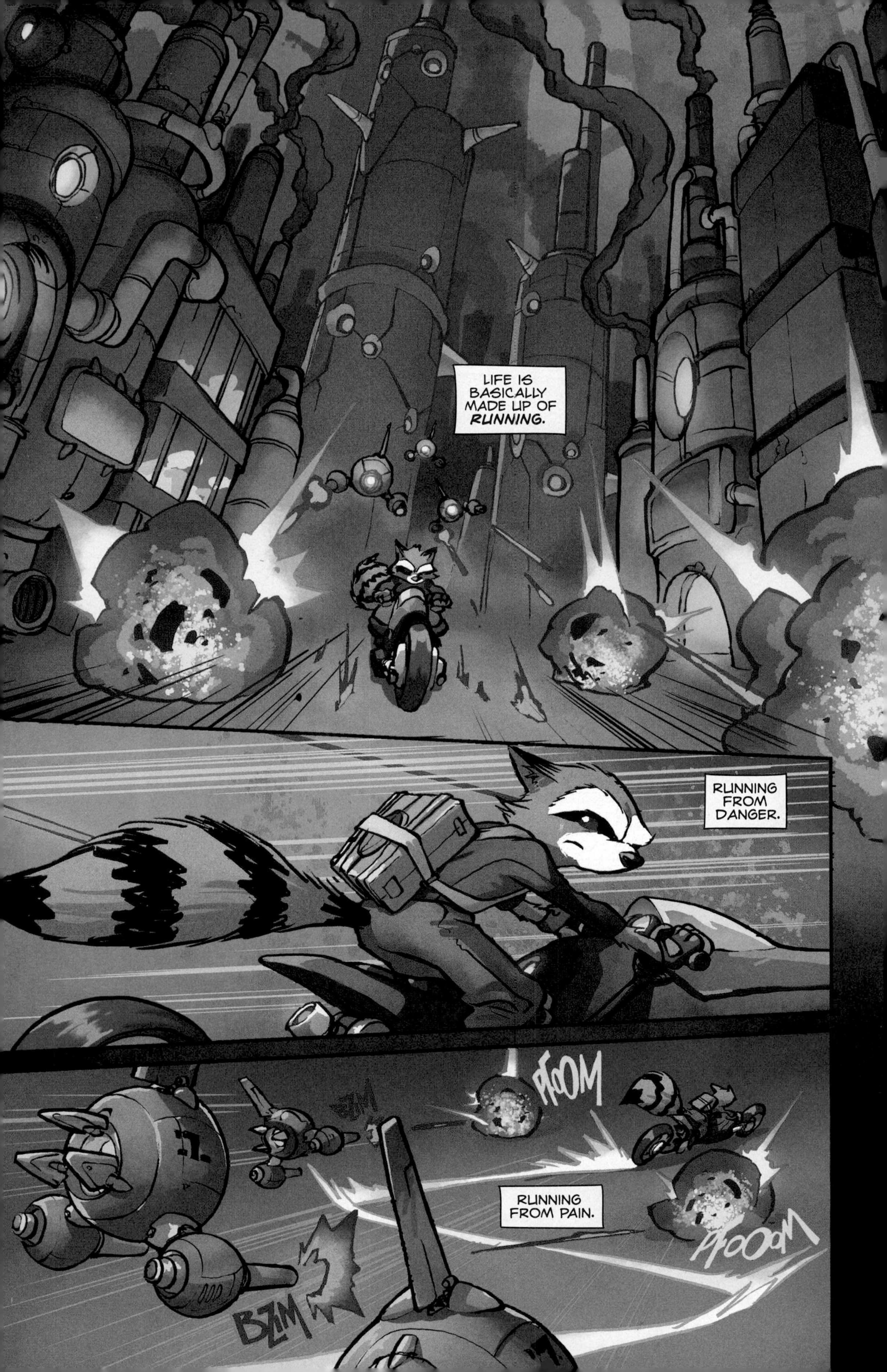
LIFE IS BASICALLY MADE UP OF *RUNNING*.
RUNNING FROM DANGER.
PFOOM
BZIM
RUNNING FROM PAIN.
PFOOOM
BZIM

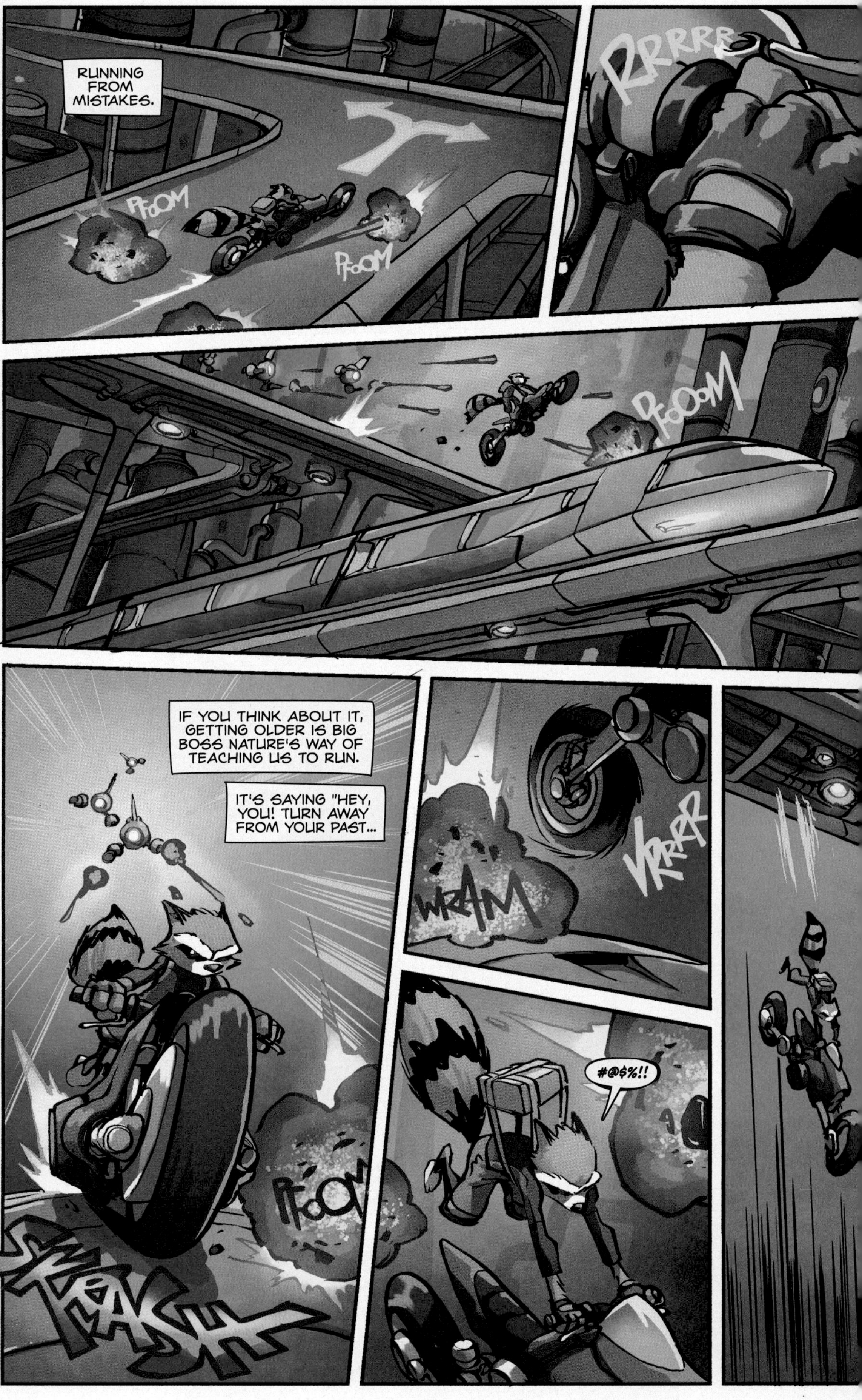
RUNNING FROM MISTAKES.
PFOOM
PFOOM
RRRRR
PFOOOM
IF YOU THINK ABOUT IT, GETTING OLDER IS BIG BOSS NATURE'S WAY OF TEACHING US TO RUN.
IT'S SAYING "HEY, YOU! TURN AWAY FROM YOUR PAST...
VRRRR
WRAM
PFOOM
SKRASH
#@$%!!

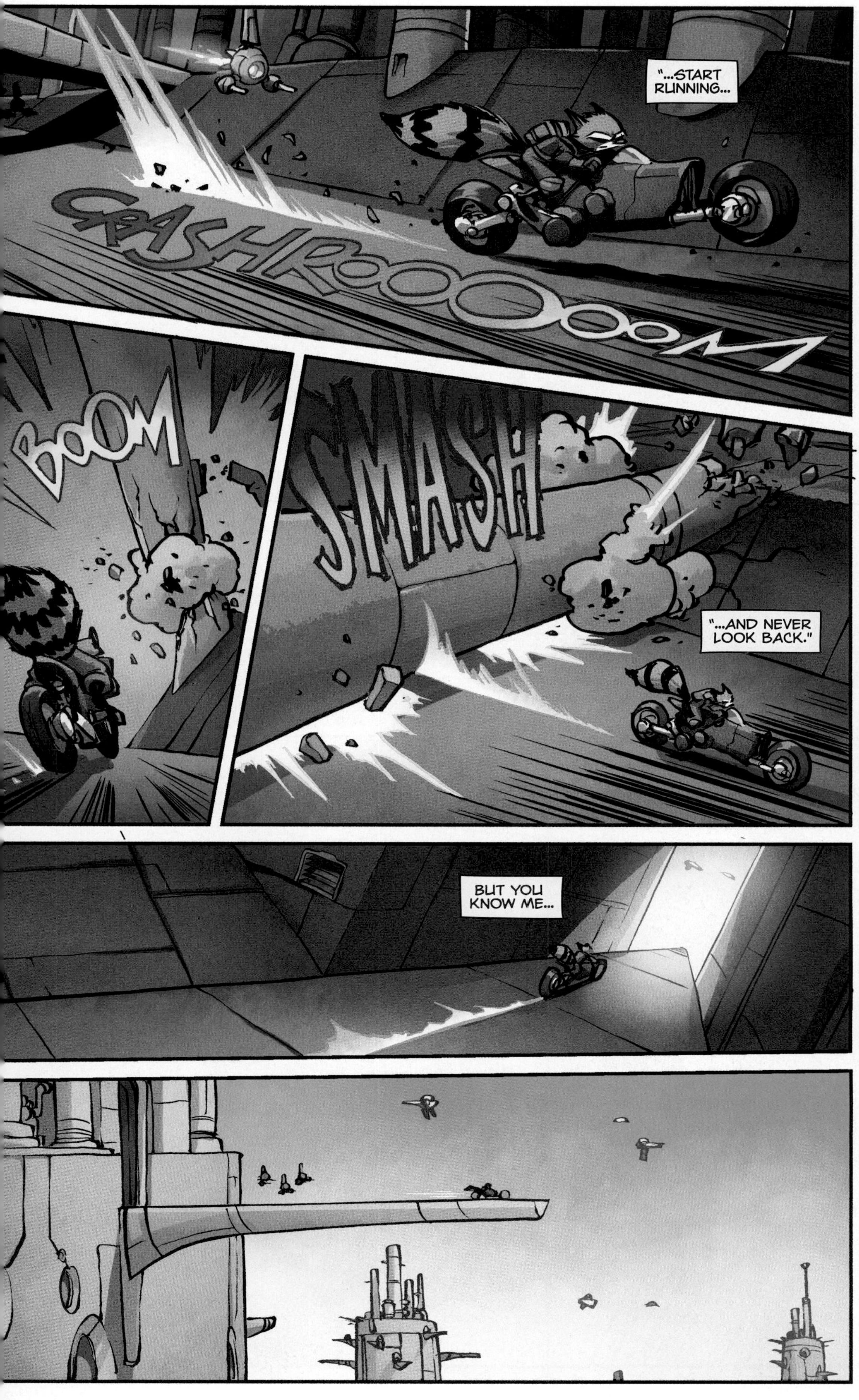
"...START RUNNING...
CRASHROOOOOOM
BOOM
SMASH
"...AND NEVER LOOK BACK."
BUT YOU KNOW ME...

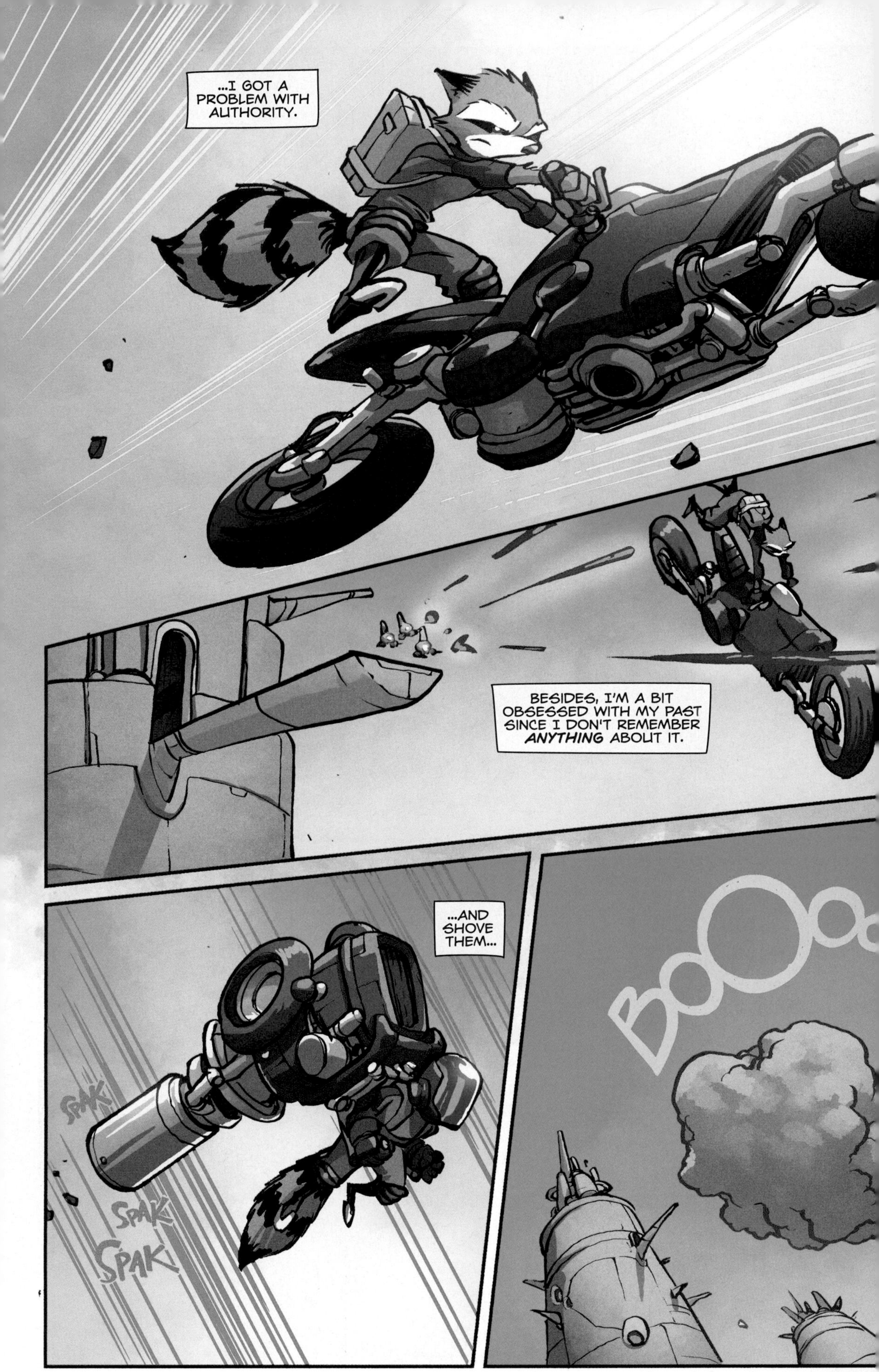
...I GOT A PROBLEM WITH AUTHORITY.
BESIDES, I'M A BIT OBSESSED WITH MY PAST SINCE I DON'T REMEMBER *ANYTHING* ABOUT IT.
...AND SHOVE THEM...
SPAK
SPAK
SPAK
BOOO

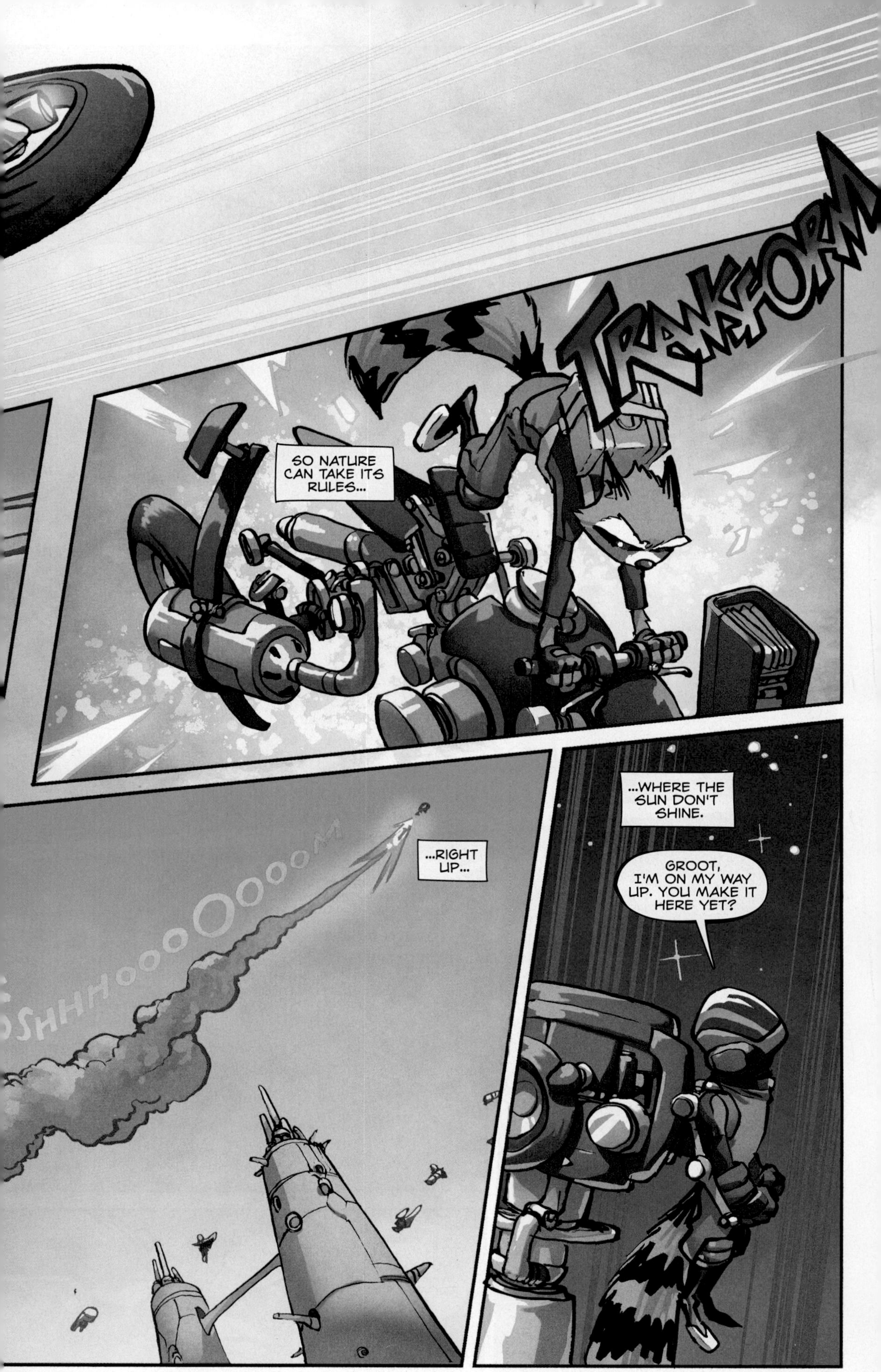
TRANSFORM
SO NATURE CAN TAKE ITS RULES...
...RIGHT UP...
...WHERE THE SUN DON'T SHINE.
GROOT, I'M ON MY WAY UP. YOU MAKE IT HERE YET?

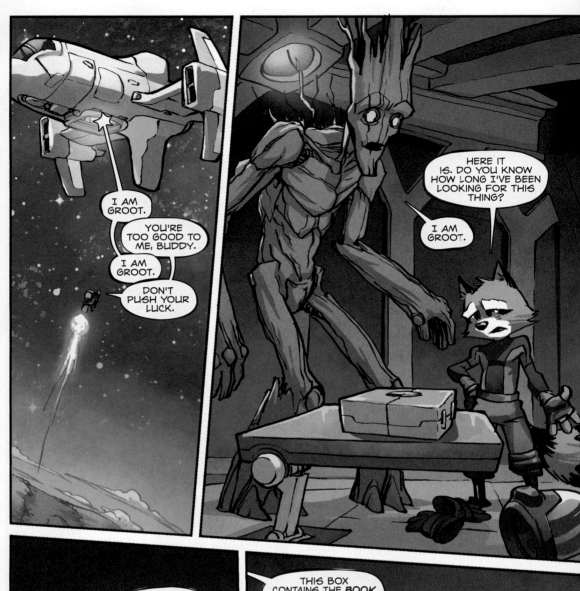

I AM GROOT.

YOU'RE TOO GOOD TO ME, BUDDY.

I AM GROOT.

DON'T PUSH YOUR LUCK.

HERE IT IS. DO YOU KNOW HOW LONG I'VE BEEN LOOKING FOR THIS THING?

I AM GROOT.

THAT WAS RHETORICAL.

THIS BOX CONTAINS THE *BOOK OF HALFWORLD.* IT'S SUPPOSED TO HAVE THE ENTIRE HISTORY OF THE PLANET.

IT *HAS* TO HAVE THE ANSWERS TO WHERE I'M FROM. *WHO* I AM.

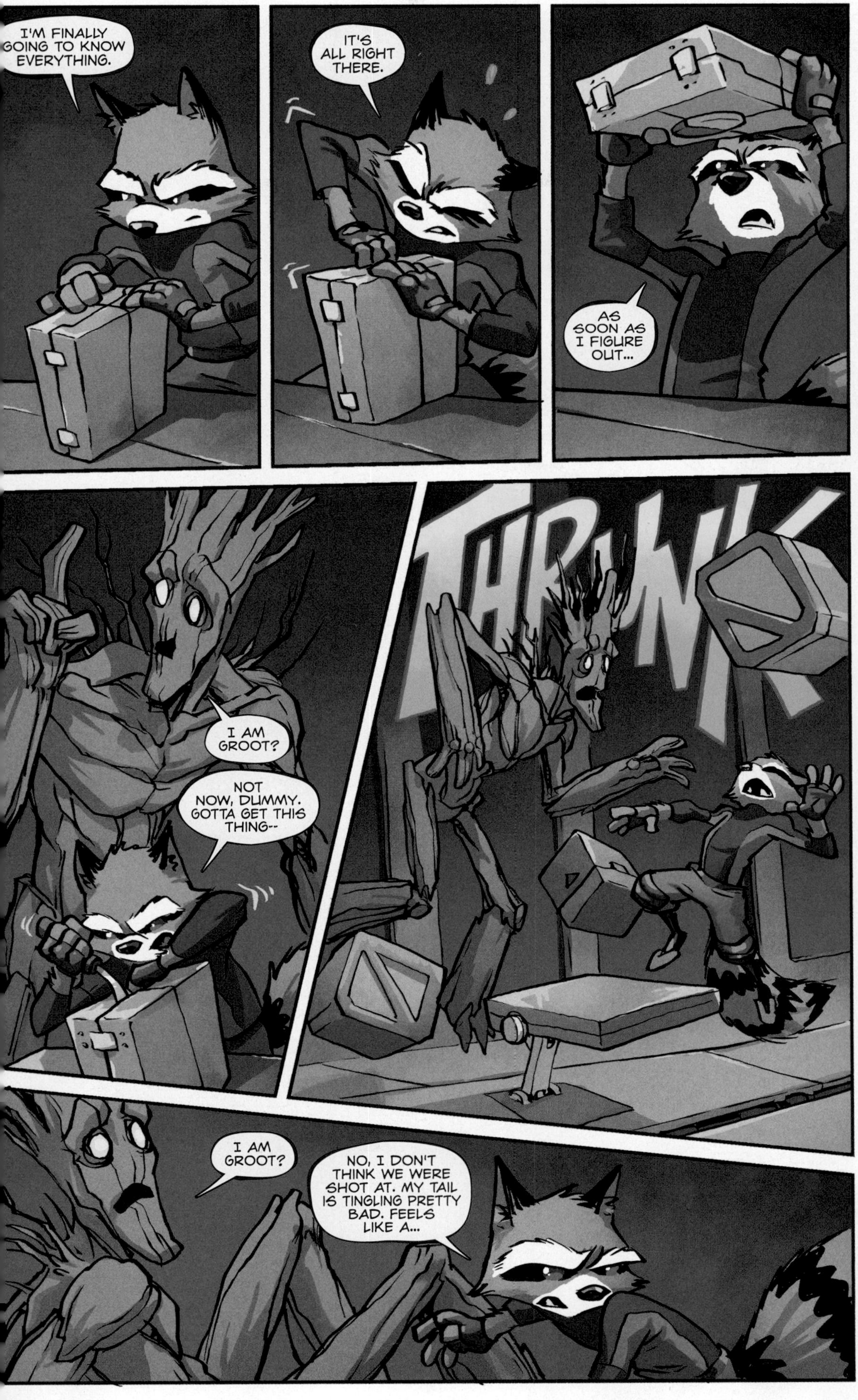
I'M FINALLY GOING TO KNOW EVERYTHING.
IT'S ALL RIGHT THERE.
AS SOON AS I FIGURE OUT...
I AM GROOT?
NOT NOW, DUMMY. GOTTA GET THIS THING--
THRUNK
I AM GROOT?
NO, I DON'T THINK WE WERE SHOT AT. MY TAIL IS TINGLING PRETTY BAD. FEELS LIKE A...

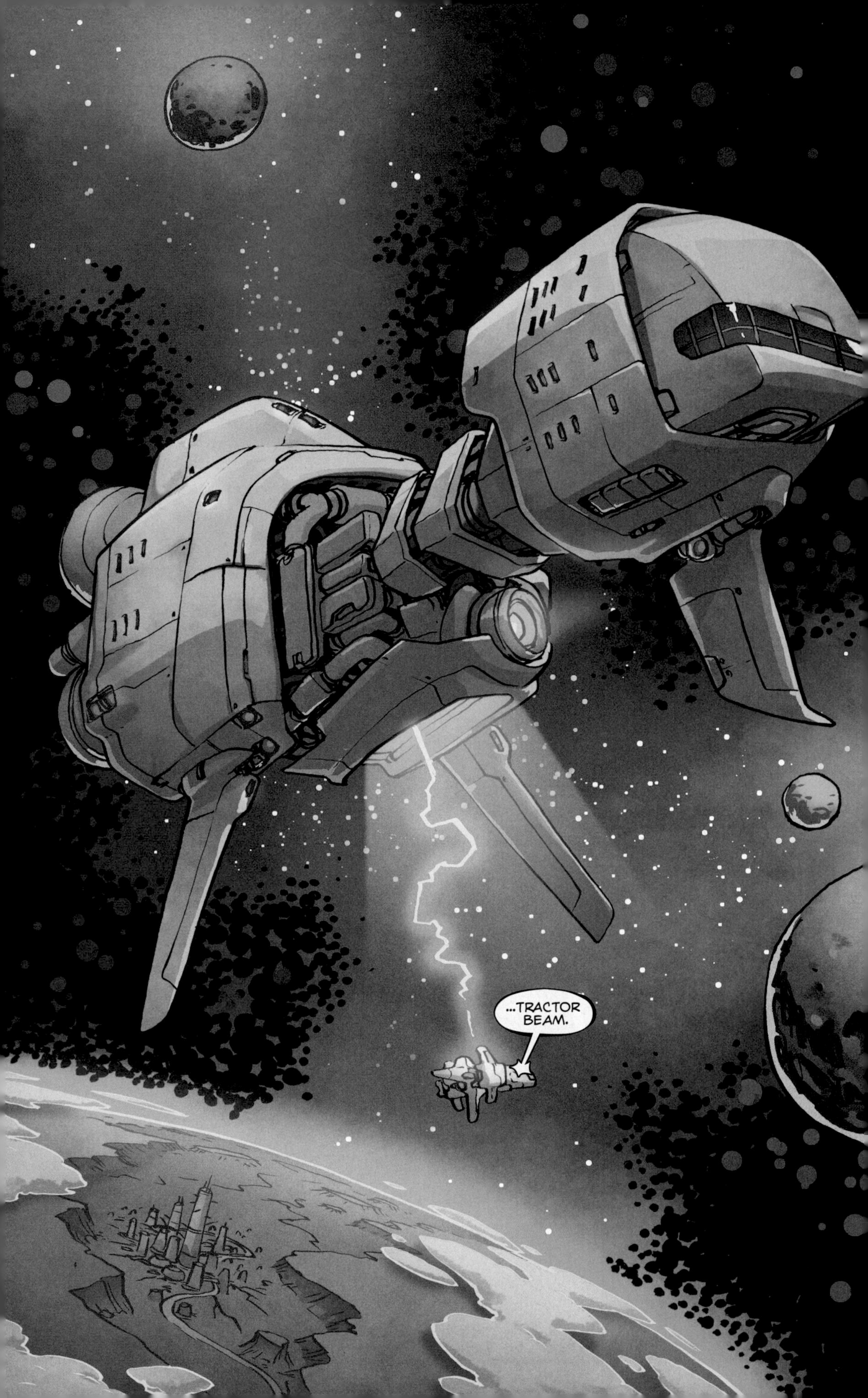
...TRACTOR BEAM.

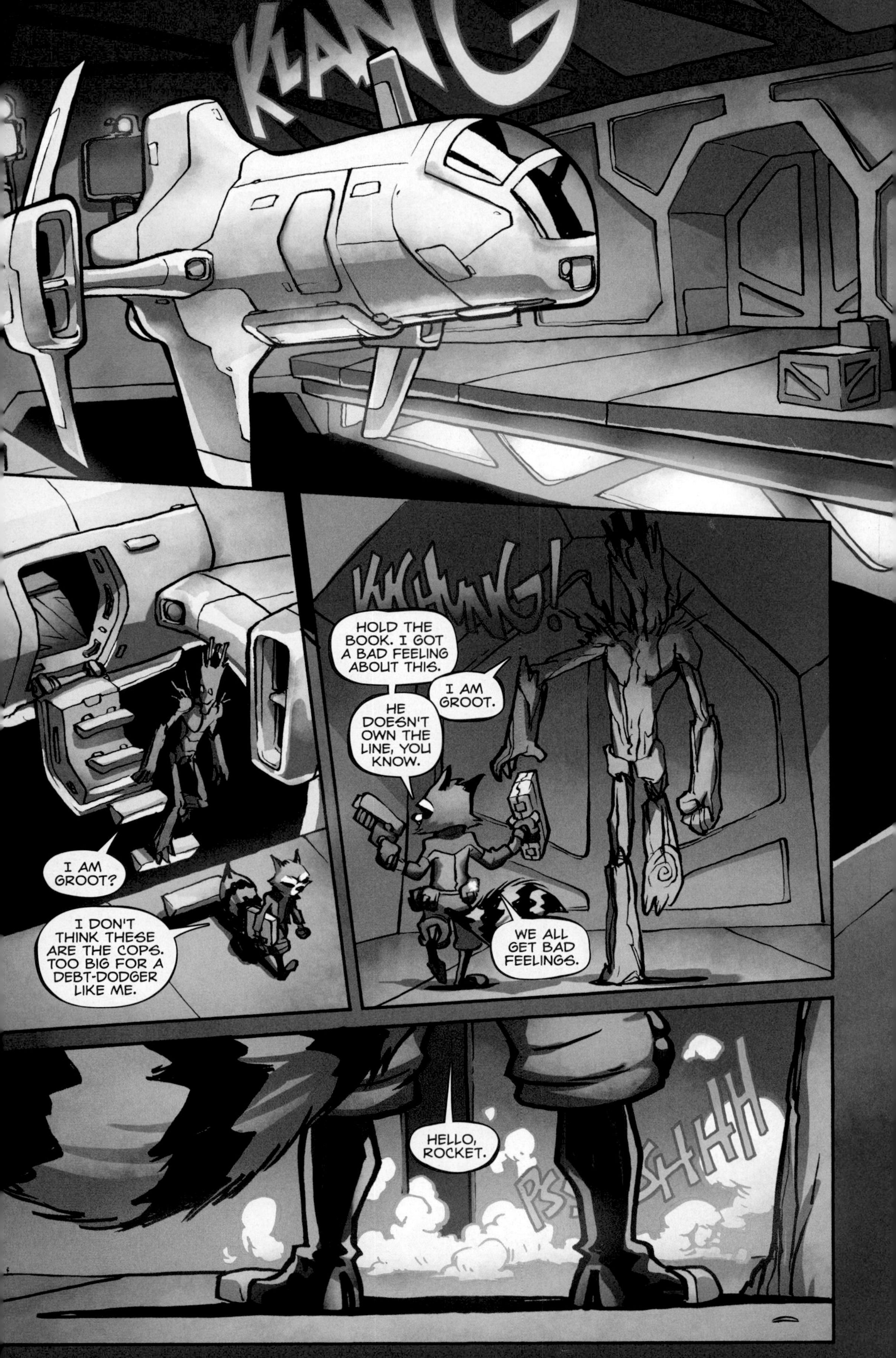
KLANG
I AM GROOT?
I DON'T THINK THESE ARE THE COPS. TOO BIG FOR A DEBT-DODGER LIKE ME.
KKCHUNK!
HOLD THE BOOK. I GOT A BAD FEELING ABOUT THIS.
I AM GROOT.
HE DOESN'T OWN THE LINE, YOU KNOW.
WE ALL GET BAD FEELINGS.
HELLO, ROCKET.
PSSSHHH

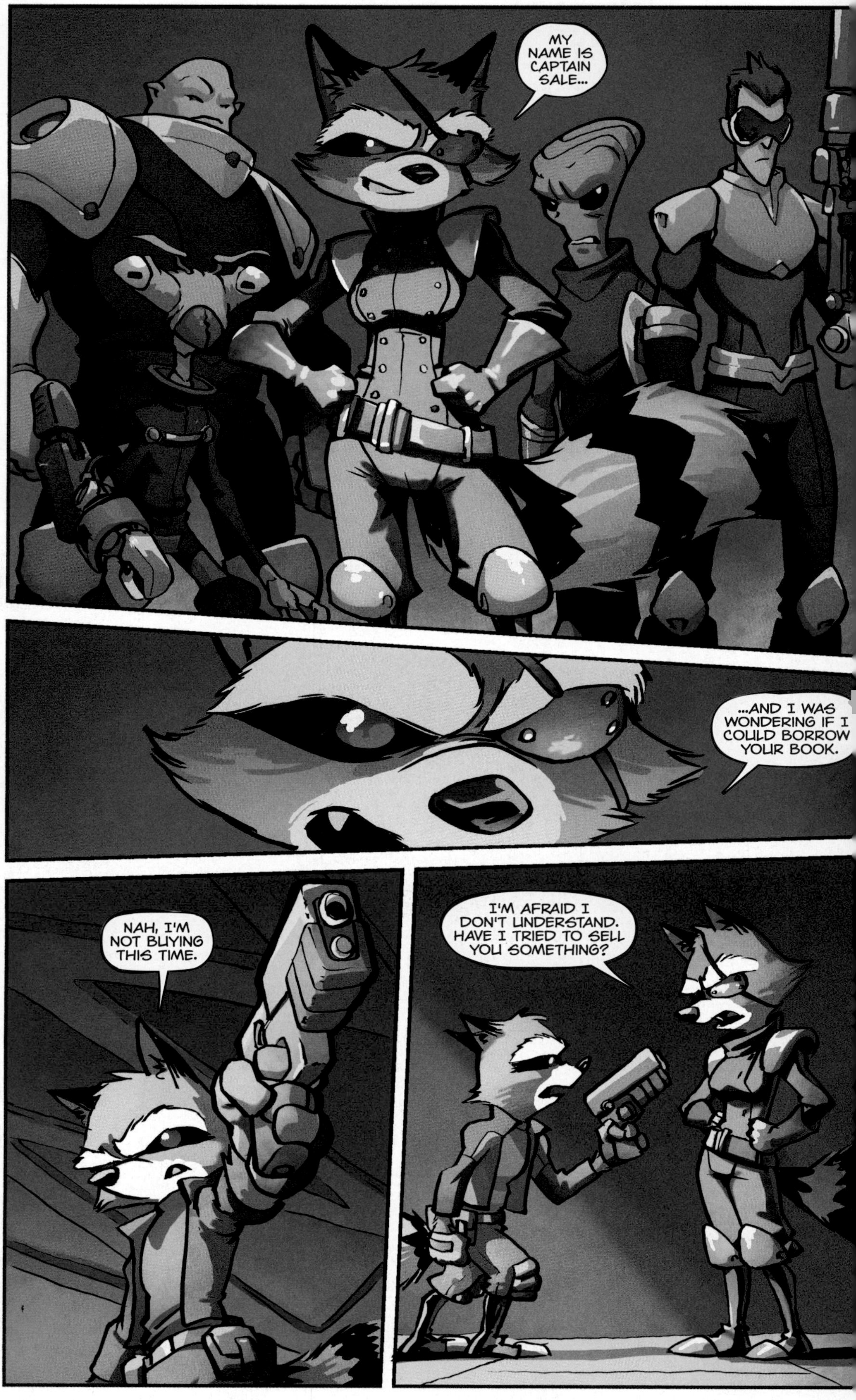
MY NAME IS CAPTAIN SALE...
...AND I WAS WONDERING IF I COULD BORROW YOUR BOOK.
NAH, I'M NOT BUYING THIS TIME.
I'M AFRAID I DON'T UNDERSTAND. HAVE I TRIED TO SELL YOU SOMETHING?

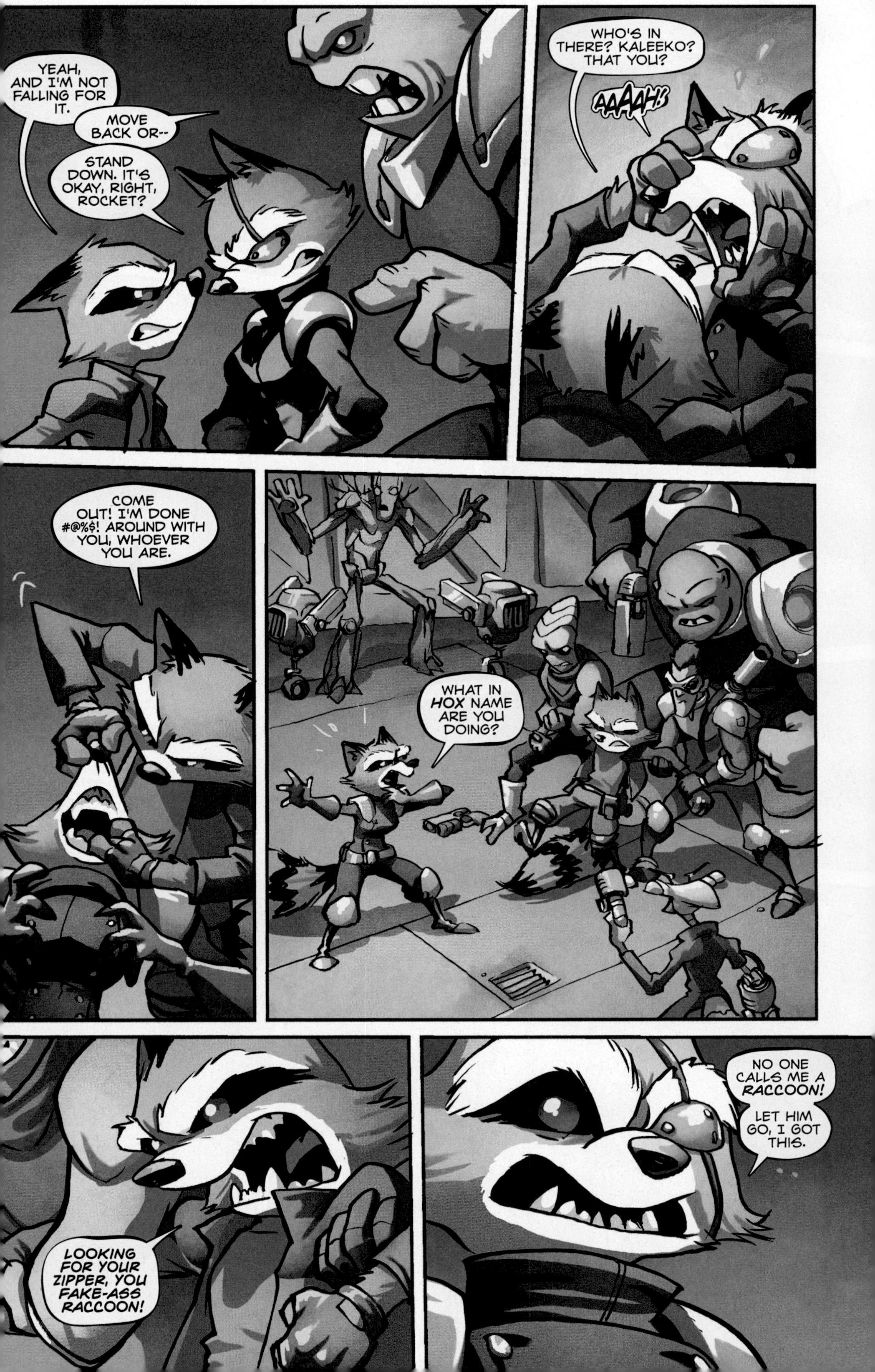
YEAH, AND I'M NOT FALLING FOR IT.
MOVE BACK OR--
STAND DOWN. IT'S OKAY, RIGHT, ROCKET?
WHO'S IN THERE? KALEEKO? THAT YOU?
AAAAH!
COME OUT! I'M DONE #@%$! AROUND WITH YOU, WHOEVER YOU ARE.
WHAT IN HOX NAME ARE YOU DOING?
LOOKING FOR YOUR ZIPPER, YOU FAKE-ASS RACCOON!
NO ONE CALLS ME A RACCOON!
LET HIM GO, I GOT THIS.

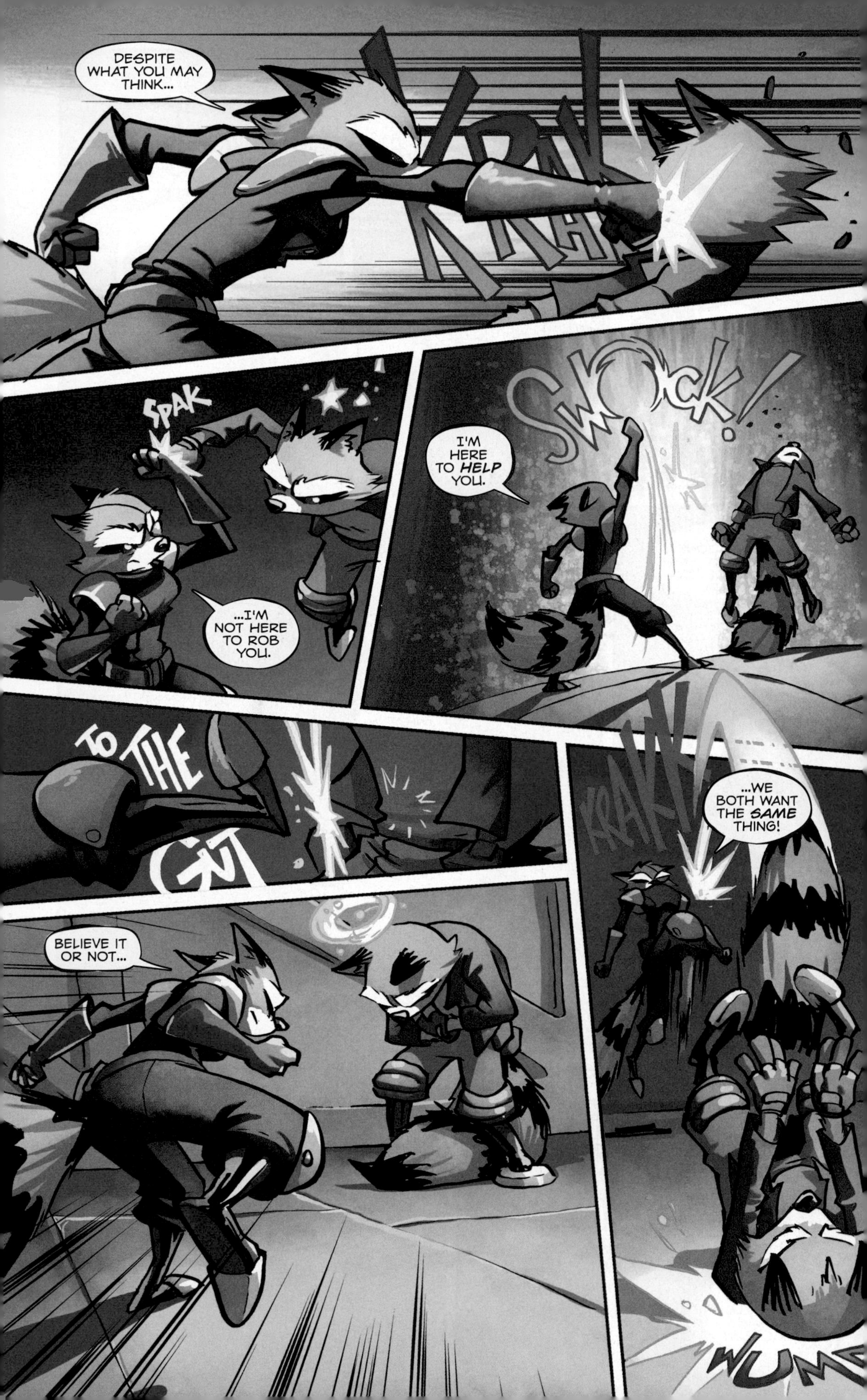
DESPITE WHAT YOU MAY THINK...
KRAK
SPAK
...I'M NOT HERE TO ROB YOU.
SWOCK!
I'M HERE TO HELP YOU.
TO THE
...WE BOTH WANT THE SAME THING!
KRAK
BELIEVE IT OR NOT...

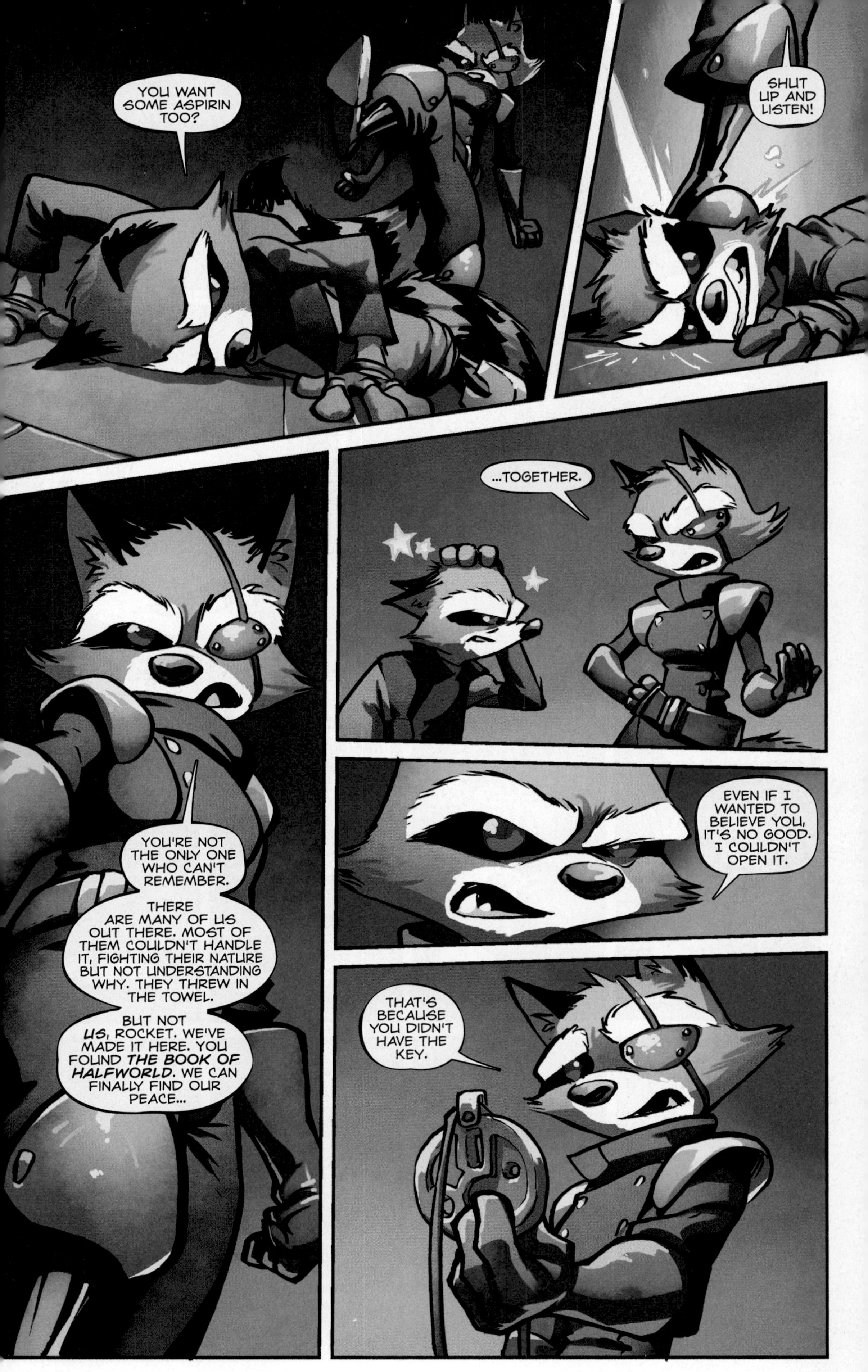
YOU WANT SOME ASPIRIN TOO?
SHUT UP AND LISTEN!
...TOGETHER.
YOU'RE NOT THE ONLY ONE WHO CAN'T REMEMBER.
THERE ARE MANY OF US OUT THERE. MOST OF THEM COULDN'T HANDLE IT, FIGHTING THEIR NATURE BUT NOT UNDERSTANDING WHY. THEY THREW IN THE TOWEL.
BUT NOT *US*, ROCKET. WE'VE MADE IT HERE. YOU FOUND ***THE BOOK OF HALFWORLD***. WE CAN FINALLY FIND OUR PEACE...
EVEN IF I WANTED TO BELIEVE YOU, IT'S NO GOOD. I COULDN'T OPEN IT.
THAT'S BECAUSE YOU DIDN'T HAVE THE KEY.

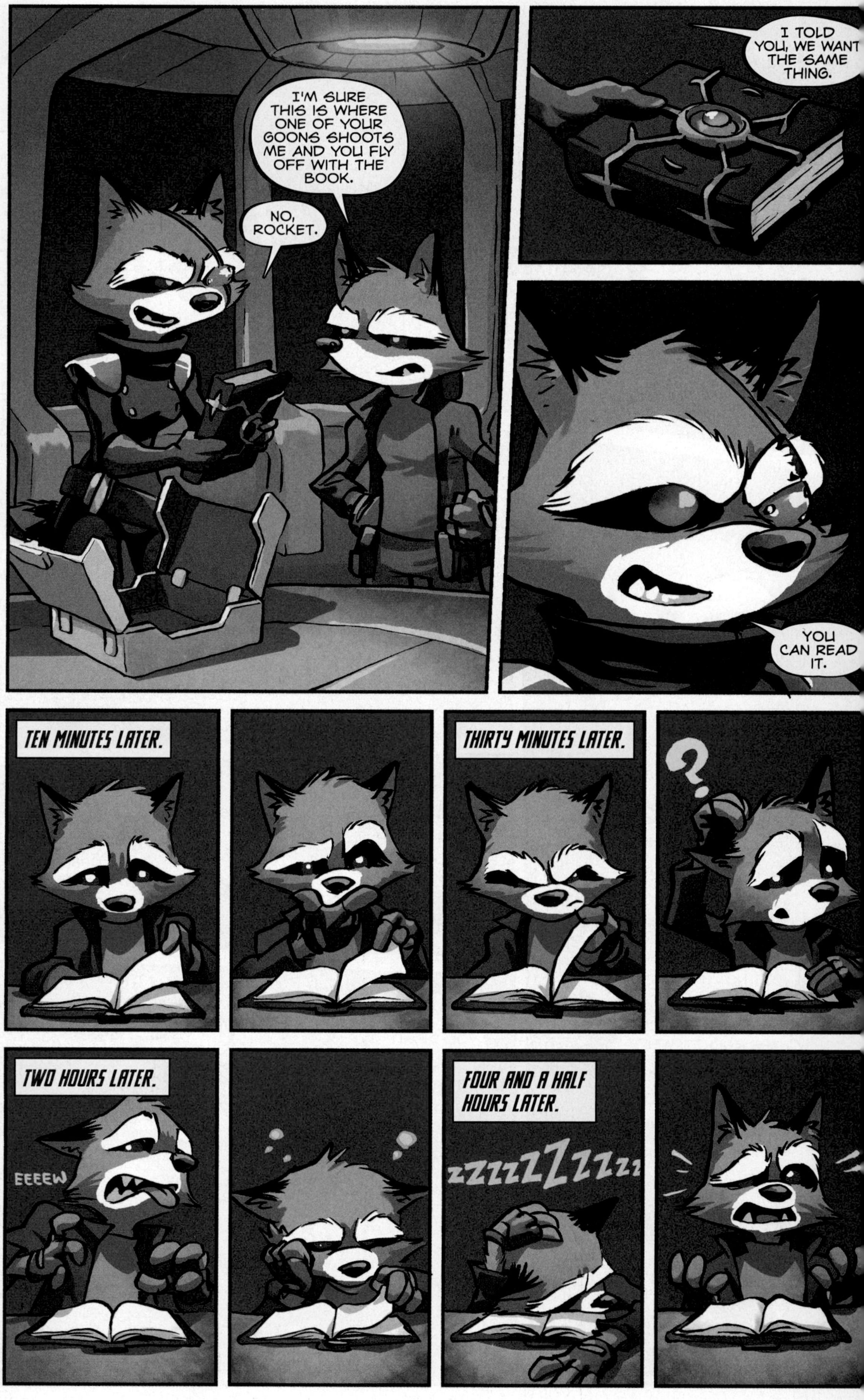
I'M SURE THIS IS WHERE ONE OF YOUR GOONS SHOOTS ME AND YOU FLY OFF WITH THE BOOK.
NO, ROCKET.
I TOLD YOU, WE WANT THE SAME THING.
YOU CAN READ IT.
TEN MINUTES LATER.
THIRTY MINUTES LATER.
?
TWO HOURS LATER.
EEEEW
FOUR AND A HALF HOURS LATER.
zzzzZZzzzz

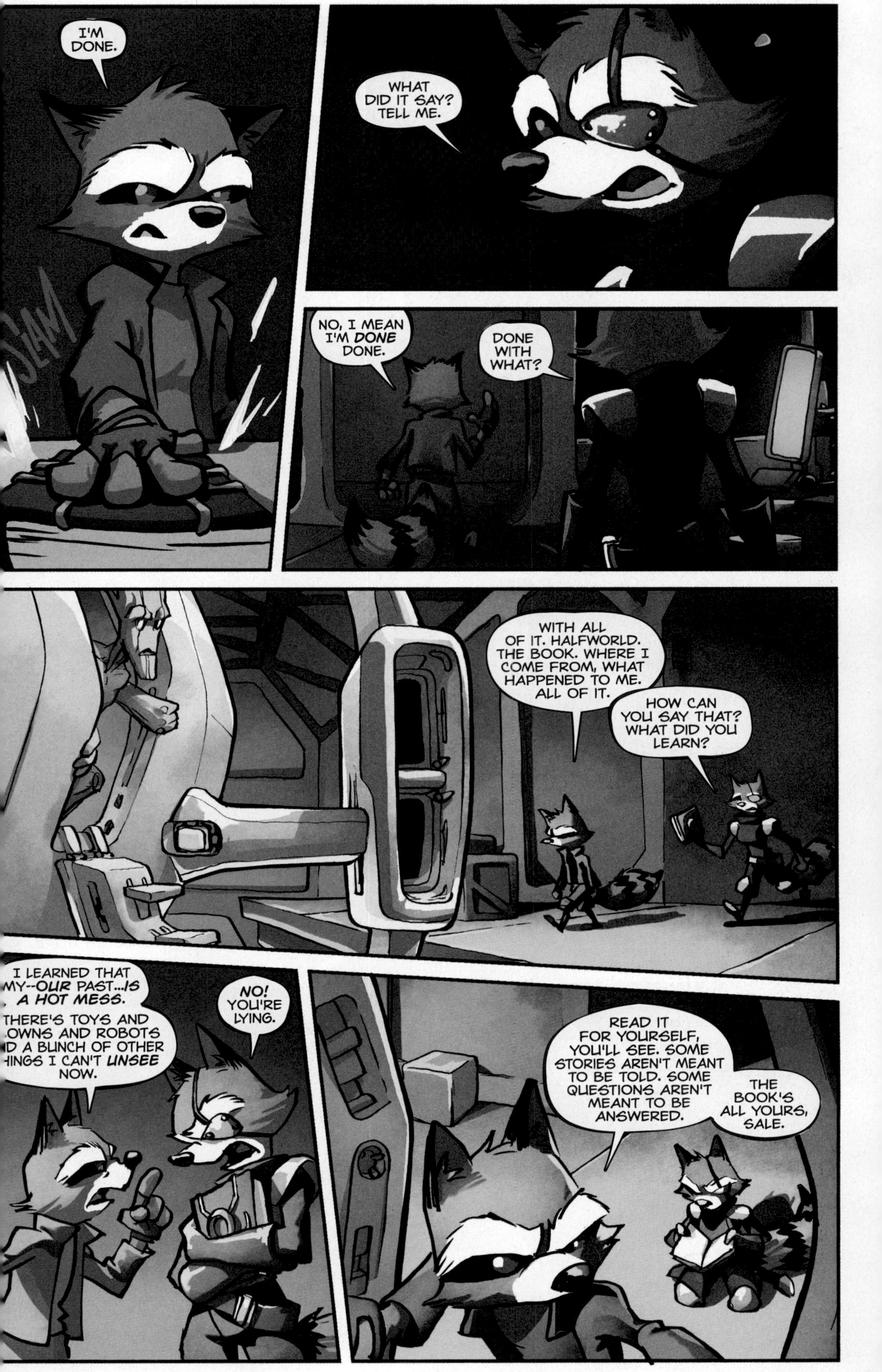
I'M DONE.
SLAM
WHAT DID IT SAY? TELL ME.
NO, I MEAN I'M *DONE* DONE.
DONE WITH WHAT?
WITH ALL OF IT. HALFWORLD. THE BOOK. WHERE I COME FROM, WHAT HAPPENED TO ME. ALL OF IT.
HOW CAN YOU SAY THAT? WHAT DID YOU LEARN?
I LEARNED THAT MY--*OUR* PAST...*IS A HOT MESS.*
THERE'S TOYS AND OWNS AND ROBOTS D A BUNCH OF OTHER HINGS I CAN'T *UNSEE* NOW.
NO! YOU'RE LYING.
READ IT FOR YOURSELF, YOU'LL SEE. SOME STORIES AREN'T MEANT TO BE TOLD. SOME QUESTIONS AREN'T MEANT TO BE ANSWERED.
THE BOOK'S ALL YOURS, SALE.

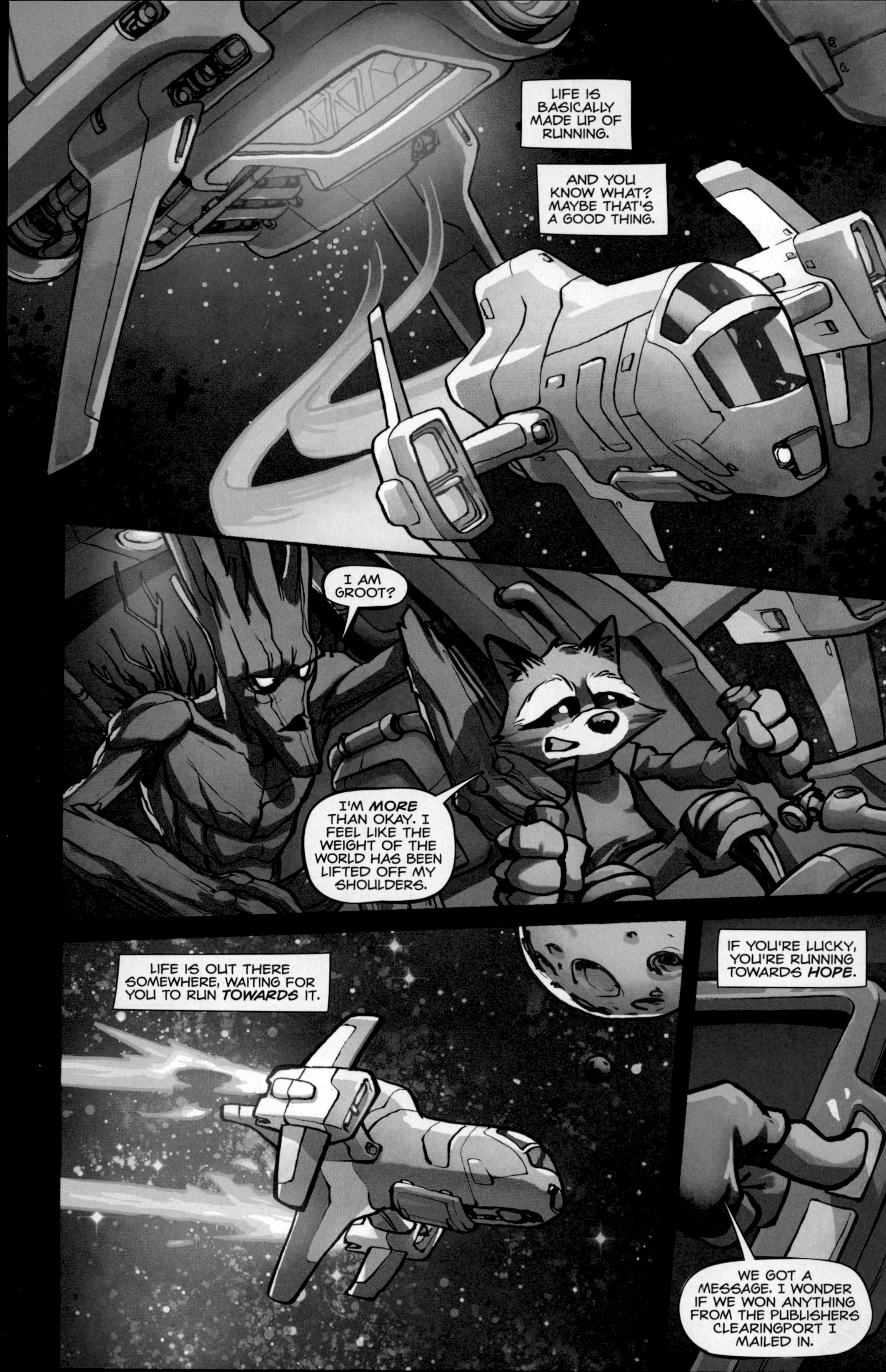
LIFE IS BASICALLY MADE UP OF RUNNING.
AND YOU KNOW WHAT? MAYBE THAT'S A GOOD THING.
I AM GROOT?
I'M MORE THAN OKAY. I FEEL LIKE THE WEIGHT OF THE WORLD HAS BEEN LIFTED OFF MY SHOULDERS.
LIFE IS OUT THERE SOMEWHERE, WAITING FOR YOU TO RUN TOWARDS IT.
IF YOU'RE LUCKY, YOU'RE RUNNING TOWARDS HOPE.
WE GOT A MESSAGE. I WONDER IF WE WON ANYTHING FROM THE PUBLISHERS CLEARINGPORT I MAILED IN.

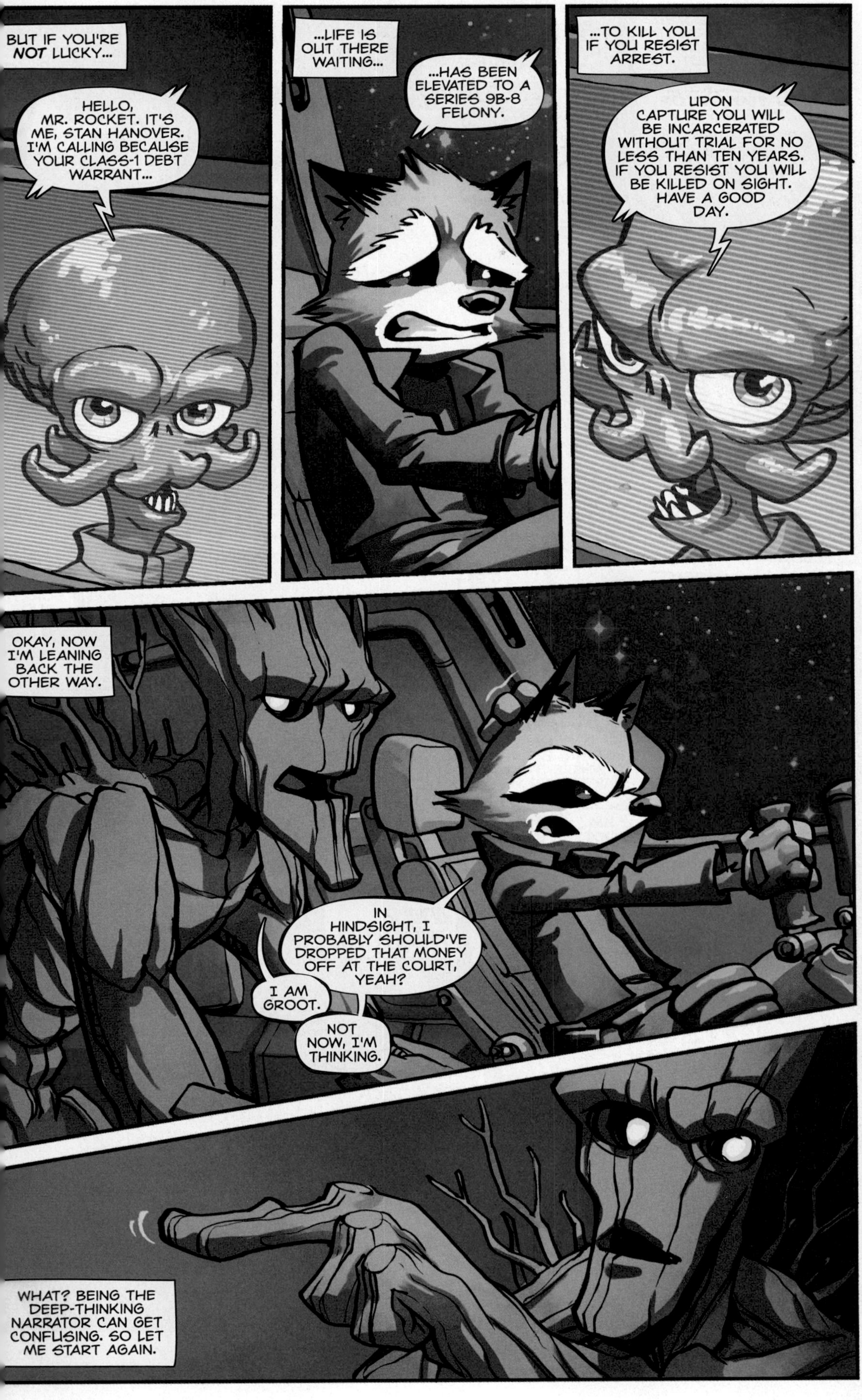
BUT IF YOU'RE *NOT* LUCKY...
HELLO, MR. ROCKET. IT'S ME, STAN HANOVER. I'M CALLING BECAUSE YOUR CLASS-1 DEBT WARRANT...
...LIFE IS OUT THERE WAITING...
...HAS BEEN ELEVATED TO A SERIES 9B-8 FELONY.
...TO KILL YOU IF YOU RESIST ARREST.
UPON CAPTURE YOU WILL BE INCARCERATED WITHOUT TRIAL FOR NO LESS THAN TEN YEARS. IF YOU RESIST YOU WILL BE KILLED ON SIGHT. HAVE A GOOD DAY.
OKAY, NOW I'M LEANING BACK THE OTHER WAY.
IN HINDSIGHT, I PROBABLY SHOULD'VE DROPPED THAT MONEY OFF AT THE COURT, YEAH?
I AM GROOT.
NOT NOW, I'M THINKING.
WHAT? BEING THE DEEP-THINKING NARRATOR CAN GET CONFUSING. SO LET ME START AGAIN.

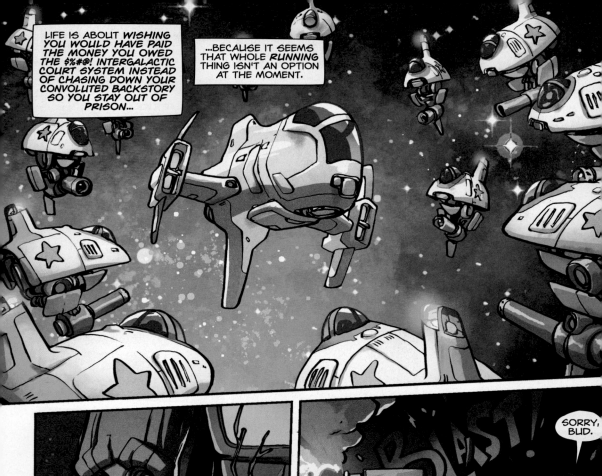

LIFE IS ABOUT *WISHING* YOU WOULD HAVE *PAID THE MONEY* YOU OWED THE $%#@! INTERGALACTIC COURT SYSTEM INSTEAD OF CHASING DOWN YOUR CONVOLUTED BACKSTORY SO YOU STAY OUT OF *PRISON...*

...BECAUSE IT SEEMS THAT WHOLE *RUNNING* THING ISN'T AN OPTION AT THE MOMENT.

LOOKS LIKE IT'S *BACK* TO WHERE IT ALL STARTED FOR ME AND YOU.

I AM GROOT?

YUP.

CHICK CHACK

SORRY, BUD.

B-LAST!

DEVIN-12. PRISON PLANET.

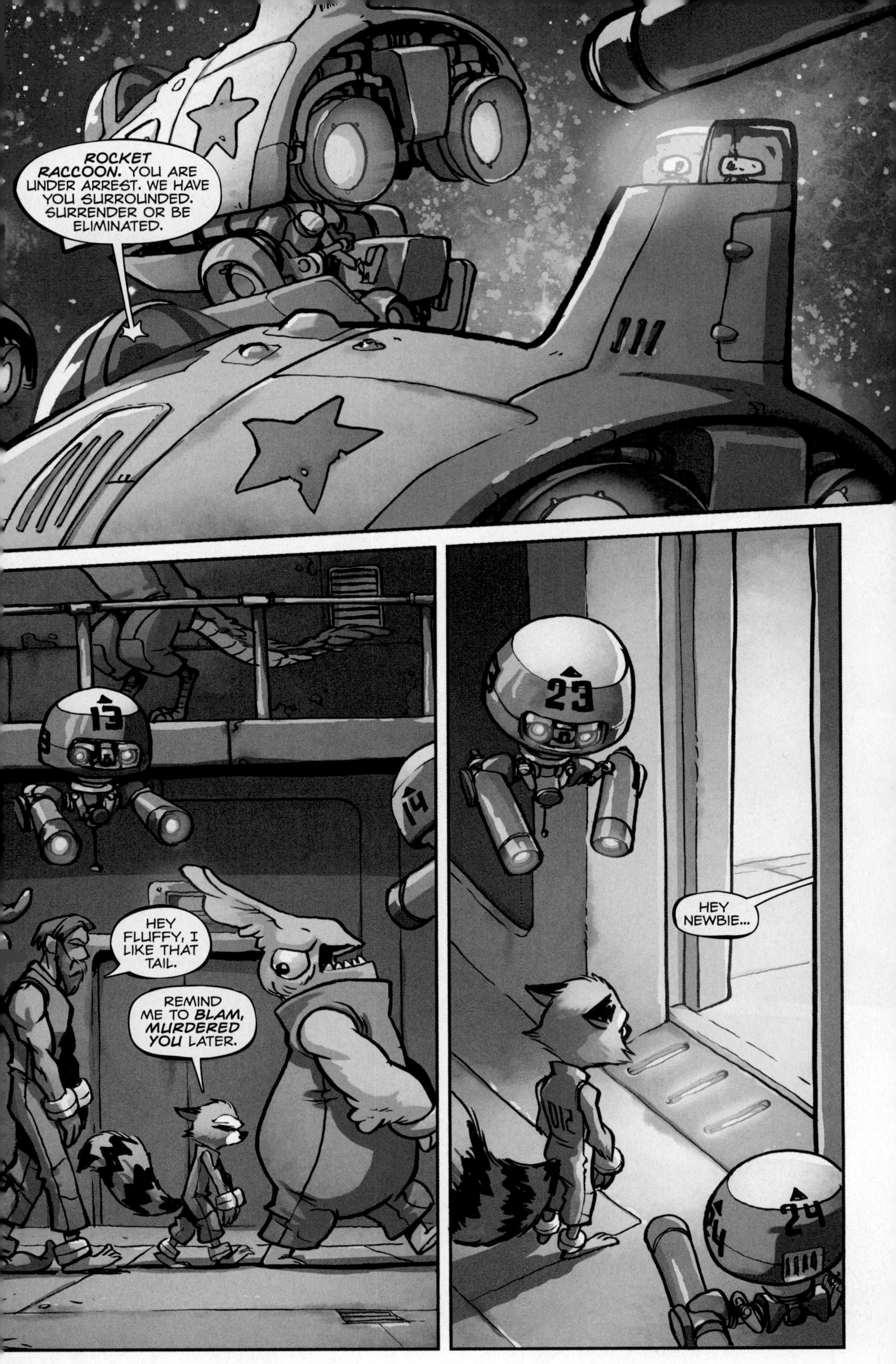
ROCKET RACCOON. YOU ARE UNDER ARREST. WE HAVE YOU SURROUNDED. SURRENDER OR BE ELIMINATED.
23
13
14
HEY FLUFFY, I LIKE THAT TAIL.
REMIND ME TO BLAM, MURDERED YOU LATER.
HEY NEWBIE...
24

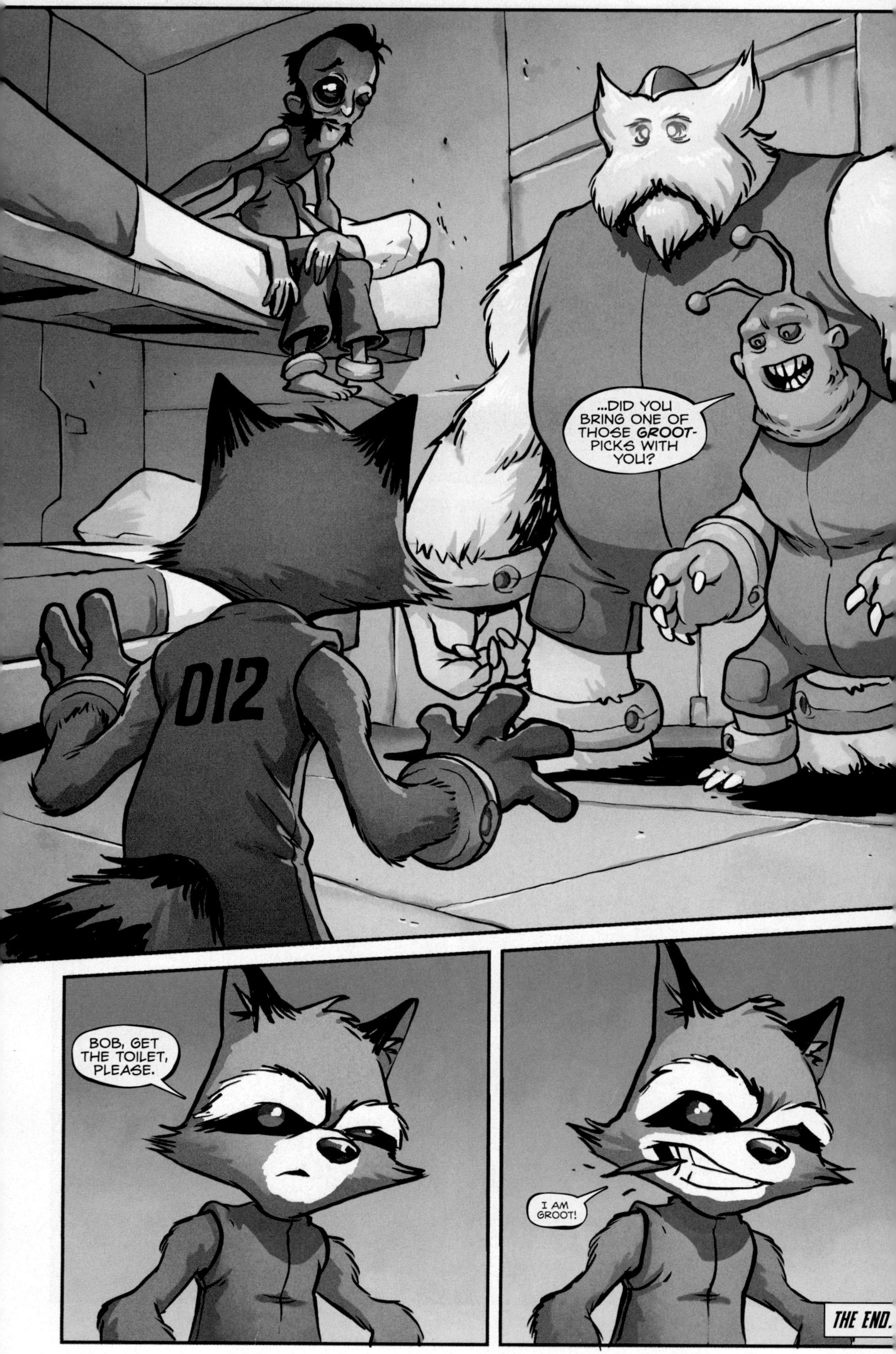

...DID YOU BRING ONE OF THOSE GROOT-PICKS WITH YOU?
012
BOB, GET THE TOILET, PLEASE.
I AM GROOT!
THE END.

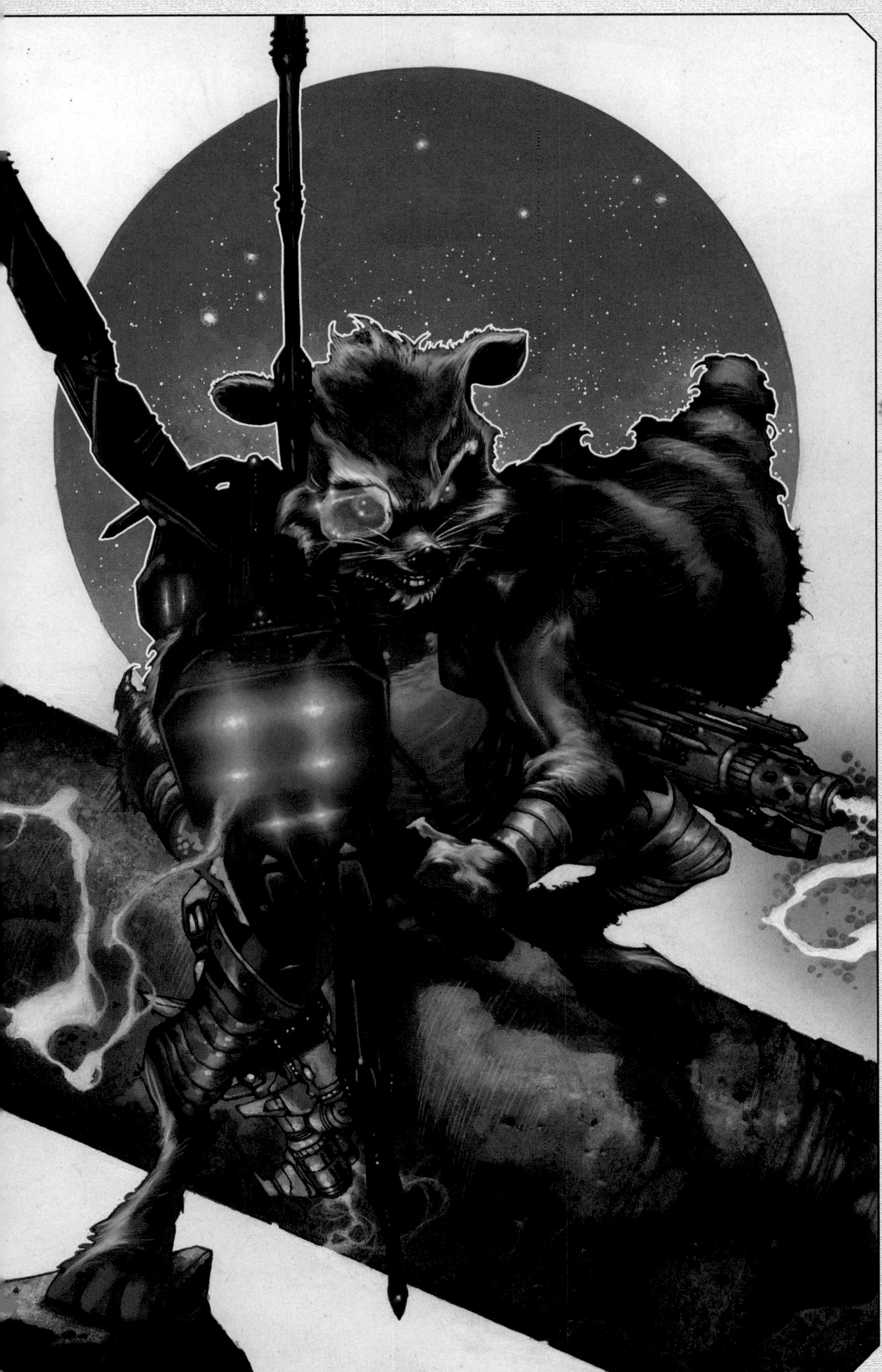

ROCKET RACCOON #7 VARIANT
BY SIMONE BIANCHI & ADRIANO DALL'ALPI

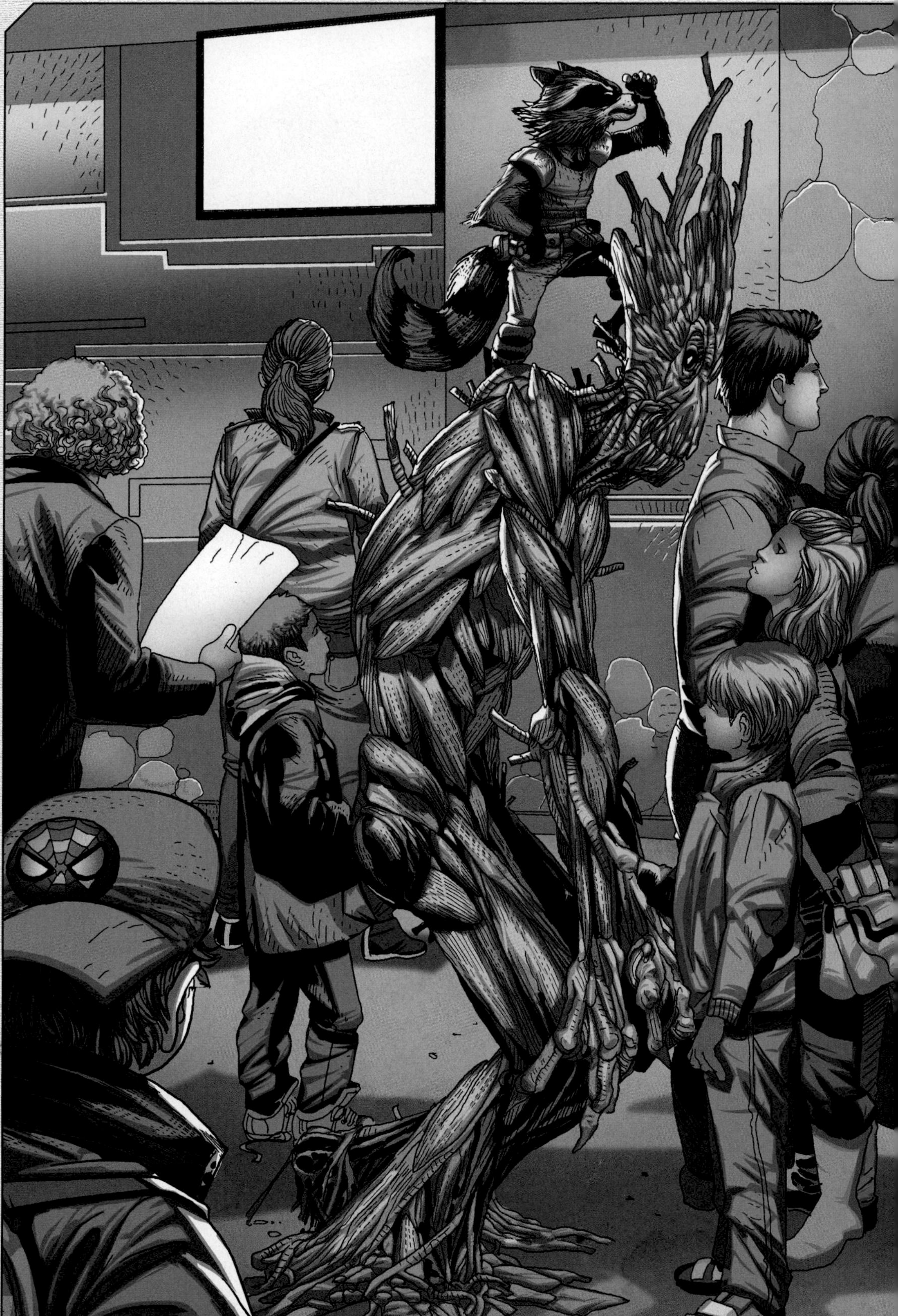

ROCKET RACCOON #7 WELCOME HOME VARIANT
BY SALVADOR LARROCA & ISRAEL SILVA

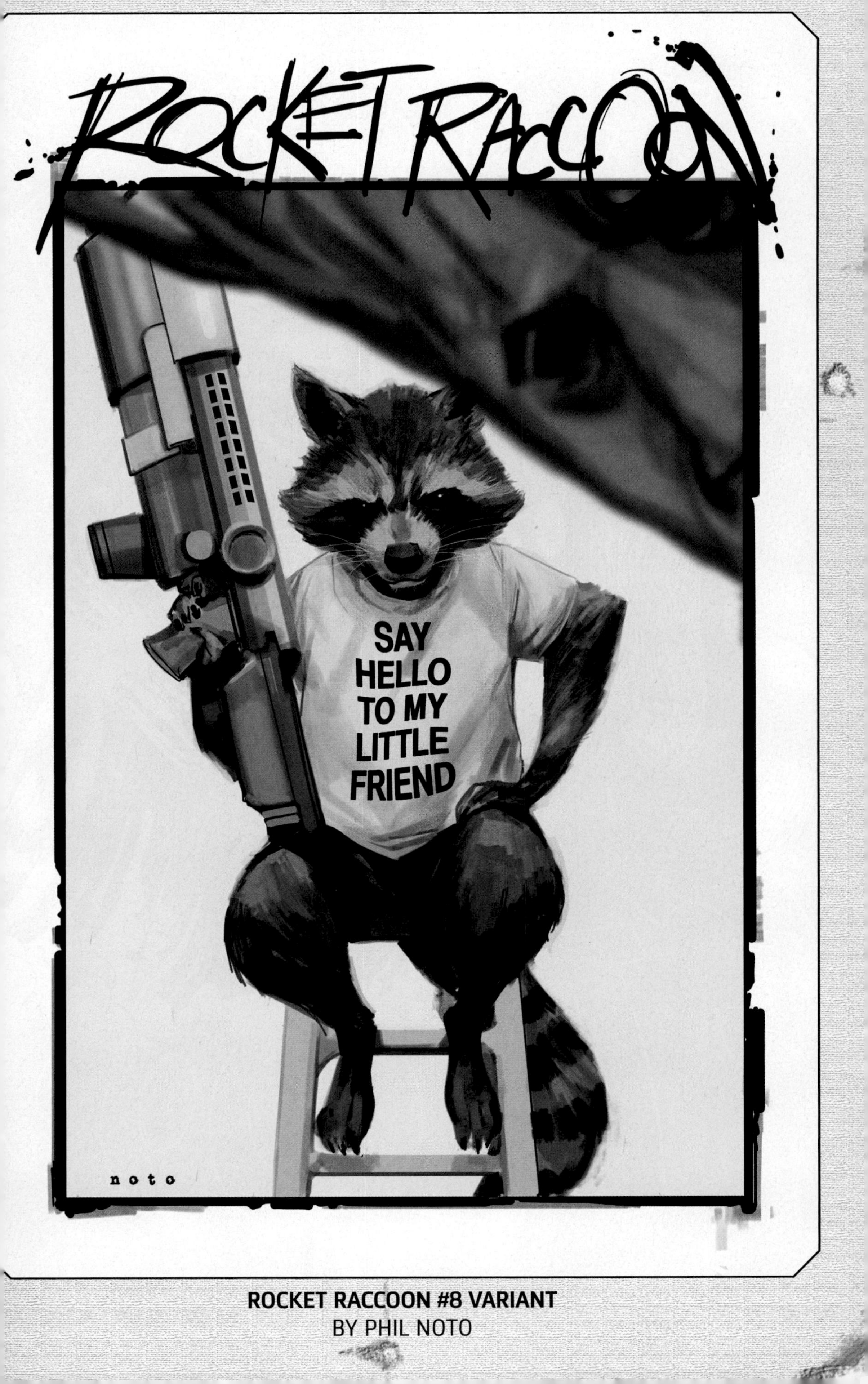
ROCKET RACCOON
SAY HELLO TO MY LITTLE FRIEND
noto

ROCKET RACCOON #8 VARIANT
BY PHIL NOTO

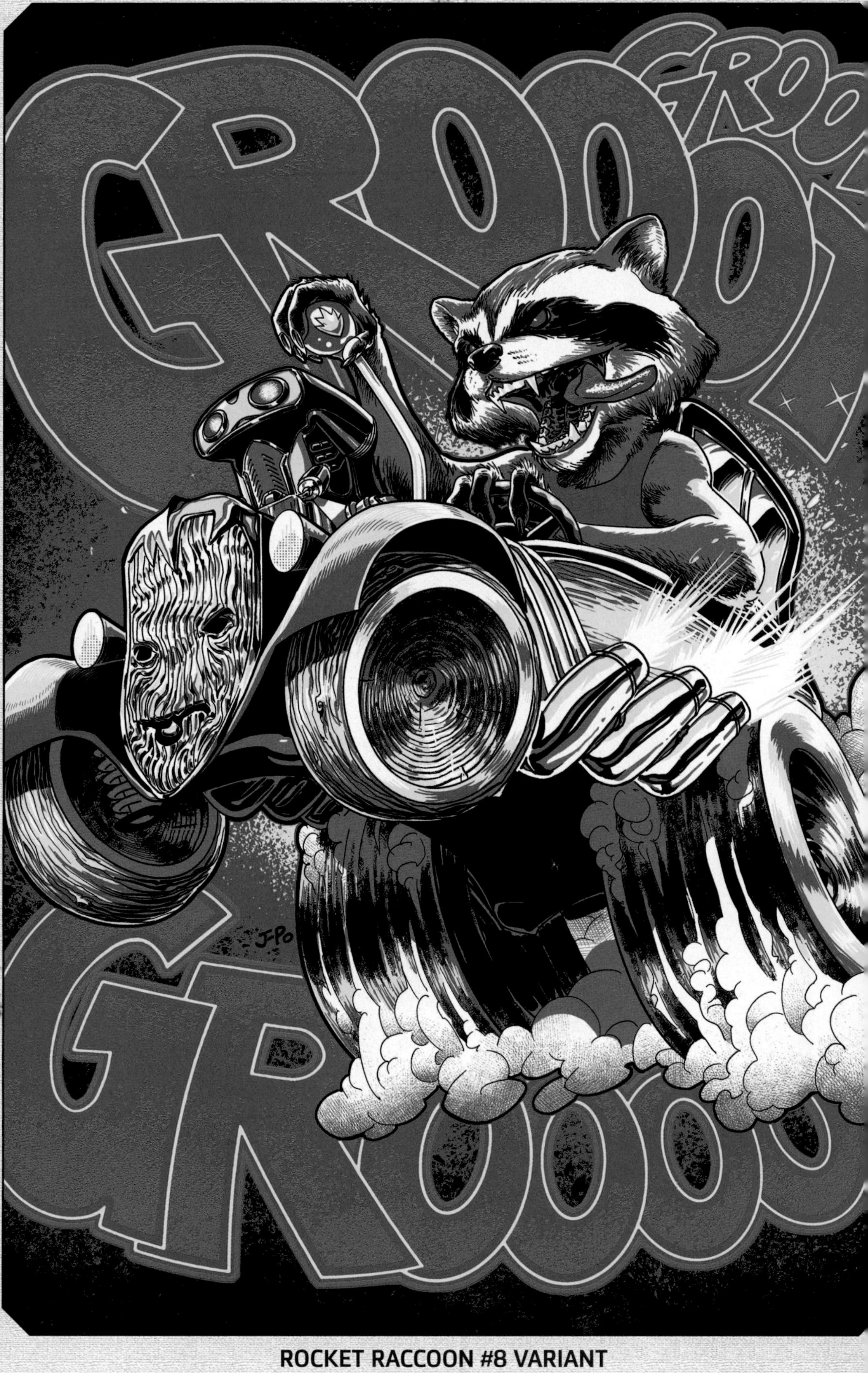
J-Po

ROCKET RACCOON #8 VARIANT
BY JUSTIN PONSOR

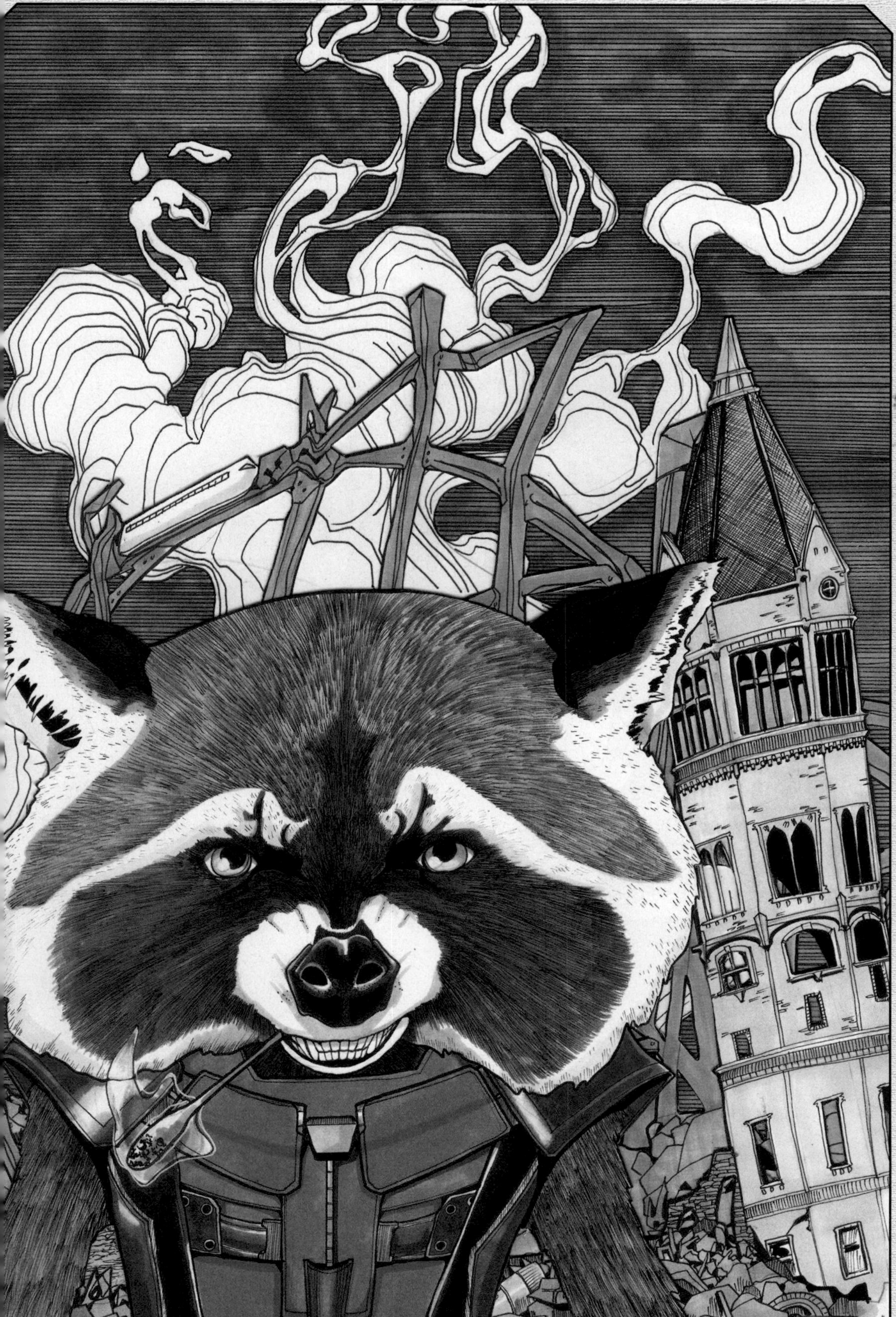
2015

ROCKET RACCOON #9 WOMEN OF MARVEL VARIANT
BY JANET LEE

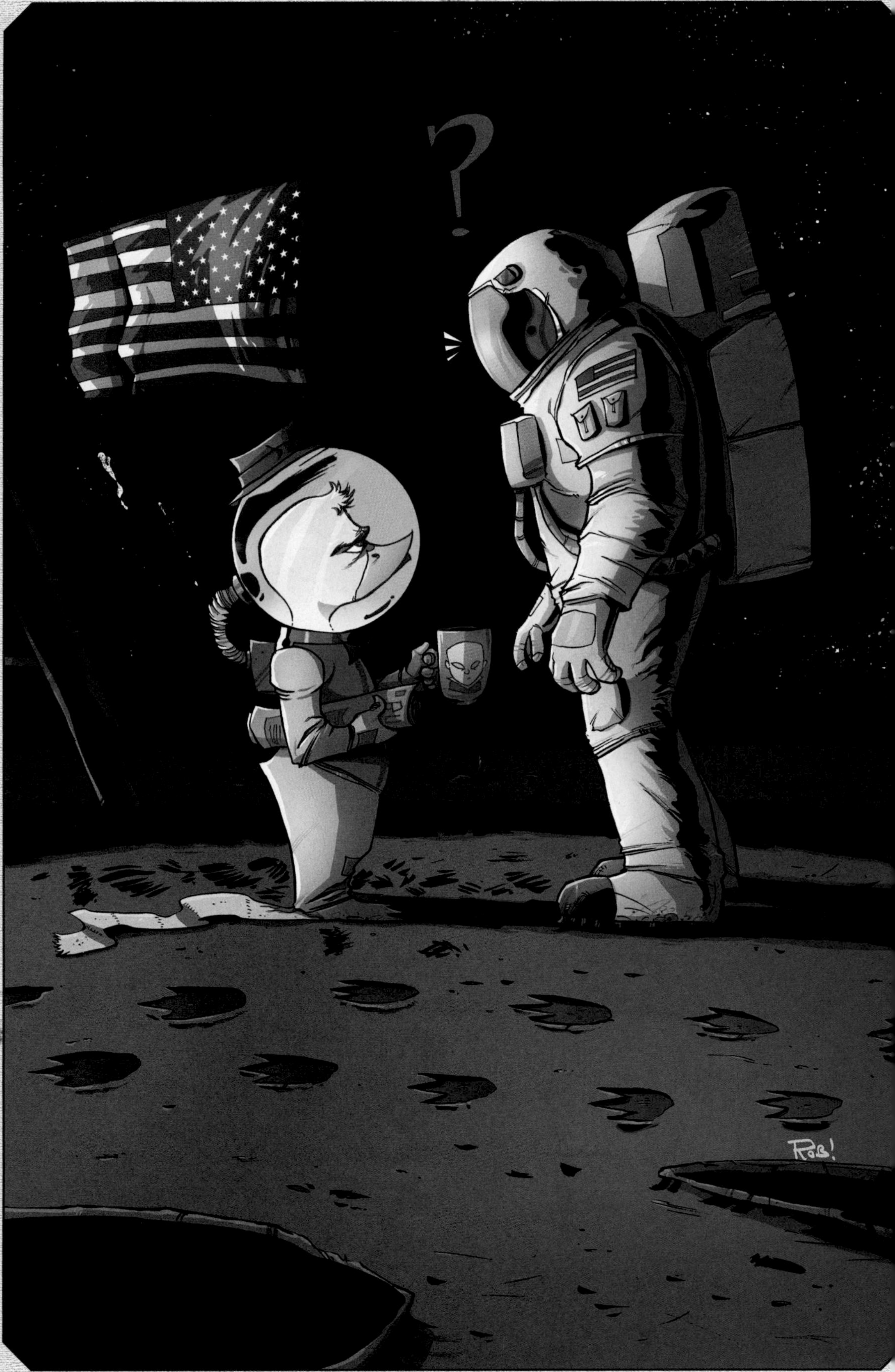
?
ROB!

ROCKET RACCOON #10 WHAT THE DUCK? VARIANT
BY ROB GUILLORY

CHARACTER SKETCHES
BY JAKE PARKER

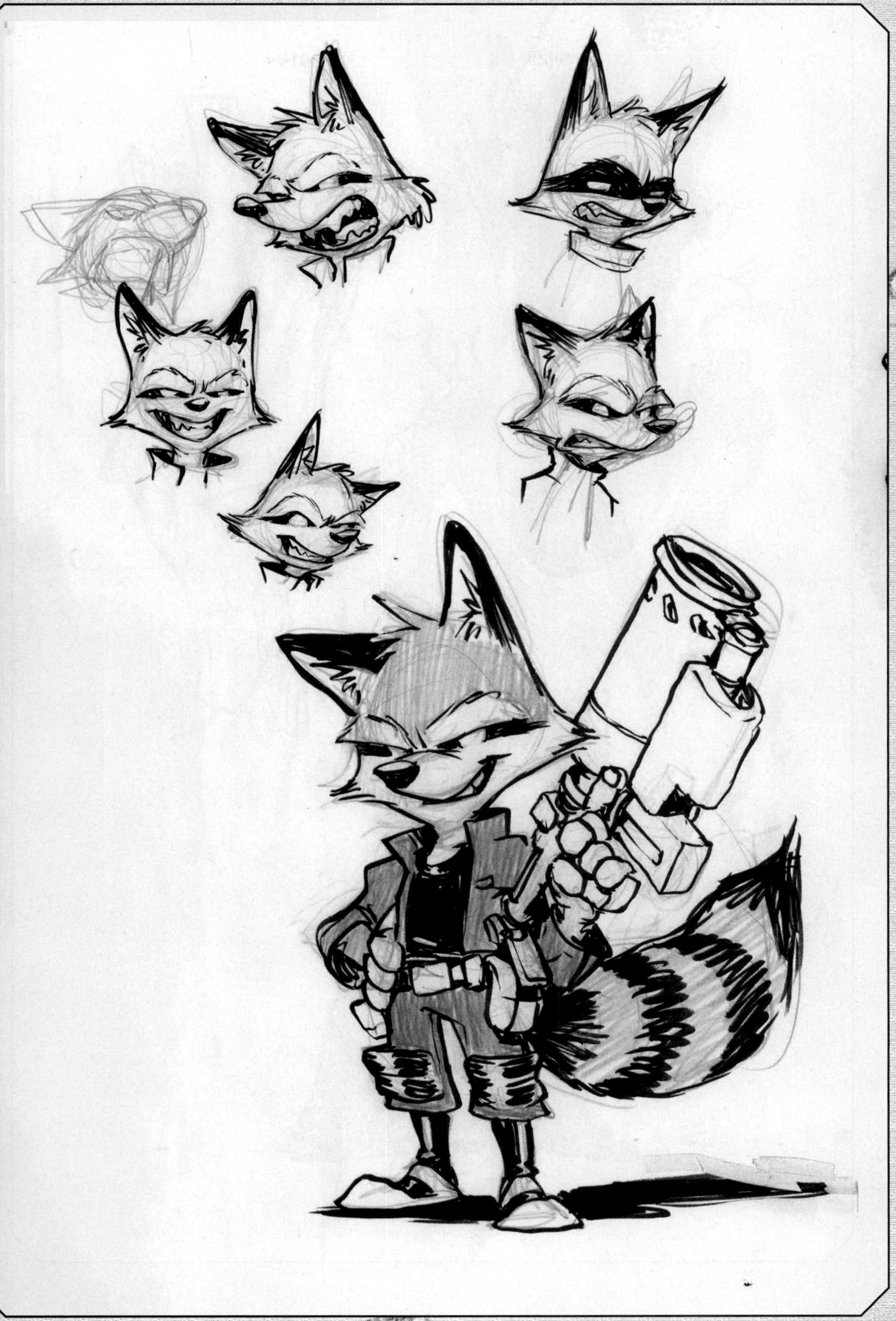

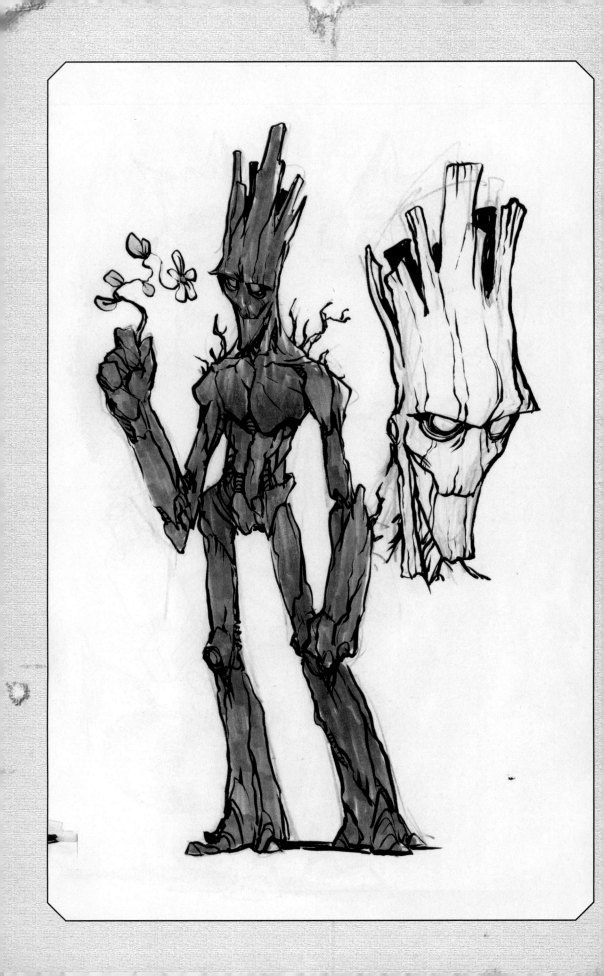

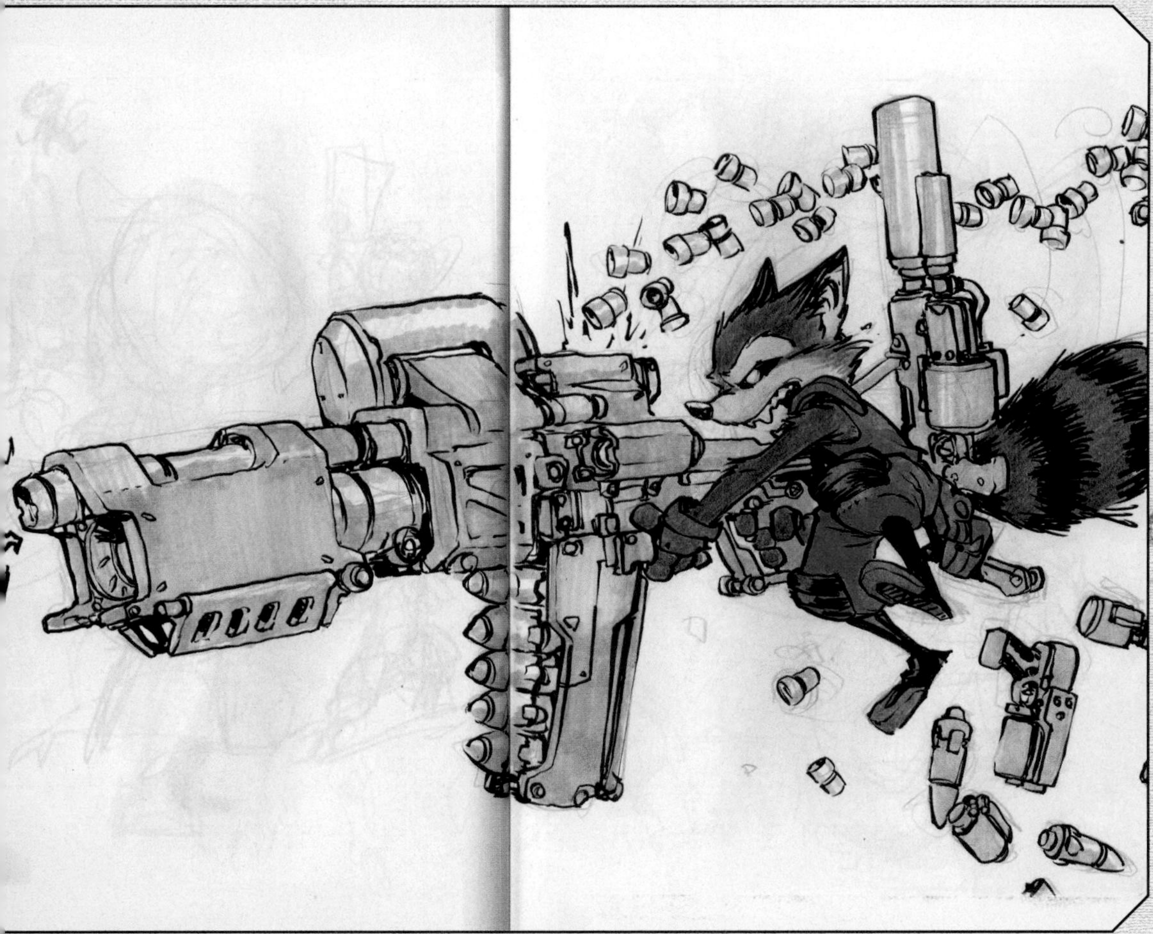
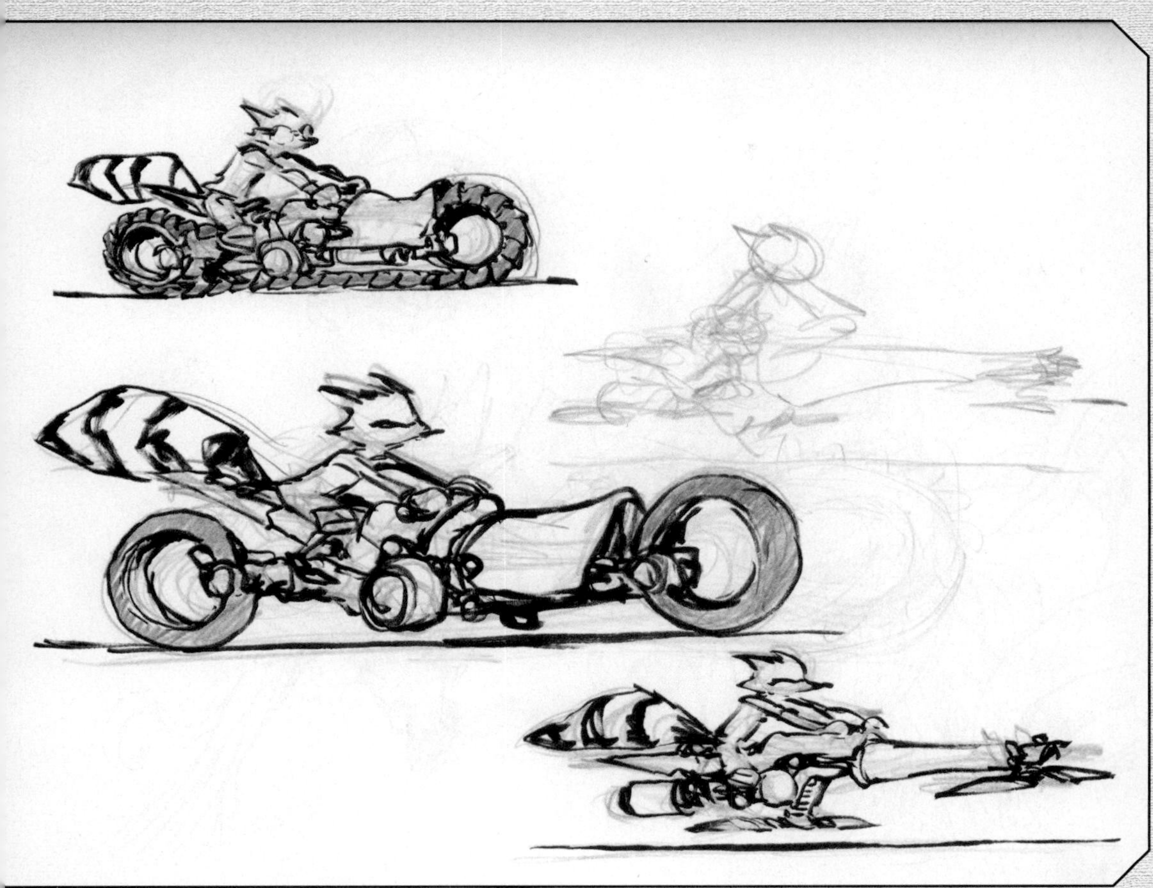

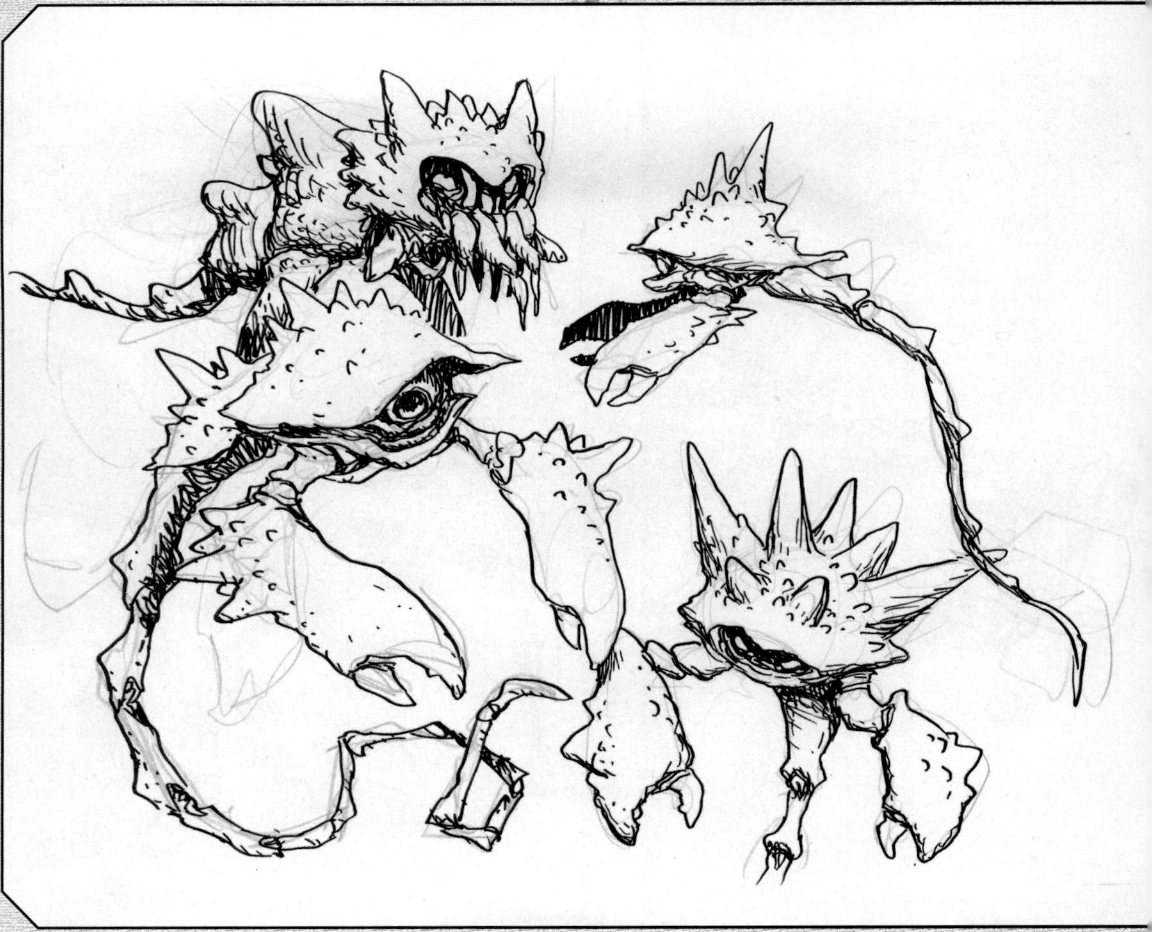

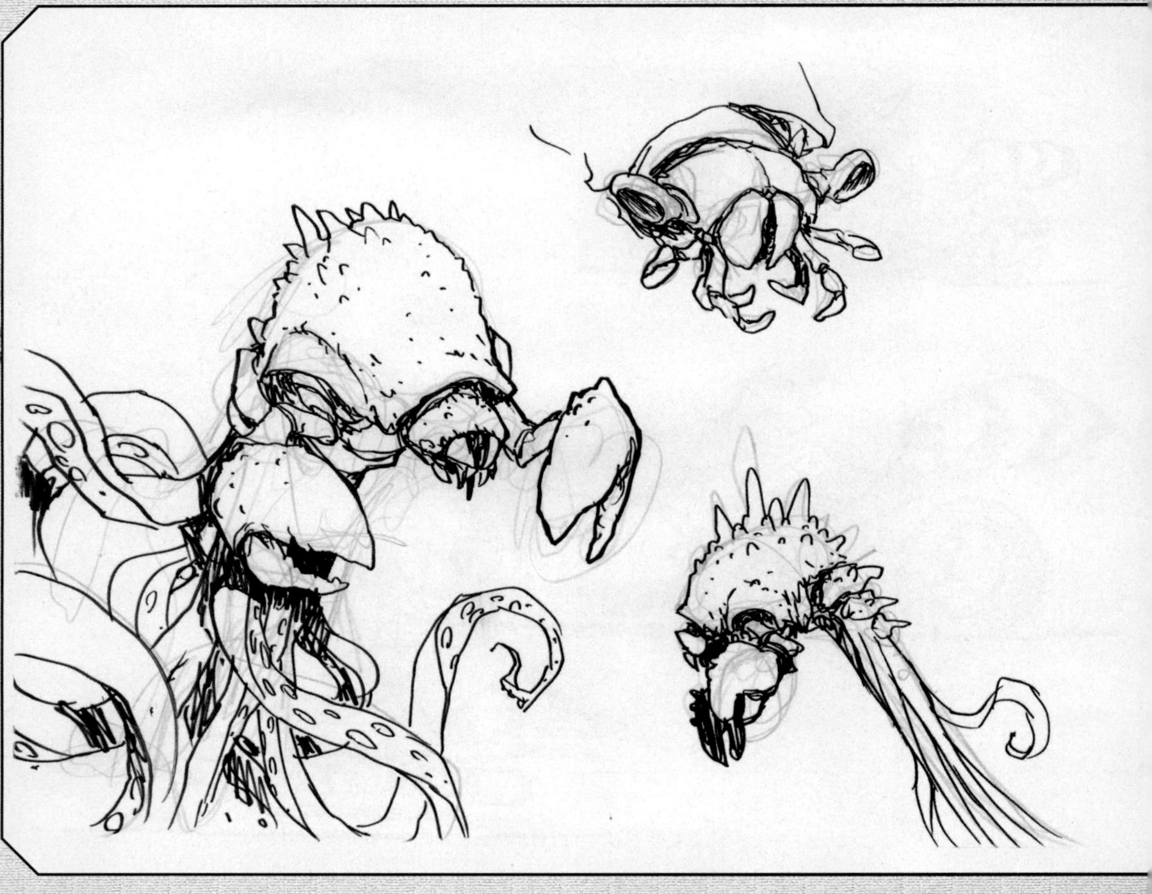

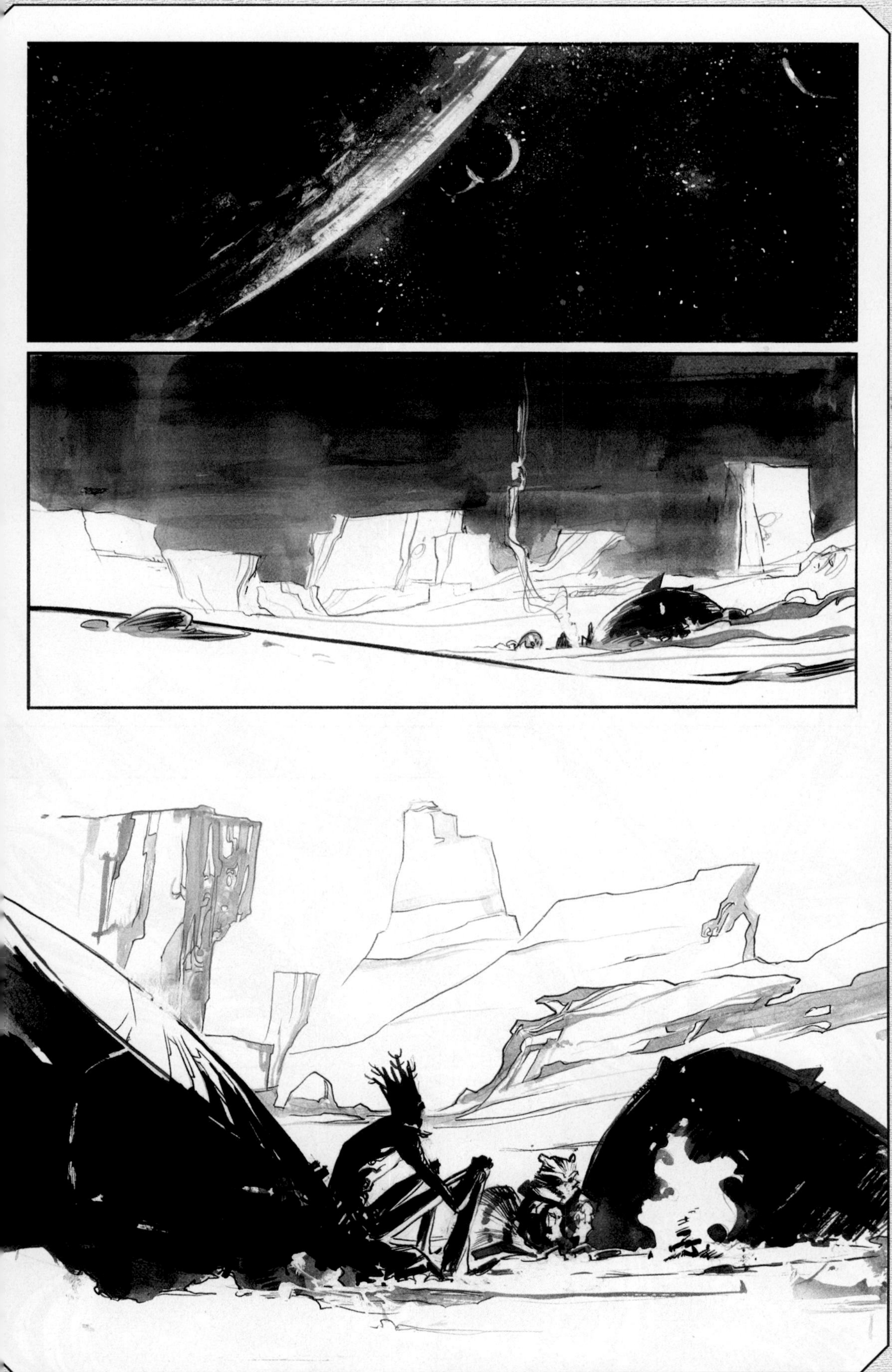

ROCKET RACCOON #7, PAGE 1 ART
BY FILIPE ANDRADE

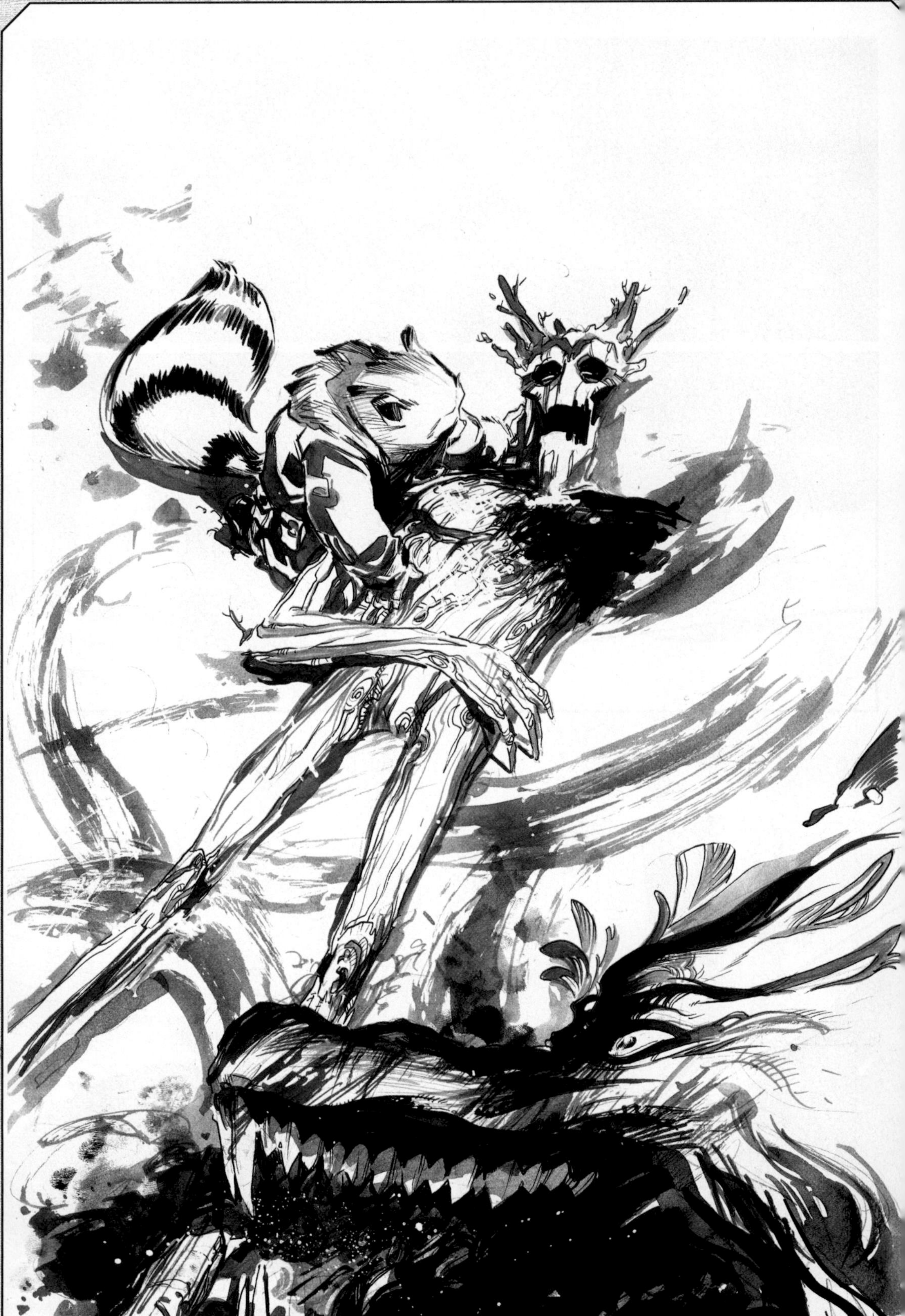

ROCKET RACCOON #7, PAGE 8 ART
BY FILIPE ANDRADE

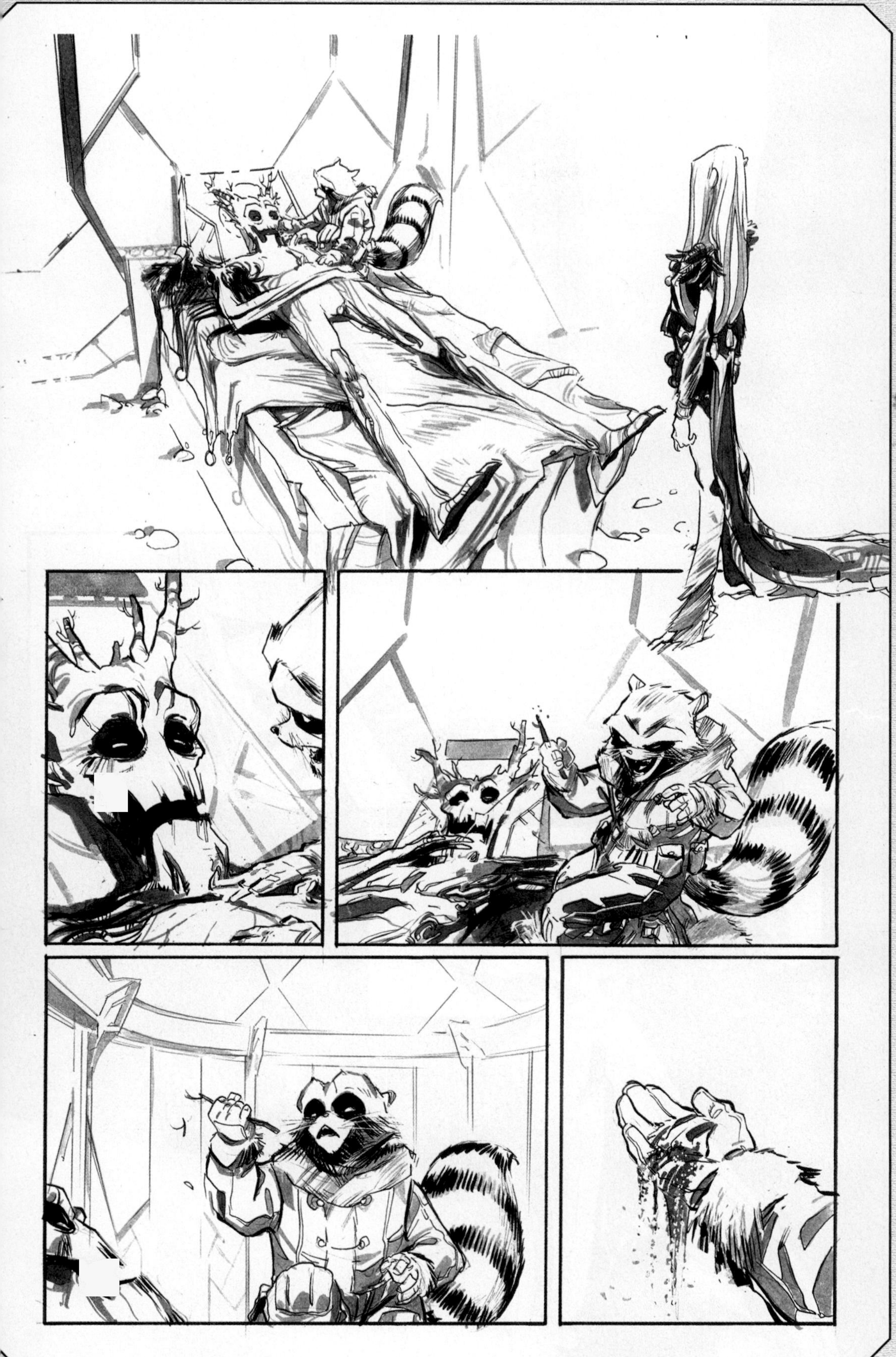

ROCKET RACCOON #7, PAGE 14 ART
BY FILIPE ANDRADE

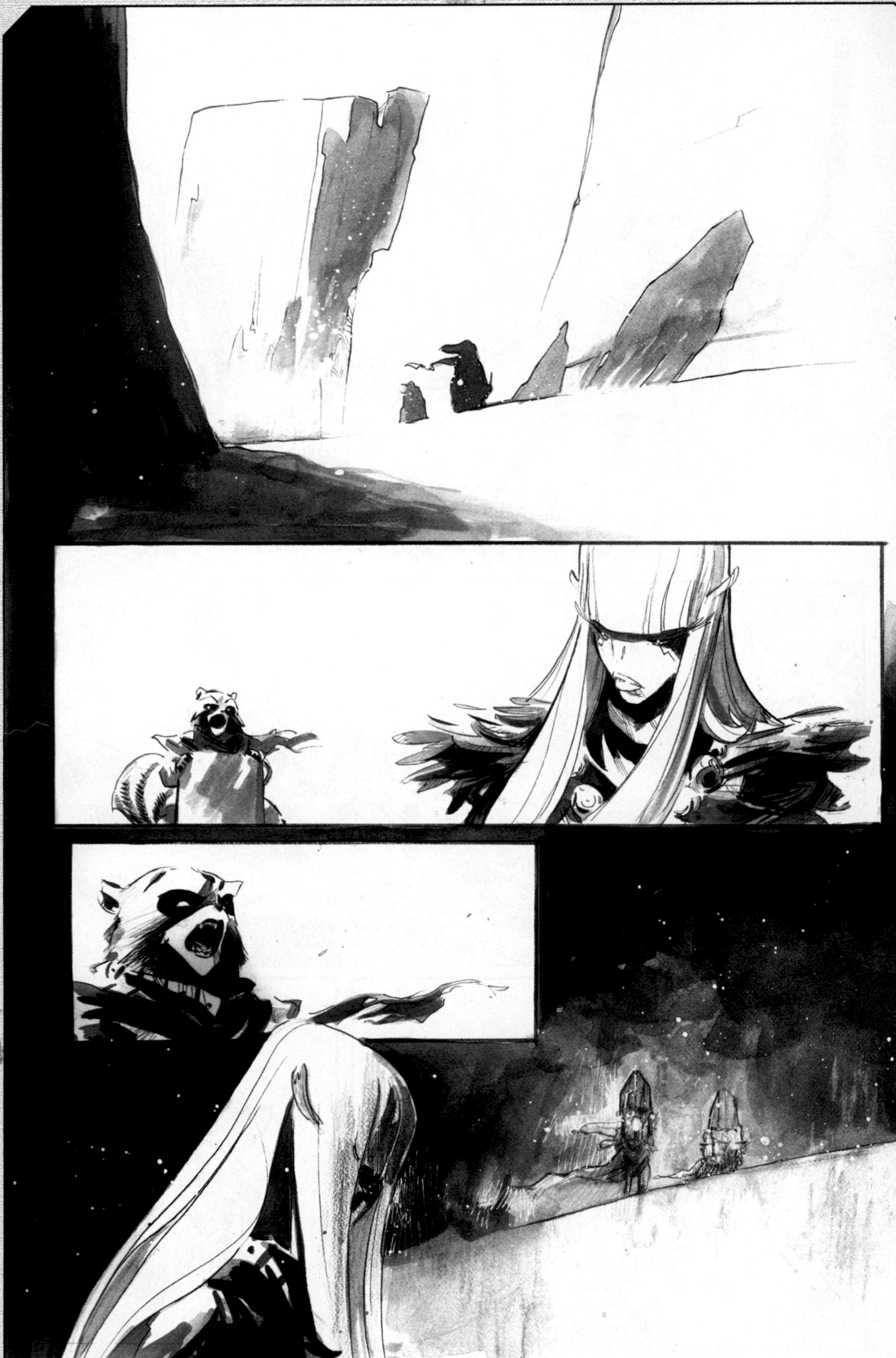

ROCKET RACCOON #8, PAGE 2 ART
BY FILIPE ANDRADE

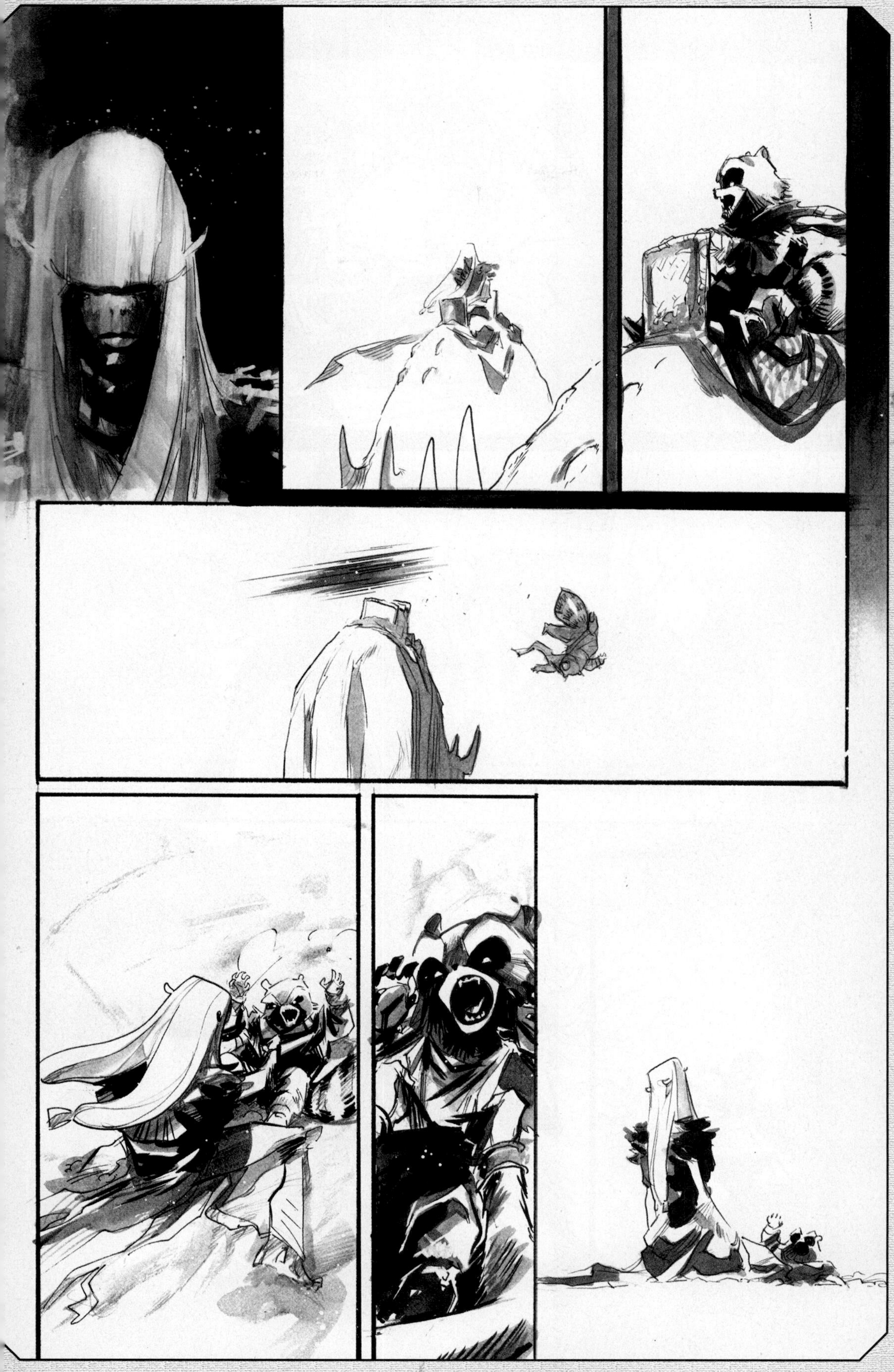

ROCKET RACCOON #8, PAGE 4 ART
BY FILIPE ANDRADE

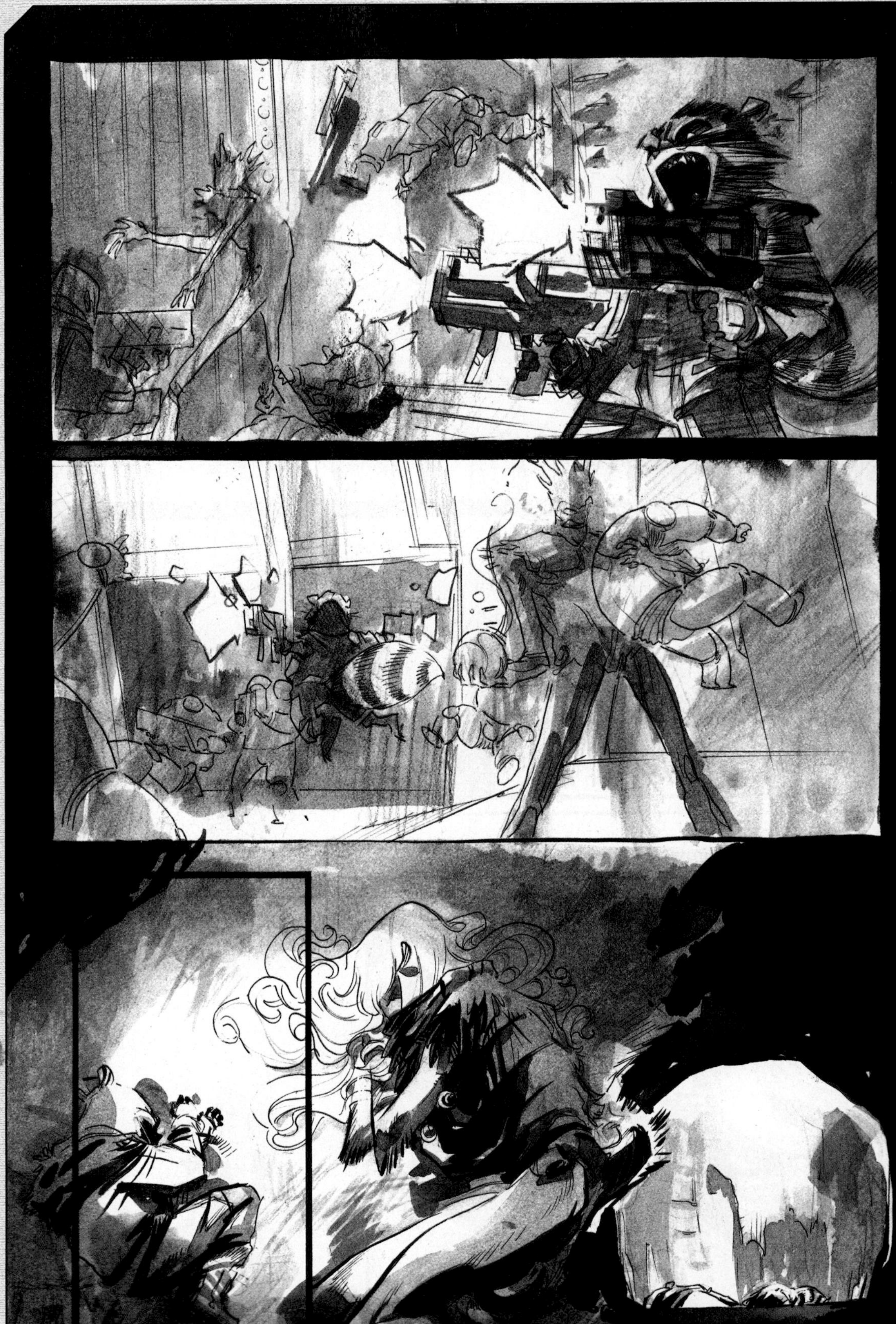

ROCKET RACCOON #8, PAGE 6 ART
BY FILIPE ANDRADE

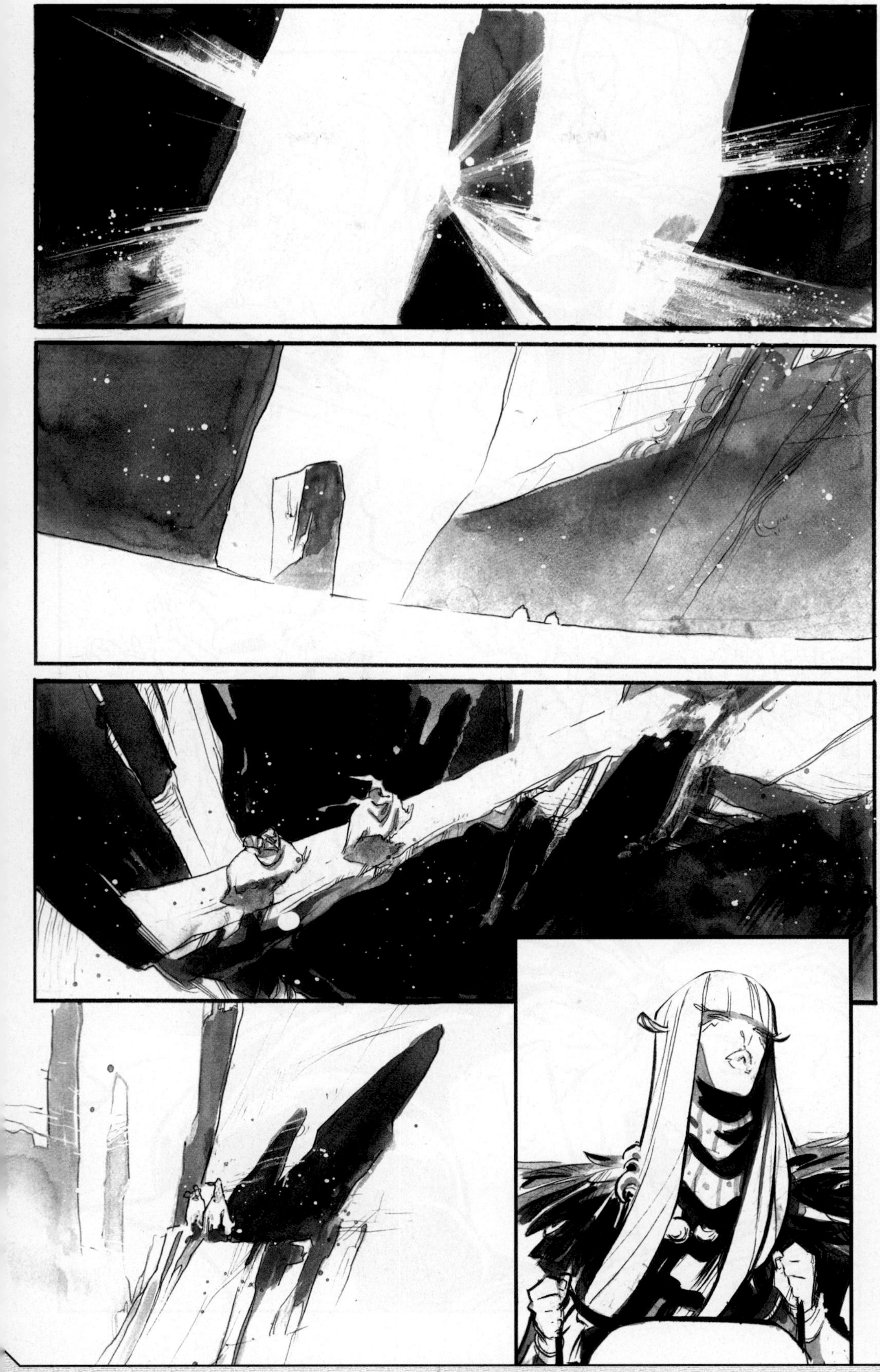

ROCKET RACCOON #8, PAGE 7 ART
BY FILIPE ANDRADE

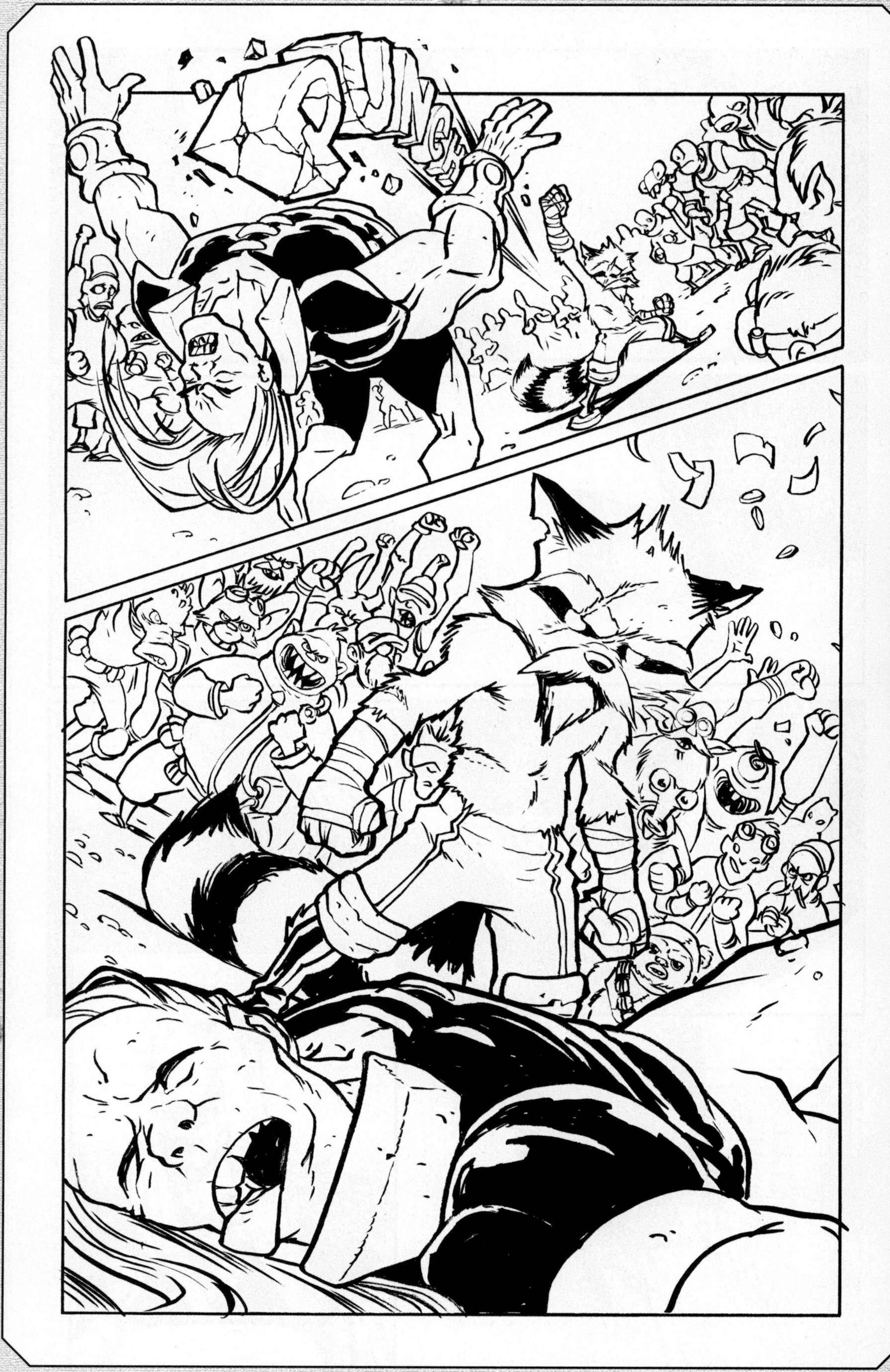

ROCKET RACCOON #9, PAGE 6 ART
BY JAKE PARKER

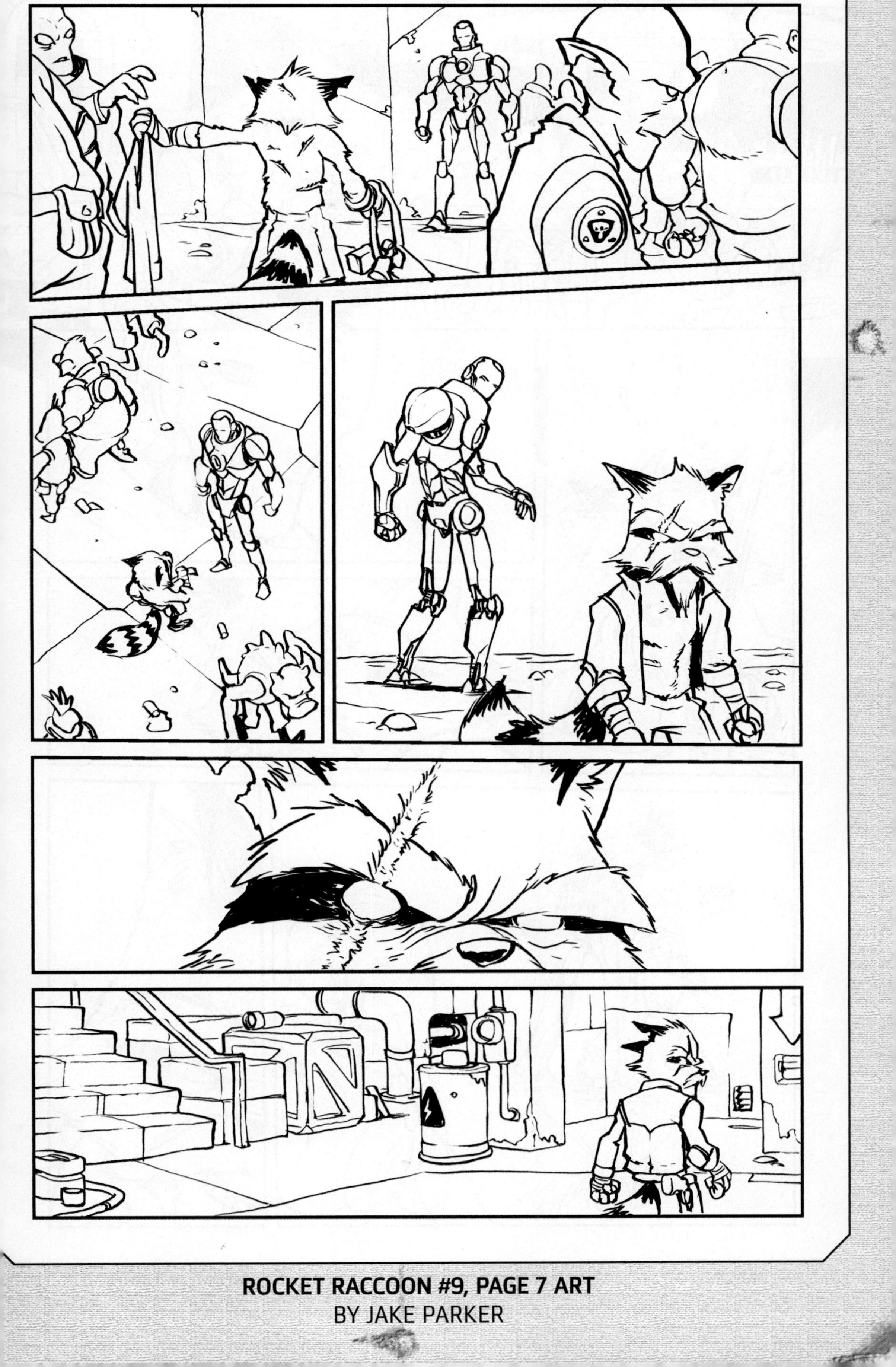

ROCKET RACCOON #9, PAGE 7 ART
BY JAKE PARKER

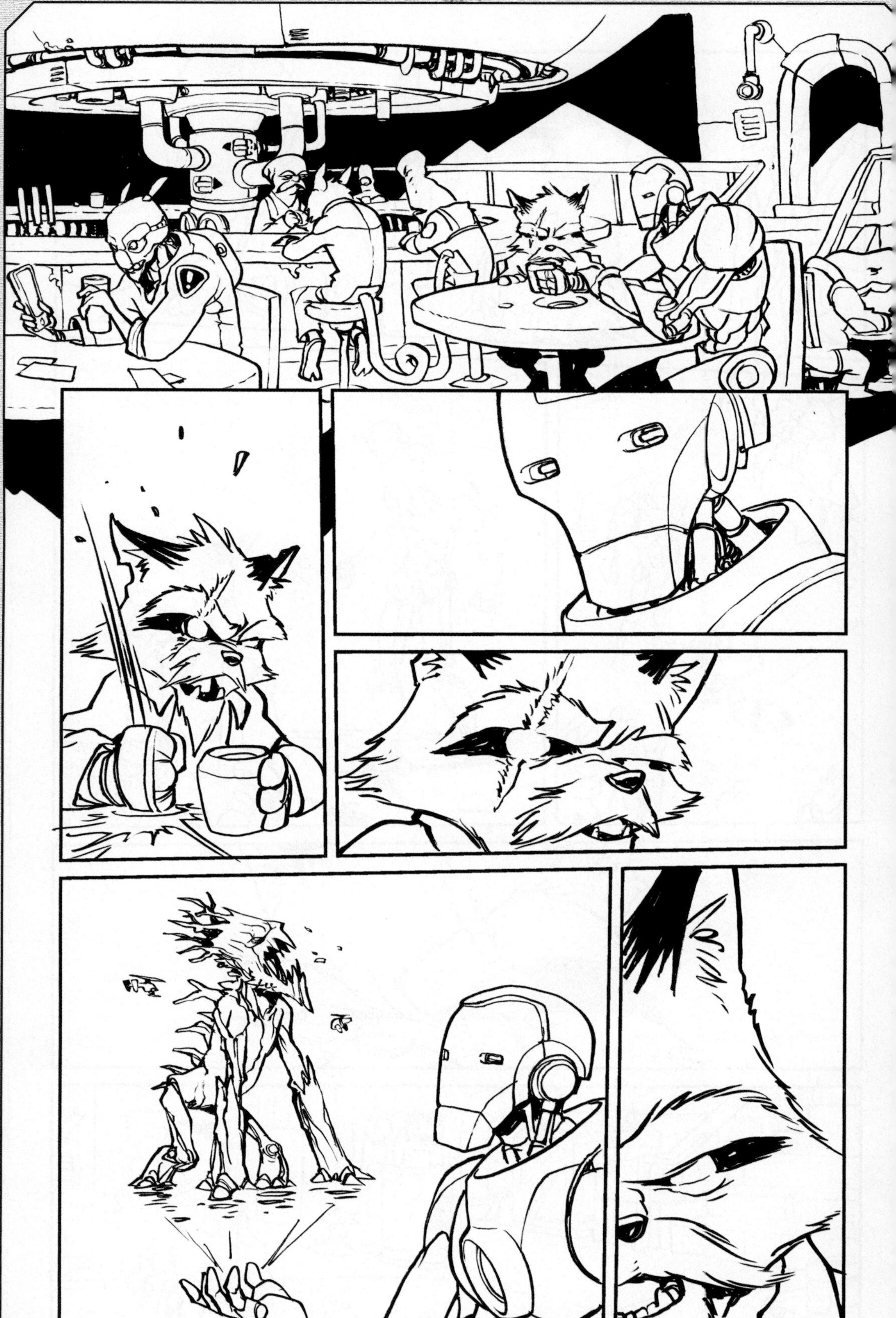

ROCKET RACCOON #9, PAGE 8 ART
BY JAKE PARKER

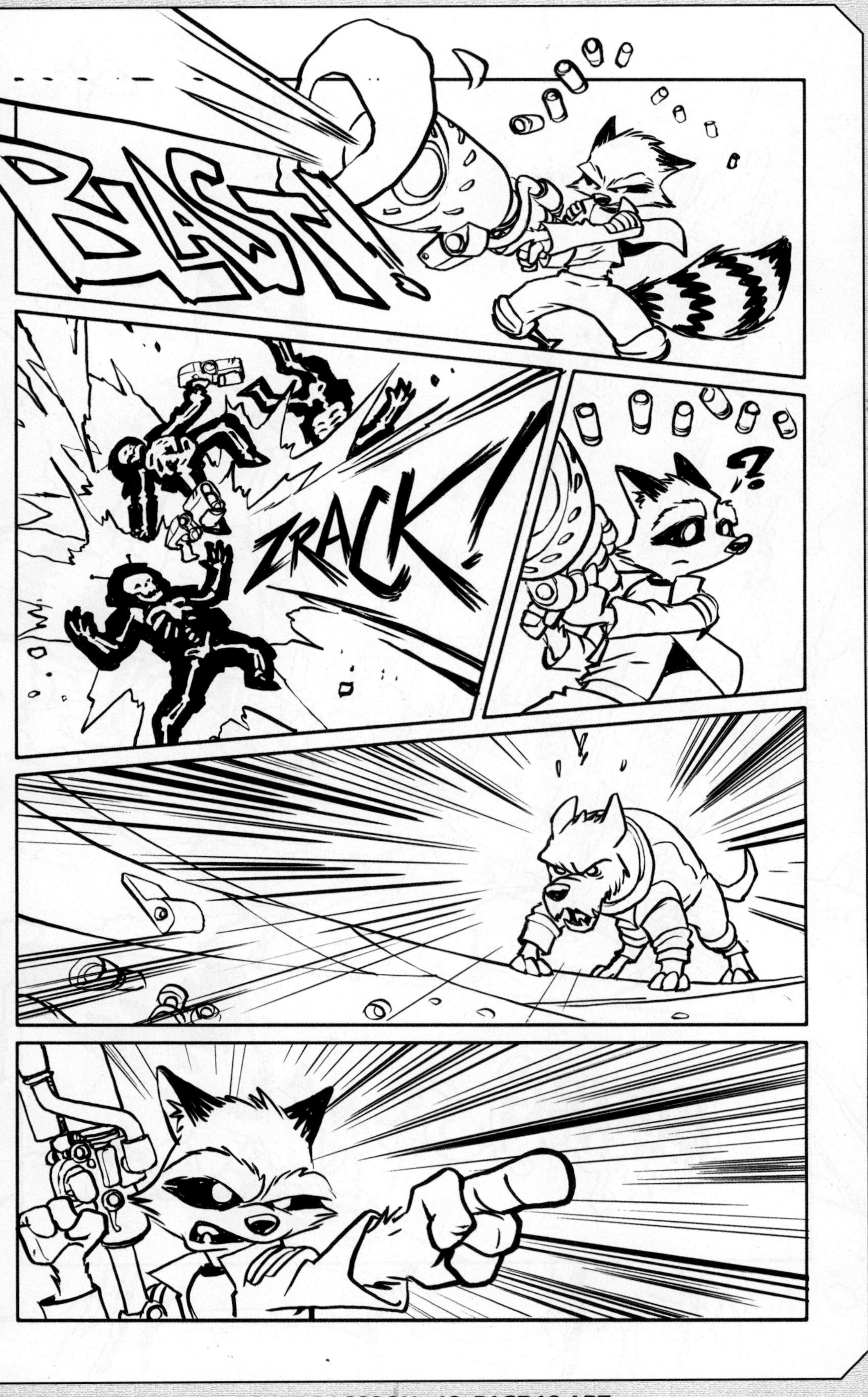
BLAST!
ZRACK!
?

ROCKET RACCOON #10, PAGE 16 ART
BY JAKE PARKER

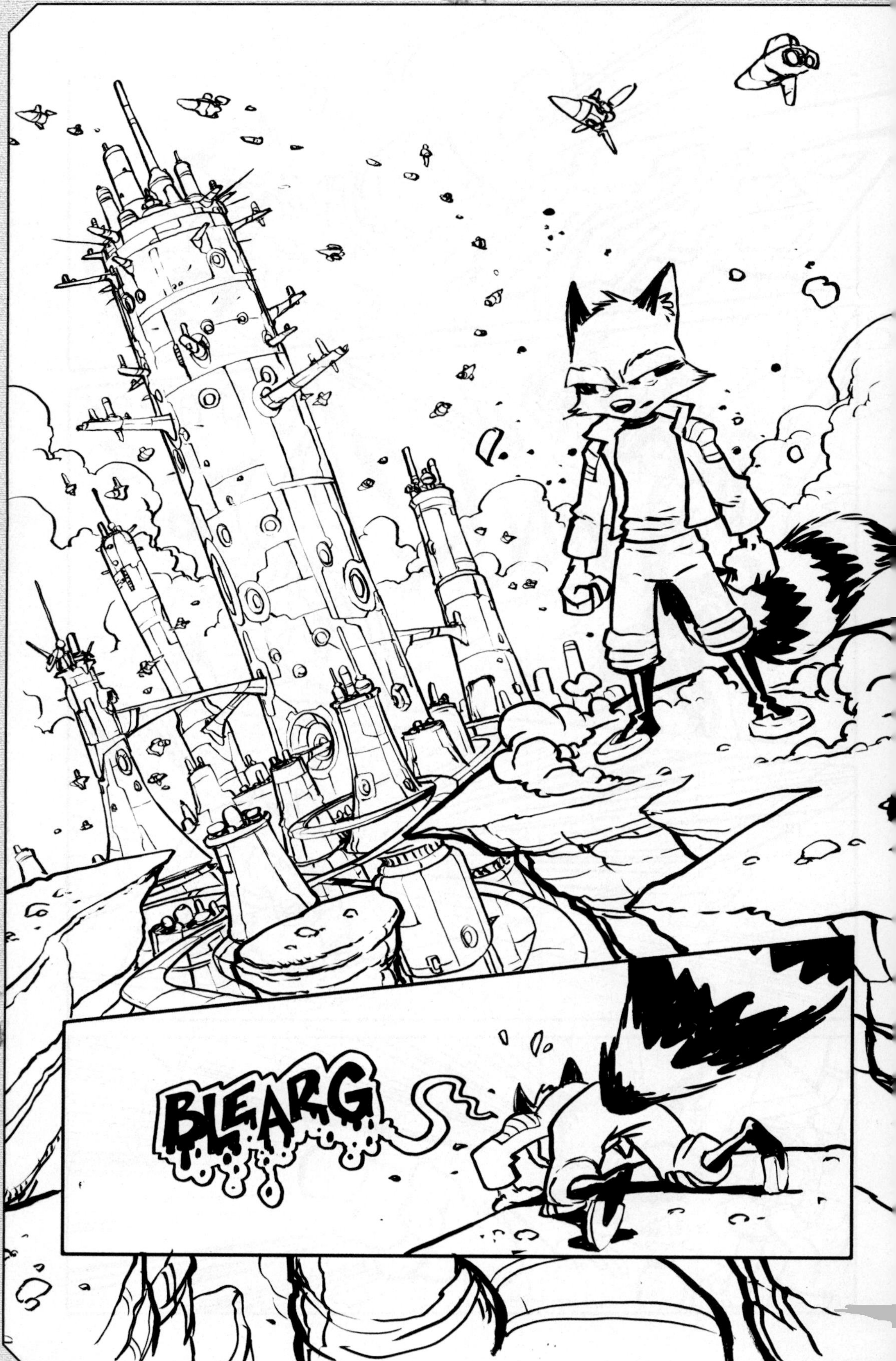
BLEARG

ROCKET RACCOON #10, PAGE 20 ART
BY JAKE PARKER

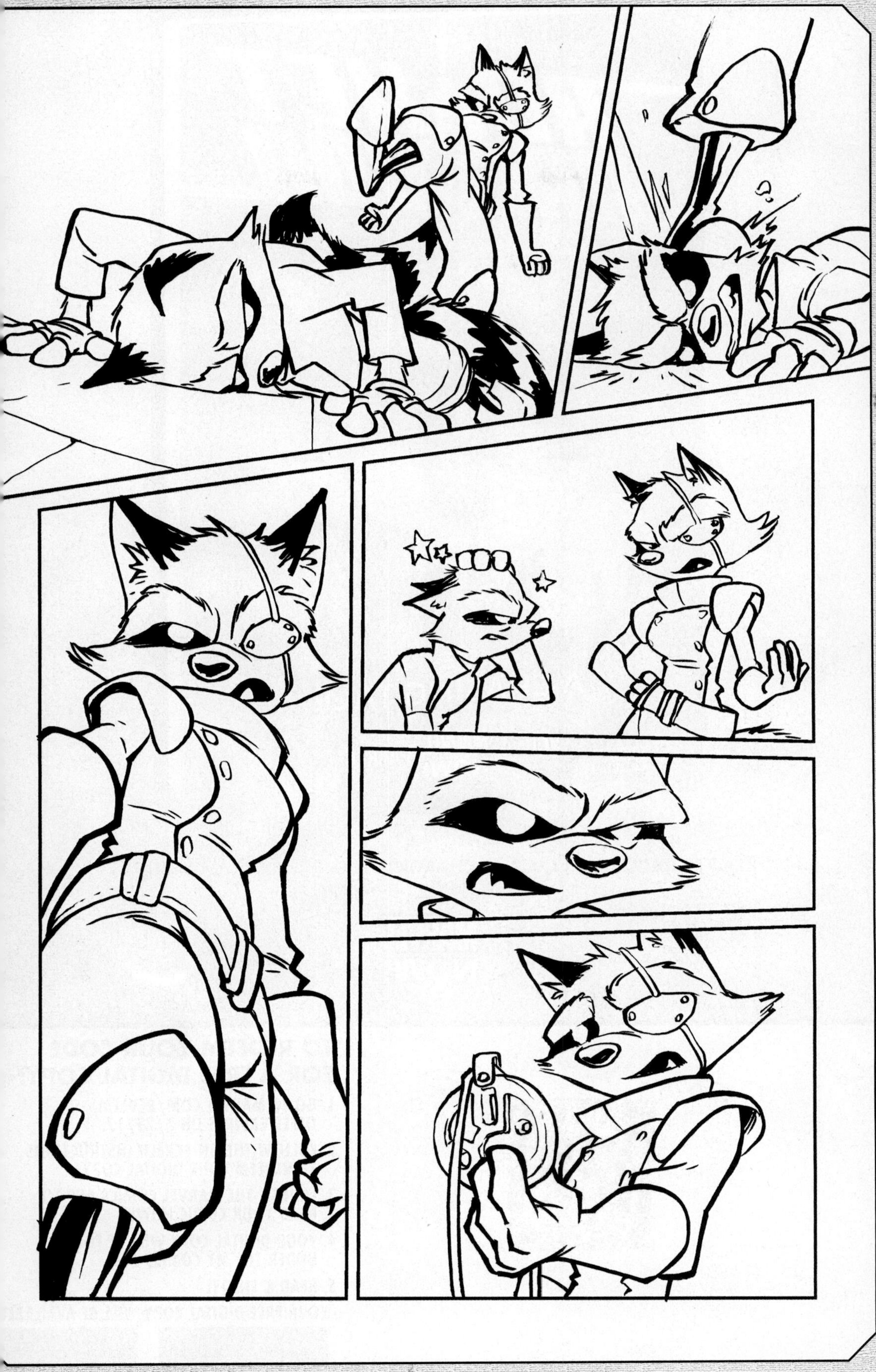

ROCKET RACCOON #11, PAGE 10 ART
BY JAKE PARKER

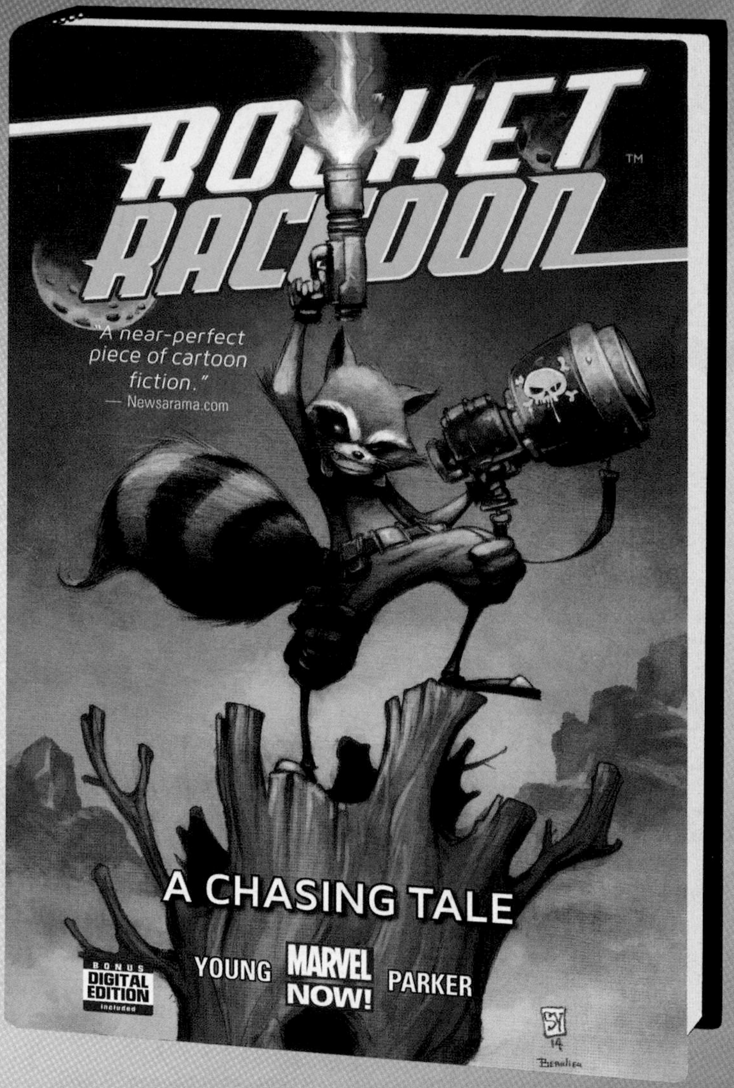
ROCKET RACCOON™
"A near-perfect piece of cartoon fiction."
— Newsarama.com
A CHASING TALE
BONUS DIGITAL EDITION included
YOUNG
MARVEL NOW!
PARKER

ROCKET RACCOON VOL. 1: A CHASTING TALE PREMIERE HARDCOVER

978-0-7851-9389-0 • NOV140861

MARVEL NOW!

TMAQAJ6F2U7H

TO REDEEM YOUR CODE FOR A FREE DIGITAL COPY:

1. GO TO MARVEL.COM/REDEEM. OFFER EXPIRES ON 7/22/17.
2. FOLLOW THE ON-SCREEN INSTRUCTIONS TO REDEEM YOUR DIGITAL COPY.
3. LAUNCH THE MARVEL COMICS APP TO READ YOUR COMIC NOW!
4. YOUR DIGITAL COPY WILL BE FOUND UNDER THE *MY COMICS* TAB.
5. READ & ENJOY!

YOUR FREE DIGITAL COPY WILL BE AVAILABL

MARVEL COMICS APP FOR APPLE® iOS DEVICES

MARVEL COMICS A FOR ANDROID™ DEVI